CAMBRIDGE LIBRARY COLLECTION

Books of enduring scholarly value

Travel, Europe

This collection of narratives contains vivid accounts of the varied landscapes, built environment and customs encountered by eighteenth- and nineteenth-century travellers in the British Isles and Europe. Some were wealthy individuals on the Grand Tour, while others were travelling on business, for pleasure, in pursuit of better health, or simply to escape trouble at home.

A Ramble in Malta and Sicily, in the Autumn of 1841

In the autumn of 1841, George French Angas (1822–86) abandoned his conventional career in the City of London for a life of art, travel and zoology. Inspired by a childhood fascination with natural history, his accounts blend detailed antiquarian descriptions of temples and palaces with picturesque notes on livestock and wildlife. Published in 1842, this work was the first of Angas' books to charm the British reading public, and its success launched his new career as a prolific chronicler and illustrator of foreign lands. Opening with the journey to Malta, Angas begins his tour in Valetta, taking in the forts of St Elmo and St Angelo and various tapestries and paintings en route. In Sicily, he continues to document Mediterranean culture, making also an ascent of Mount Etna. Illustrated with fourteen engravings, this book displays the charm and diversity that defines the best nineteenth-century travel writing.

Cambridge University Press has long been a pioneer in the reissuing of out-of-print titles from its own backlist, producing digital reprints of books that are still sought after by scholars and students but could not be reprinted economically using traditional technology. The Cambridge Library Collection extends this activity to a wider range of books which are still of importance to researchers and professionals, either for the source material they contain, or as landmarks in the history of their academic discipline.

Drawing from the world-renowned collections in the Cambridge University Library and other partner libraries, and guided by the advice of experts in each subject area, Cambridge University Press is using state-of-the-art scanning machines in its own Printing House to capture the content of each book selected for inclusion. The files are processed to give a consistently clear, crisp image, and the books finished to the high quality standard for which the Press is recognised around the world. The latest print-on-demand technology ensures that the books will remain available indefinitely, and that orders for single or multiple copies can quickly be supplied.

The Cambridge Library Collection brings back to life books of enduring scholarly value (including out-of-copyright works originally issued by other publishers) across a wide range of disciplines in the humanities and social sciences and in science and technology.

A Ramble in Malta and Sicily

in the Autumn of 1841

GEORGE FRENCH ANGAS

CAMBRIDGE
UNIVERSITY PRESS

CAMBRIDGE UNIVERSITY PRESS

Cambridge, New York, Melbourne, Madrid, Cape Town,
Singapore, São Paolo, Delhi, Mexico City

Published in the United States of America by Cambridge University Press, New York

www.cambridge.org
Information on this title: www.cambridge.org/9781108054683

© in this compilation Cambridge University Press 2013

This edition first published 1842
This digitally printed version 2013

ISBN 978-1-108-05468-3 Paperback

A RAMBLE IN MALTA AND SICILY

BY

GEORGE FRENCH ANGAS.

Designed, & Drawn on stone, by George French Angas

Printed in Colors by M & N, Hanhert

A RAMBLE

IN

MALTA AND SICILY,

IN THE AUTUMN OF 1841.

BY

GEORGE FRENCH ANGAS.

Illustrated with Sketches

TAKEN ON THE SPOT, AND DRAWN ON STONE BY THE AUTHOR.

"It is a strange thing that, in sea voyages, where there is nothing to be seen but sky and sea, men should make diaries; but in land travel, wherein so much is to be observed, for the most part they omit it, as if chance were fitter to be registered than observation. Let diaries, therefore, be brought into use.—LORD BACON.

LONDON:
SMITH, ELDER, AND CO., CORNHILL.
———
1842.

To

Her Most Gracious Majesty

Queen Adelaide

The following Pages

are, by Her Majesty's permission

most respectfully dedicated by

Her Majesty's

most obedient &

obliged humble Servant

George French Angas.

INTRODUCTION.

To write a Preface, which shall display neither vanity nor egotism, has ever been acknowledged to be a task of great difficulty, even by experienced writers. I trust, therefore, that I shall be excused for evading it with this my first and very juvenile work, merely saying that I have endeavoured to make it as true as my powers of observation would permit, describing only those scenes which I have personally visited, and sketching the various characters whose evidences of "life and manners" have been accidentally brought under my notice.

I can but feebly express my gratitude for the encouragement and honour which I have received, in being permitted to dedicate the following pages to Her Most Gracious Majesty Queen Adelaide, illustrating scenes so recently visited by Her Majesty, and which retain such memorials of Her Majesty's piety and benevolence.

I also beg to return my sincere thanks to my numerous Subscribers, who have thus so kindly assisted and encouraged me, especially when I remember that the following pages are compiled from my daily journal, and form but the descriptive detail of my sketches, which I trust may be found creditable evidences of the undeniable truth of Mr. Waterhouse Hawkins's new and infallible system of teaching drawing, as I had been the professional pupil of that gentleman but for four months when I made my sketches from nature, and on stone, as they now appear.

London, September 20th, 1842.

CONTENTS.

CHAPTER I.

CHAPTER II.

CHAPTER III.

CHAPTER IV.

CHAPTER V.

CHAPTER VI.

CHAPTER VII.

CHAPTER VIII.

CHAPTER IX.

CHAPTER X.

CHAPTER XI.

ILLUSTRATIONS.

A RAMBLE, &c.

CHAPTER I.

" Oh who can tell?—not thou, luxurious slave,
 Whose soul would sicken o'er the heaving wave—
 Nor thou, vain lord of wantonness and ease,
 Whom slumbers soothe not, pleasures cannot please
 Oh who can tell,—save he whose heart hath tried
 And danced in triumph o'er the waters wide,—
 Th' exulting sense, the pulse's maddening play,
 That thrills the wanderer o'er the trackless way ? "

August 16, 1841.—It has been justly said, that there are three distinct pleasures enjoyed by travellers of which those who constantly dwell within the narrow limits of their own homes can form no competent idea. They are the pleasures arising from anticipation, realization, and retrospection; all of which are in themselves separate sources of enjoyment to the observant mind. The first of these I had already cherished with the most enthusiastic visions of hope; and the realization of my expected gatification from the second, commenced, when bidding farewell to my home and friends for awhile, I embarked for Malta in the beautiful clipper schooner " Prospero." The bustle and excitement of departure being over, I was anxious to leave St. Katharine's Docks without delay, that we might sail down the river, and float freely over the broad bosom of the sea.

But disappointments, like the clouds which mar an April sunshine, mingle themselves with our most pleasing moments; and thus it proved to me; for by an unavoidable tardiness caused by the brokers of the vessel, we were compelled to remain in our close quarters for one night, and part of the succeeding day. At nine P.M. the noisy, thundering bell of the Docks sounded the hour of repose, when all lights are ordered to be put out, under a penalty of ten pounds. But this curfew of modern times did not prevent our burning a candle "on the sly," as the sailors term it ; and covering the skylight with a tarpaulin, and locking the cabin-door, we sat very comfortably without molestation until ten o'clock. By-and-by, the custom-house officer came down, and after the old gentleman had fastened the doors, he stretched himself on the sofa immediately below my berth, and commenced snoring most famously, (as only a custom-house officer can,) until the same thundering bell proclaimed the hour of six on the following morning. My sleep was frequently broken by the nasal music of this gentleman of the "customs," which combined with many new and strange sounds, such as the dog's feet patting up and down the deck overhead ; the distant "pulley hoy" of vessels going out by the night tide, and the gentle ripple and plash of the water just level with my head, filled my sleep with strange and singular nautical dreams. The morning was unusually warm, and the weather calm and settled. About one, P.M, we left St. Katharine's Docks, and were towed by a steam-tug down the river towards Gravesend, where we put the officer ashore. After passing this place, the river became much wider, and as the shades of evening gathered in, the low distant shores melted away in the twilight haze, and the numerous vessels scattered here and there looked like black specks on the surface of the quiet water. Before us was the Nore light, and to the left, the lights of Southend sparkled brightly in the distance ; while on our right, the lamps of Sheerness, in the Isle of Sheppey, were equally visible. A few young porpoises, and a solitary sea-gull, gave token of our approach to the ocean, and about nine o'clock we cast anchor one mile to the westward of the Nore.

Aug. 18.—At five o'clock this morning we got under weigh. The atmosphere was hazy, and after we had passed the Reculvers, in sight on our starboard side, we were becalmed for several hours. The glassy waters around were smooth and placid as a lake, and at noon it was oppressively hot. On looking over the stern of the vessel, I observed numbers of medusæ rising through the water. After several attempts, I succeeded in catching one in a basket let down by a rope ; and when I had made a coloured sketch of the creature, I again committed him to his watery home. I was not a little amused when the captain and sailors positively assured me that it was "only the strength and filth of the water ;" and I could not persuade them that it was an organized and created being.

By-and-by the breeze again sprang up, and as we tacked about, Margate and the surrounding shores were frequently in sight. At seven o'clock we cast anchor in the Downs, and the wind blowing strongly from the south-west, gave us a pretty fair tossing. Here our pilot left us, by whom I sent letters ashore. The sky looked wild and stormy, but the stars shone brilliantly between the dark masses of cloud, and our little vessel rose and fell on the surging water, as we lay moored off Deal for the night.

Aug. 19.—The morning rose bright and serene, and before I went upon deck we were passing the Straits of Dover. The white cliffs of the South Foreland presented a fine effect, with the morning sunshine upon them, and the picturesque town and castle of Dover were interesting objects from the water. The scene was still more enlivened by numerous vessels of all sizes lying scattered over the gently sparkling waves. The morning haze that hung like a veil over the south, prevented our seeing much of the French coast, but the heights of Calais were distinctly visible. About noon we were again nearly becalmed. The towns of Folkestone and Hythe, with Romney, and the entrance to its extensive marshes, successively presented themselves to our view. Towards dusk, we rounded that long promontory of shingle, Dungeness, nearly at the extremity of which is the well-known and conspicuous lighthouse. The waters were like a sheet of glass; the last gentle breeze had died away, and we lay motionless on the sea. The sails hung silently aloft, whilst above us shone down through the cloudless sky thousands of stars whose brilliancy, mingling with the bright lustre of one glorious planet upon the waters, gave additional loveliness and magnificence to the whole scene. The beauty of the night tempted me to linger on the deck till long after the last wild fowl had sailed past us on his flight to the marshes; and it was with reluctance that I exchanged the landscape of sea and starlight, for my close cabin quarters below.

Aug. 20.—At seven o'clock this evening, we had a brisk breeze; all sails are spread, we are now off the Isle of Wight, and I am only wishing for a pair of wings to enable me to revisit that delightful spot. I have watched its rugged cliffs until distance and the mists of evening shrouded them from my sight, and the flame of St. Catherine's lighthouse was the only spot discernible in the horizon.

Aug. 21, four, A. M.—The breeze during the night has increased, and it is now blowing violently against us with a heavy sea. I remained on deck all day, and securing myself with a rope to the lockers, weathered wind and waves. Notwithstanding several good duckings from the spray, I enjoyed the novelty of my situation, and preferred it greatly to lying in my bed-cabin. At two o'clock we passed Purbeck Island, and I had a fine view of that barren and rocky coast. At five o'clock we tacked out to run towards the French shore; but as the weather became more stormy we were driven back, and put in for shelter into the Portland Roads, where we cast anchor along with a little fleet of forty or fifty vessels, all weather-bound like ourselves.

Aug. 22.—We rode at anchor all night, and this morning I went on shore at Portland Island with some of the sailors, who took casks with them to obtain some fresh water. This remarkable promontory or bill, as it is called, is connected to the main

land by a ridge of sand several miles in length, forming an excellent shelter for vessels
from the westerly gales.   On reaching a small village on the western side of the rock,
I got some letters conveyed to the post ; and after exploring the barren place, and
providing ourselves with some watercresses for tea, we returned on board, though
even in this sheltered bay the waves were so rough that our boat was very nearly
capsized.   We dined off a fresh leg of mutton that we brought from London, and this
will probably be the last fresh meat we shall taste until we arrive at Malta.   Three,
P. M.; as the wind appeared rather more favourable we set sail again ; but before we
had well got clear of the harbour, it blew with greater violence than ever.   We had
now to pass through the Race of Portland—a dangerous place—with the sea running
very high and the waves standing up almost perpendicularly, resembling those pictures
we occasionally meet with of Moses dividing the waters of the Red Sea.   The captain
desired Mrs. B. and myself to go below whilst we were passing through the Race, but
before we could well do so the waves swept completely over us.   At six o'clock we
turned in to our berths, but not to sleep, for it soon blew a heavy gale which continued
raging from seven until twelve o'clock, accompanied with torrents of rain.   At midnight it suddenly fell a dead calm.   During the storm the waves ran mountains high,
and the wild confusion of the elements produced a sound like the tumult of a mighty
mob.   This dreadful discord was only broken at intervals by the shouts of the captain
giving orders to the crew, and the noise and bustle of the sailors securing the sails and
other moveables on the deck.

Aug. 23.—Early this morning the waves still rolled very high from last night's
gale, and we have been out of sight of land all day until eight o'clock when we made
Dartmouth.   To-day I turned cook, and made some dumplings for our dinner, which
we partook of upon the cabin floor.   My dumplings were more fortunate than King
Alfred's cakes, as they turned out very good, and the captain and mate did them
ample justice.

Aug. 24.— Off Plymouth, in sight of the Eddystone lighthouse.   To-day we took
our departure from the Lizard, distant about twenty-five miles north.   The mainsail, as it flapped in the wind, knocked the captain's hat overboard, and he is now looking very grand in an old " southwester."   As a winding up, the Channel sent a
mighty farewell wave, which swept all over the decks, and not one of us escaped without a good ducking.

Aug. 25.—We are now clear of the Channel, where we have been tossing about
a whole week.   Yesterday we bade adieu to the land, and to-day not a single sail has
appeared in the horizon.   The only objects are a few sea-gulls skimming over the
waves.   We dined on the cabin floor off a miserable fowl, very lean and boiled to
atoms.   I attribute its emaciated condition to melancholy, and sorrow at leaving its
native land, and being shut up during the past week in the long boat.   Even as I am

writing I hear dreadful screams on the deck, which assure me that a second unhappy creature is being sacrificed to our voracious appetites. As they pine so fast we are to dine upon them every day, till not one remains to tell its tale of woe! Half-past eleven, P. M.,—I had no sooner retired to my berth than the mate called me up again to see a shoal of porpoises playing around the vessel; they had a most curious and beautiful appearance, being quite luminous; their phosphorescent brightness was indeed so great that they resembled fishes of fire, as gliding along swiftly they left a shining track of light behind them. In the wake of the vessel thousands of bright sparkling animals were constantly in motion, lighting the curl of every wave.

The water in the Bay of Biscay is extremely clear and translucent, and of a deep blue colour. On looking over the stern of the vessel, I could frequently discern her keel, and clearly see the smallest objects that were many feet below the surface. The depth of water in the Bay has never been ascertained, and it is said to be fathomless. One of the sailors gravely assured me that it had no bottom at all, and extended quite through the globe to the other side, where it is known by the name of the Chinese Sea!

Aug. 27.—This morning was ushered in by a thick fog, through which the sun in vain endeavoured to penetrate. We are now approaching latitude 45°, where strong winds and doubtful weather so generally prevail that they have become proverbial amongst seamen. We are one hundred miles distant from Cape Finisterre, running on with all sails spread. Towards evening, the wind increased until seven o'clock, when it blew very strong, but fortunately in our favour, from the east, and we flew along over the waves instead of meeting them. The captain reefed the sails, and even then we ran at the rate of ten knots an hour. The waves were very magnificent, and on a much larger scale than in the Channel; they appeared sometimes as though they would overwhelm the vessel, when suddenly each mountainous billow sank as quietly as it rose, and was soon succeeded by another of equally terrific magnitude. As the wind blew the spray from their foamy crests, the sun shining through them formed myriads of small rainbows, which were as evanescent as they were beautiful. Whilst gazing with delight at these beautiful prismatic reflections, a tremendous wave came sweeping along the side of the vessel, and breaking directly over me wetted me thoroughly to the skin. Nor was this the only misfortune that befell me, for soon afterwards Mrs. B. and I went down to tea in the cabin below; we had no sooner poured it out than the vessel gave a heavy lurch, and precipitated tea-pot, cups and saucers, with all their scalding contents, into our laps. We were in this miserable condition when the captain came down, and added to our trouble by scolding us well for not having our tea as usual upon the floor.

Aug. 28.—We passed Cape Finisterre, the north-western extremity of Spain, during the night, though at a considerable distance. The morning is charming, it breathes of a southern climate : the air is fresh, but so soft and warm as to render it quite luxurious. At nine o'clock the thermometer stood at 87° in the shade, and on deck the sun was quite scorching. We are now sailing in a southerly direction, about twenty-five miles from the coast of Spain ; and were it not for the haze, or "loom of the land," as the sailors term it, we should be able to see it quite plainly. In the morning a large shoal of porpoises played around the bows of the vessel. The harpoon was got out, and the mate at the first thrust plunged it up to the hilt in the body of one of them, which probably might measure about eight feet. Unfortunately the harpoon snapped in two with the struggles of the animal, and giving a tremendous leap out of the water, the poor creature darted down again like lightning through the water, bearing the barbed weapon deep within him, and for a considerable distance the waves were red with its gushing blood. All the other porpoises in the shoal followed it immediately, as the sailors said, to make a meal on their unhappy companion as soon as his dying struggles were over. During the day we saw several whales, at a short distance from the ship, spouting up water like a fountain, and blowing with a noise resembling that of an elephant. Four, p. m.—We are once more becalmed ; the Spanish coast is visible at a great distance, with a yellow haze resting upon it. Thousands of the most venom- ous little flies imaginable have entered the cabin, and are stinging us most cruelly. We have tried to kill them, but they are so uncommonly lively, and come in such numbers, that it is utterly impossible to get rid of them. The captain affirms that he can hear them swearing and growling at him because he will not let them have a chance of biting him. Our feet and hands are stung all over from their furious attacks. Mrs. B. has accounted for their appearance in a very philosophic manner. She sup- poses them to be the flies we brought from St. Katharine's Docks, who having just recovered from their sea-sickness, are come out with very keen appetites. The sunset this evening was peculiarly beautiful. From a cloudless sky of the purest blue the sun sank majestically in the west, bathed in a flood of the most vivid scarlet, gradually melting off into orange and yellow, till at last it produced that warm glow of atmo- sphere so much admired in the works of Claude Lorraine. The moon, too, was brighter and clearer than in more northerly climates, and being nearly at the full, it renders the evenings on deck very pleasant and delightful.

Aug. 29.—During the day the sea has been nearly a perfect calm and the air very hot. The evening brought no breeze, but the moon and the stars shone brightly, and only a few fleecy clouds stole almost imperceptibly along the sky. Several huge black fish rose within a few yards of the vessel, and made such a noise with their blowing, that the dog we had on board commenced barking at them, believing, no doubt, that they were nightly intruders come with dishonest intentions.

Aug. 30.—The early morning was hazy, but the sun soon burst out with an unusual degree of warmth, and not a breath of air fanned the sleeping surface of the waters;

the thermometer stood at 82°. Whilst lying thus becalmed, three very large whales rose near us, blowing at a dreadful rate, and lying with their backs above the water. Towards evening the Farilhœns rocks appeared in sight, bearing s. s. e. They seem to rise perpendicularly out of the sea, not unlike the Bass rock, or Ailsa, in Scotland. The sailors term them the "haystacks," which they greatly resemble. The Berlingas or Borlings, are several small barren islands lying south of the Farilhœns, about five miles from Cape Carboeyro on the main land. These we passed in the night, lat. 39° 26′, long. 10° 4′.

Aug. 31.—We have been now a fortnight at sea, and if our progress is no quicker than it has hitherto been, we shall make a long and very tedious voyage. There appears no hope of our getting on; it is a dead calm, and the vessel sleeps upon the sheeted water; indeed the sultry state of the atmosphere makes crew and captain equally drowsy, and we long for a breeze to invigorate us. The coast of Portugal is in sight, but so hazy from the heat, that I can make but little of it, even with the aid of a telescope. I long to be on shore, tasting some of their delicious grapes, as the water we have on board is too lively to tempt us to drink it, however extreme our thirst may be; and would form a better subject for microscopic exhibition and wonder among the marvels of that marvellous place, the Polytechnic Institution.

I have been trying my fishing lines, but they have proved unsuccessful; the stormy petrels skim around the hooks, and dexterously carry off the bait, without being able to secure them. To add to the mortification, shoals of sardinias, pursued by a whole troop of albicore, have approached within a boat's length of the vessel. During the day, as we lay becalmed, the captain put off the jolly-boat, and three of the men went out to endeavour to catch some from among the numerous shoals of fish that were rising from the deep water in every direction around us. When the boat approached within less than one hundred yards of a fine troop of albicore in full play, they provokingly disappeared, and, to use the sailors' phrase, "made fools of them." A second excursion for the same purpose proved equally unsuccessful, and the boat was hauled again on board in despair. We saw several sharks for the first time, and the sea-fowl and storm-birds became more numerous. It is a very interesting sight to watch the last-mentioned little birds, for ever on the wing, skimming swiftly over the surface of the water. They resemble a swallow, but are somewhat larger, and have a conspicuous white patch of feathers above the tail; sometimes they skim within a few inches of us, as they fly across the deck, but are so dexterous as never to be captured, even by the most expert hands. The sun shining upon the Portugal coast, rendered it rather more conspicuous; and in the afternoon we could discern the town of Ereceira, and on the summit of a high hill, the famous convent of Mafra, which is very conspicuous from the sea. Five, p.m.—A Portuguese fishing-boat has just passed us with four men and a boy in her.

As we observed them busily pulling up their lines, the captain thought that we might get a little fish, and called out to them, "Any pisco?" but the only thing they held up was a dog-fish; at this our captain shook his head, and muttered some words that savoured of the Portuguese, when they departed. Capo Rocca, or the rock of Lisbon, is in sight, bearing s.s.e, and distant about twelve miles; behind it the land suddenly rises up into a mountainous ridge, extending a considerable way to the eastward. The summit is very uneven, having on it a number of detached eminences; this is the mountain of Cintra, and beyond it is the city of Lisbon.

Sept. 1.—The morning was stormy, accompanied by rain and thunder; but it soon cleared off, and a steady breeze sprang up in our favour, and carried us along briskly. In the afternoon land appeared again in sight, and before six o'clock we rounded Cape St. Vincent, running at the rate of ten knots an hour. The sea is once more curled up into long sweeping waves, on whose snowy crests the full moon is shining with a flood of silvery light. The evenings begin to draw in very quickly, which is owing to the latitude we are in; the sun sets at half-past six, and in a few minutes night closes in, the duration of twilight being shorter than in England. Cape St. Vincent, the south-western extremity of the coast of Algarva, in Portugal, lies in north latitude 37° 3', and on its summit stands a convent of Augustine friars. About twenty fathoms from the foot of the Cape stands a large isolated rock, and the intervening channel is wide enough for ships of heavy tonnage to pass through. In the distance rise the mountains of Monchique, which are visible at sea for twenty-five leagues.

Sept. 2.—Very hot weather, with a clear, cloudless sky of the purest azure. The thermometer in the shade is 81°. We have had a fresh breeze all day, which will carry us nearly to the coast of Africa, from which we are about sixty miles distant. The sunset was most gorgeous; it filled the western horizon with a wide atmosphere of golden light, shining against the deep indigo blue of the Atlantic ocean. The effect of the sun's refraction was remarkably beautiful; just as it seemed to touch the water its orb appeared elongated, and seemed drawn downwards in a cylindrical form into the sea. Ten, P.M.—The breeze has freshened, and the lights of Cadiz are in sight, bearing N.E.

Sept. 3, Two o'clock, A.M.—The thermometer in the cabin stands at 83°. This degree of heat effectually prevented my sleeping, so I arose and went upon deck. We were entering the Straits of Gibraltar, and by the light of the moon I could discern Cape Trafalgar on the European, and Cape Spartel on the African coast. The ruddy hues of morning soon began to appear streaking the eastern sky, and I was amply repaid for my vigils, not only by a beautiful sunrise, but by an excellent view of the coast on each side of the Strait, which is one of the boldest and most romantic I ever beheld. At first it broke upon me like a dream, and I could hardly persuade myself that I was really, for the first time in my life, gazing upon the shores of Africa. The whole scene was bathed in the rosy light of morning. The Spanish hills, covered with vines and olive-trees ; the blue and crisped waters over which we were speeding, and the high and rugged mountains of Barbary with their lofty peaks glittering in the sunshine, formed altogether a panorama too strikingly grand and beautiful ever to be forgotten. The rock of Gibraltar stands at the eastern extremity of the Straits, and directly opposite to it, on the African side, is the town and fortress of Ceuta, the only remaining Spanish possession in the Moorish territories. These are the famous pillars of Hercules, the western gates of the world, according to the ancients. A little to the west of Ceuta, rises the lofty and singular mountain called Sierra Bullones, or Ape's Hill, with its summit wrapped in clouds. Vast numbers of monkeys are said to inhabit this spot, and there is a vulgar belief current among many that they cross and re-cross to the rock of Gibraltar opposite by a subterranean passage below the sea. To the right of Ceuta are the remains of Old Ceuta, probably Carthaginian. On the Spanish side, the town and lighthouse of Tarifa, the town of Algeçeiras, and on the opposite extremity of the bay the rock and fortress of Gibraltar, rising abruptly to the height of 1400 feet above the level of the sea, are all objects worthy of notice. The wind continued to blow strongly from the westward ; we were soon carried through the Straits, and were sailing over the bosom of the Mediterranean at the rate of nine knots an hour.

Sept. 4.—This morning it is a calm, and the long swell from yesterday's breeze rocks us to and fro like a cradle on the subsiding waves. The thermometer at noon in the cabin was 100° ; and we have not a breath of air to fan the sultry atmosphere. Numerous dolphins have been playing around the vessel ; the sailors attract them with a spoon suspended by a line over the bows of the ship, which they move to and fro in the sun, to resemble the motion of the flying fish.

Sept. 5.—A number of fine bonitoes have accompanied the vessel all day, and a troop of flying-fishes have just risen from the water, skimming over the waves like little bladders blown along by the wind. I observed, also, a large fish jump out of the sea, and up rose another cloud of these timid little creatures, escaping from their voracious enemy into another element, till their little wings becoming dry they sank exhausted into their native brine. Quarter past six, P. M. ; the sun has just gone down over the African coast at Cape Tenez ; a few scattered clouds have caught the reflection of the glowing sky upon their fleecy forms, and are exhibiting the most fairy-like appearance imaginable, being tinted with a pure rose colour of exquisite brilliancy, whilst the wide western heavens are radiant in molten gold, and streaked with broad belts of vermilion cloud.

Sept. 6.—To-day we have seen large numbers of the Portuguese men-of-war, those small marine animals so frequently noticed by seamen in warm latitudes. They are of a deep blue colour, and as they float upon the surface of the water they raise their thin transparent gauze-like sail, which catches the wind. I fished up several in a basket, and made drawings of them. I found it quite useless to attempt preserving them in alcohol, as it immediately changed their colour to a bright red, exactly in the same way as litmus paper, or any other vegetable blue is affected by being brought into contact with an acid. One of the sailors harpooned a bonito, which we cooked for our supper; but I did not relish it much, it was too oily and rank.

Sept. 8.—The Balearic Isles are in sight, but the wind continues directly opposed to us, and we are compelled to tack about in a zig-zag direction, so that we only gain twenty miles in every 100. The sea is running very high, and the sun shining brightly. Four, P.M.; the high mountains of Africa are again in sight, somewhere in the neighbourhood of Algiers; for a short time we thought we saw the city itself, with its white buildings, in the distance, but upon a nearer approach it proved to be nothing but sand-hills. The city of Algiers lies about ten miles to the east, and is hidden from our view by a projecting cape.

It was near sunset, and the deep indigo sea curled into a thousand snowy waves. A beach of yellow sand, backed by wild and picturesque rocks, sloped gradually down to the water's edge, beyond which the hills arose rapidly till the scene was flanked in by lofty mountains, so distant that they almost vanished in the warm hazy glow that overspread the African landscape. The herbage appeared small and scanty, and near to the water's edge there projected out a bold rock crowned with a ruined castle, whilst around it grew magnificent aloes with their lofty flower stalks rising to a great height; but I could detect no trace or vestige of any human beings in this glorious wilderness of nature. The French have carried their usurpation and arms into this devoted land, where Carthage once reared its hundred palaces, and where, in the middle ages, the Moorish hosts swept down from its mountains like some wild tumultuous sea, carrying their conquests into the very heart of Gaul. But now,

> " Only the wandering Arab's tent
> Flaps in the desert blast."

Lions and other wild beasts abound in these unfrequented recesses; and even the Arab himself is as fierce and untameable as they. After dark we have several times observed large fires on the hills, which we conjecture were made by some bivouac to keep out nightly intruders.

Sept. 11.—This morning it is a perfect calm, and very sultry; the thermometer in the shade being 85°, and the burning sun pours down its beams upon as blue a sea as ever garnished the brightest visions of fairyland. The water was so extremely clear that we resolved to try some experiments. We lowered a basin with a line into the sea, and at the depth of thirty-two fathoms it was distinctly visible. We next sank an empty bottle, strongly corked and sealed over; on being drawn up it was found filled with water, with the cork inverted. Thinking that I might make known to the world our condition, I wrote on a slip of paper the name of the vessel, with full particulars of the latitude and longitude where we lay becalmed, and all other necessary information; this I enclosed in a bottle, and sealing it well up, threw it overboard. Two large dragon-flies played all day around our top-masts; and our rigging was rendered lively by a bevy of small birds, that had ventured from the shore and taken up their abode with us.

Sept. 12.—To-day we spoke the schooner " Petrel," thirty-eight days from Newcastle, laden with coals for Corfu. The heat is greater than yesterday, but as there is scarcely any wind, we have put up the awning over the quarter-deck, which provides us with a pleasant shelter from the glare of the sun.

Sept. 14.—Wind contrary; I could not sleep during the night for the violent motion of the vessel, and the extreme heat of the cabin. I was in constant fear of being precipitated out of my berth on to the floor; and whilst the vessel was on her southerly tack, my berth was about as easy a place of repose as the side of a pyramid. Our salt butter was turned into oil, and our cabin was hot enough for a furnace.

Sept. 15.—In the dead of the night we were all thrown into a state of great consternation by the alarm of pirates. It was a sudden calm, our vessel lay motionless, and the sails hung silently from the yards. The dew was falling like rain as we all assembled upon deck, aroused by the cry of the watch, and by the starlight we distinctly saw four boats making directly towards us, and soon afterwards we heard the plash of their oars, and a confused sound of voices on the still night air. The captain ordered all hands to prepare for combat, and when our fire-arms were mustered, we found them to consist of two blunderbusses, five or six pistols, two cutlasses, and a large axe. Armed with these, we considered that we could make a tolerably stout resistance. For half an hour we stood awaiting their approach, whilst poor Mrs. B. paced the deck almost frantic with terror. At the end of this time they seemed to alter their course from some unknown cause, and in twenty minutes we quite lost sight of them. At the same time a light breeze sprang up, and we stood out to sea without encountering any more Algerines.

Sept. 16.—During the morning the African island of Galita was in sight. In the offing we saw a troop of large white animals, somewhat resembling whales, but which the sailors affirmed to be grampuses; they were of a delicate cream colour, with a dark line running along the back; and they reminded me of white asses. During the night the waters were unusually sparkling and vivid; the medusæ resembled masses of green fire as they rolled over in the foam of the waves. Whilst amusing myself by fishing up some of these creatures on the larboard side of the vessel, I was witness to a strange and brilliant atmospherical phenomenon. The heavens had hitherto been as clear as azure, and the wind for a fortnight past had been easterly; on a

sudden, a globe of fire as large as a cannon-ball arose in the south-west, (the direction
of Africa,) and whirling violently along through the air, broke almost directly over our
heads, whilst at the same moment it exploded into a thousand atoms, exhibiting a
brilliant display of natural fire-works.   The flash of light was of a blue colour, and so
intensely vivid that our eyes were for a time quite dazzled by it.   Several persons
on board, who only saw the glare of the light, imagined that our vessel was on fire.
The electricity produced by its passage through the air was so great, that the mag-
netic needle of the compass was whirled several times very rapidly round before it
regained its true position.   Immediately afterwards, dark clouds spread over the horizon from the quarter whence the fiery ball had arisen, and a strong wind (in our
favour) bore us rapidly along at the rate of eight knots an hour.

Sept. 17.—The fair wind has continued blowing all the day, and Maritimo, the
most westerly of the Ægadean isles, off the coast of Sicily, has been in sight since
five o'clock.   This island is used as a place of banishment for the Sicilian nobles.
Since sunset the lightning has been uncommonly vivid, and the sheets of electric
vapour every now and then illuminate the whole eastern side of the horizon, whilst
between the clouds the forked lightning shoots down in golden streams into the dark
sea.   The wide track of foam around the vessel as she glides on her way, shines like
a silver fringe gemmed with countless stars, rendering it beautifully luminous, and
contrasting finely with the blackness of the surrounding waters.

Sept. 19.—At sunrise the captain called me on deck to witness a most magnificent
spectacle.   The sun rose surrounded with long rays, forming a complete glory of most
dazzling brilliancy, whilst the scattered fleecy clouds shone like burnished gold upon
the exquisite light blue of the morning sky.   On our left was the coast of Sicily,
with Mount Etna towering proudly above it, at the distance of 120 miles ; and
far before us, cradled in the Halcyon seas, the Maltese islands themselves appeared like dark specks on the horizon.   We saw several turtles floating on the surface of the water, and not being able to resist the temptation of so inviting a prey, the
boat was lowered and sculled silently along to the nearest of them, but when it had
reached to within an arm's length of the prey, the wary creature swiftly and silently
sank beneath the water.   Soon afterwards another one appeared, sleeping, with his head
towards the sun.   This one they succeeded in catching, and we all made ourselves
happy at the prospect of dining on turtle soup.   At sunset the sailors killed the
creature, after which I saw no more of him.   The temperature of the atmosphere was
greater to day than yesterday, the thermometer in the shade at noon was 87°.
Eight o'clock.—The new moon is shining with great brilliancy, and a Sicilian speronaro
has just passed us.   The lights of Valetta are visible, distant about fifteen miles.
Eleven o'clock.—One of the native Maltese boats has come alongside to put a pilot
on board ; the moment he neared us, he jumped upon deck without any ceremony,

leaving his companions in the boat to keep up with us in the best manner they could. He appears to be a pleasant little man, and speaks English very tolerably.

Sept. 20.—Long before daybreak a crowd of small boats surrounded us, whose crews begged that they might tow our vessel into the Grand Harbour. We are now fast approaching it, pulled along by about a dozen of them. With this extra assistance we soon neared the Maltese shores, which speedily became visible through the dim light of early morning. It was a truly pleasant and refreshing sound, after a five weeks' tedious voyage across the briny sea, to hear the murmuring of the waves as they dashed at intervals against the rocky shores, a sound to whose gentle music we had been strangers ever since we had watched the sweeping breakers hurry confusedly along the Race of Portland. As the water rapidly deepens at the distance of a few yards from the shore, we sailed along close under the land, and the first ruddy hues of morning discovered to our view the towering fortress of St. Elmo, with its impregnable buttresses and turrets, bristling with cannon. The moment we rounded the promontory of St. Elmo, all was gaiety and animation. Myriads of little boats were darting in every direction across the harbour, and the graceful polacchi and speronaros with their curved latine sails, the men of war lying at anchor, and the crowd of yachts, schooners, and other vessels, rendered the waters of the Grand Harbour a very lively scene. On the Valetta side, the dark green foliage of the feathery trees, and the broad spreading leaves of the bananas, the sombre cypresses contrasting strongly against the unstained purity of the white buildings as they rose up one above another from the water's edge, and the line of domes, turrets, and varied fortifications, added to the bright sky and strangely foreign air of the whole scene, bursting at once upon the sight, produced a fairy-like panorama,—a real picture with all the vivid novelty of some city seen in dreams; and the charm was not a little augmented by its contrast to the monotonous but silent grandeur of the ocean, where all around, as far as the eye can reach, nothing breaks the distant horizon but a sail dimly seen, or a solitary sea-fowl skimming over the restless waves.

CHAPTER II.

" For many a night, and many a day,
  The ship held on her weary way ;
  At last she reached those radiant isles
  Where pleasant summer always smiles,
  And the blue waters at their feet,
  Murmur in music soft and sweet."

As the morning gun was fired from the castle of St. Elmo, our schooner cast anchor in the Grand Harbour, surrounded by the numerous boats that had formed our escort. The Maltese boats are very different from ours, and always attract the attention of a stranger. They are flat-bottomed, and both the stem and stern have an appendage of an upright piece of wood which projects about a foot above the level of the boat. They are painted with all the colours of the rainbow, and as they are exceedingly numerous, they present a very gay appearance, skimming in all directions over the waters of the Grand Harbour. The pleasure-boats (caico) have a canopy over them, which can be taken down at pleasure, and is generally a most necessary appendage to protect and screen the traveller from the great heat of the sun. Ferry-boats (barca del passo) are constantly crossing over to the town of Vittoriosa, on the opposite side of the harbour : the proper fare by these boats is one penny, though the boatmen are always ready to impose upon foreigners. The fishing boats (farilla) go out every morning before sunrise, and generally return laden with excellent fish, which is sold directly it is brought on shore. The Maltese boatmen always row standing, and are remarkably expert in avoiding the waves which often threaten to swamp their little boats.

The castle and fortress of St. Elmo stand on the right shore of the Grand Harbour as you enter it. It is surmounted by a lighthouse; and beyond, in a southerly direction, lies the city of Valetta. The Marina, lined with stores and crowded with vessels from all parts of the world, extends along the water's side for about a mile. The houses rise one above another, so that almost the whole city can be seen from the water, interspersed with churches and gardens, which have a remarkably pleasing appearance. At the extremity of the harbour lie the British men-of-war. The "Howe," the "Indus," and the "Vanguard," were there on my arrival; but the "Revenge" (to one of the officers of which I bore a letter of introduction) was unfortunately at Tunis. On the left side of the harbour lie the towns of Borgo (Vittoriosa) Birmula, and Senglea, called also Isola, guarded at the entrance by the towers of Fort Ricasoli, and further in, by the stupendous fortifications of St. Angelo.

When we had arrived in the harbour, the health officer came alongside, and took our ship's papers in a pair of tongs. After asking us the usual questions we were ordered to the Pratique-office, where we stood guarded by a wooden barrier for some time, till at length we got Pratique, and were permitted to enter the city. The barrier was then removed, and the officers shook us most cordially by the hand. On returning to the vessel, to get my things ashore, I found it crowded with Maltese, who had come on board with various articles for sale. It was quite amusing to witness the various characters: ship-chandlers soliciting custom; the carpenter, the butcher, the baker, and even the hair-dresser made their appearance, to say nothing of other worthies who were very desirous of driving a bargain for fruit, liqueurs, cigars, canary-birds, and shells. Josef Soler, a young Spaniard, very kindly took me ashore in his boat; and as I was possessed of a letter of introduction to an English gentleman residing at Valetta, we proceeded to his house. The atmosphere in the streets somewhat resembled that of an oven, but as the houses are very high, and the streets narrow, it is easy to walk in the shade, sheltered from the heat of the burning sun. We first visited the store of M. Pietro Paolo Agius, whence I wrote a letter to England, as I was anxious to send it by the steamer, which left at twelve o'clock. I went through this gentleman's maccaroni works, which are very extensive, and there I saw the various processes employed in the preparation of this substance, which is one of the chief articles of food in the south of Europe. The mills for grinding the corn are turned by mules, and numbers of miserable looking men and women are employed in forming the paste into an infinite variety of shapes, which is then dried in the sun, and afterwards packed up for exportation. A great deal of the bread made here is sent to Alexandria, where it realizes a good price. Above the houses on the Marina is a delightful terrace, commanding a wide and extensive view of the harbour and the opposite fortifications, with the various vessels taking in their respective cargoes, among which the speronaros and polacchi, with their long curved latine sails, had a very pleasing and attractive appearance, from their uncommonly picturesque style of rigging. On a platform just above the Marina, stands a bronze statue of Neptune, holding a trident in one hand; it is the work of Giovanni Bologna, a pupil of Michael Angelo, and serves as the centre of a fountain, around which the fish-market is held.

Passing through a long excavated passage called the Lascaris Gate, you enter the Strada Levanté, and cross a drawbridge over a second fortification, beneath which is a small garden filled with orange, lemon, and cypress trees, whose cool greenness forms an agreeable contrast to the white dusty glare of the streets on first entering the city. The houses are all built of stone, of three or four stories in height, and most of them have an interior court open to the air above, (after the eastern fashion.) This forms a cool and shady retreat, and is often ornamented with spreading trees and shrubs growing in pots. Here the Maltese females generally sit and spin, or employ themselves in needle-work. The floors, even of the bed-rooms, are all paved with tiles or flag-stones, and the roofs of all the houses are flat and without chimneys; and in the cool of the evening after sunset, the people often resort to the housetop to enjoy the sea breeze, and pass the time in conversation. In front of the dwellings there are generally one or two balconies jutting out into the street several feet from the wall. These are sometimes furnished with glass windows, and sometimes screened with blinds made of India matting, which form a characteristic feature in the houses of Malta. The streets, though regular, from the declivity on which part of the city is built, are so steep as to be composed of stairs, which Byron recollected with no very pleasant feeling in his lines entitled, "Farewell to Malta." At night the city is badly lighted; a small lamp fixed in the corner of every alternate street being the only guide for passengers; but the inhabitants retire to rest so very early, that comparatively few persons are seen in the streets after dark.

I found Mr. S. at his residence in the Strada Zecca, and, after a little conversation, he recommended me to take lodgings with an English family who resided in an adjoining street, and I proceeded thither, accompanied by Josef Soler, who being able to speak English pretty fluently was of great service to me, and by informing me of the price of provisions, &c., saved me from frequent imposition. Finding that the lodgings I was in search of were all engaged, I was recommended to try those kept by Signor Fabreschi, a Leghornese merchant in reduced circumstances. Here I engaged a bedroom only, as I found it to be the most convenient method to take my meals at the café, or restaurateur in the adjoining street. I soon found in this family all that I could wish for, as they did every thing in their power to render me comfortable, and make my stay in Valetta as agreeable as possible.

On my arrival, one of the first pieces of information I heard was, that there had been no rain in Malta for four years, and that water was in consequence extremely scarce. Indeed, the country in most parts resembled a barren desert, the fields being so parched up that not a single blade of grass was to be seen; and the constant glare of the burning sun upon the white rock, and the clouds of dust that arose on every breath of wind, rendered it extremely unpleasant to the eyes. There was, however, still some water in the public fountains in Valetta, and on passing any of these I was generally sure to see some twenty or thirty poor creatures gathered around with small water barrels to take home this valuable necessary to their wives and families.

All were of course eager to be served first, which gave rise to endless quarrels and contentions, in which the strongest party was of course victorious. In many of the casals or villages, the people are obliged to buy their water at the rate of one half-penny a gallon; this is supplied to them by water-carts from the aqueduct, built by the Grand Master, Wignacourt, A.D. 1610.

The principal street of Valetta is Strada Reale, which extends from the gate of the same name as far as the castle of St. Elmo; a distance of three quarters of a mile. The city is closed by three gates; Porta Reale, which is the chief entrance from the country, and the suburban town of Floriana; Porta Marsamuscetto, from the quarantine harbour; and the Marina gate, from the Grand Harbour.

Before the arrival of the order of St. John, the capital of the island was the Citta Notabile, or Civitta Vecchia, as it is generally called. The first stone of the new city was laid by the Grand Master, La Valette, on the 28th March, 1566, and the whole was completed by his successor, Pietro de Monte, in May, 1571. The population of Valetta, including Floriana, is estimated at about 30,000, and that of the whole island at 120,000. Gozo contains 18,000 more, consequently it is one of the most thickly populated places on the face of the earth. The Maltese are generally of an ordinary stature, strong, robust, and of a sallow complexion; the country people are very tawny, and are said to bear extreme heat better than any other nation. They have large black eyes, and those you see in the towns are occasionally handsome; they are full of fire, and endowed with a warm and lively imagination, and in their love and hatred, as well as in their general opinions, they are tenacious and affectionate. Notwithstanding the natural fertility of the island beneath a sky of almost continued serenity, the population is so dense that a large portion of the supplies of grain, fruit, vegetables, &c., on which most of the inhabitants subsist, is constantly brought over in boats from Sicily. Many of the overplus population find an asylum in the Barbary states, in Egypt, Syria, and Turkey. The language is certainly a dialect of the Arabic; and in many of the villages, and particularly in Gozo, its original is preserved almost pure. In Valetta most of the better classes understand Italian, and some few speak English, though not nearly so many as I should have supposed. In the town, there is a normal school, attended by about 500 children, as well as several private schools for the children of the better classes. Education is, however, chiefly in the hands of the priests. The Government University is a large building, and is attended by about 90 students; in the Lyceum, there are nearly 100. It is governed by a rector, and has professors in the four faculties of arts, theology, law, and medicine. There is a confessor appointed for the youthful pupils, who pay 2s. 6d. per month each; those of the Lyceum pay 1s. per month, and both have the use of the extensive library belonging to Government.

D

CHAPTER III.

" There is a glory in the setting beams
  Of heaven's bright sun at even,
  When, through a bank of purple clouds,
  He streaks the western sky
  With many coloured radiances,
  Of amber and of gold,
  Till one ineffable brightness
  Pervades the wondrous scene ;
  And, like an orbed glory
  Steeped in vermilion light,
  He rolls his chariot-wheels away
  Along a path of fire."

126, Strada Dominico.

I HAVE just returned from a pleasant walk in the country, where I have been to see Mr. Agius's villa and farm, accompanied by his two sons, Antonio and Tancredi. We left the city by the Marina gate, and walked along the shore of the Grand Harbour to Marsa, where there is a pillar erected on the beach. This spot commands a fine view of the harbour and the surrounding country. As we strolled along, the music from the men-of-war sounded cheerfully across the water, and broke the calm and pleasing stillness of the evening. The air was delicious ; indeed the only time in this warm climate, suitable for walking, is either at sunset, or else very early in the morning. When we had gained the summit of the hill, the sun was just setting behind a bank of resplendent clouds. The whole western horizon was tinged with a deep orange-yellow, and small clouds scattering their golden light along the sky, contrasted their exquisite beauty with the blue of the surrounding heavens. Occasionally we could see the gleaming lightning shine between the clouds, whose darkened edges became in an instant vividly bright, and added a glorious and impressive grandeur to the prospect. On passing the walls of Pieta, we encountered a most remarkable-looking personage, whose appearance strongly reminded me of the idea I had formed of a ghost in my younger days. He was dressed wholly in white, with a thick veil covering his head and face, and two holes left for his eyes ; in one hand he held a small box for money, and my companions explained to me that he was a religious beggar called the "Fratello dell' anima Justiziate," or brother of the souls in purgatory. By and by we reached the farm, but it only resembled an English farm in name. We entered beneath a portly archway, painted with divers strange representations of camels, goats, and birds, and other creatures whose names I was unable to divine; above every door-way was a cow's head, carved in stone, and painted to resemble life. The cattle, of which there were nearly 300, were all tied up in rows outside long stone sheds, into which they are put at night, and in wet weather. These creatures were all under-going the process of fattening, and some of them were really handsome : those from Barbary and Sicily I admired most, as the native Maltese cattle are all of a small size. It is from this farm that most of the men-of-war calling at Malta are supplied with beef. These animals are fed chiefly on hay, and other supplies brought from Sicily, as the present excessive drought has put a stop to almost all cultivation in the island. By far the greater part of the cattle consumed in Malta are brought over from the Barbary states, and yield very good beef. The sheep are also from Barbary, and of a very different breed from our own; they are frequently black and spotted; with long legs, and wool almost approaching to the structure and consistence of hair. But the most numerous and valuable animals which the Maltese possess are their goats, of which it is computed there are about 12,000 on the island; they are handsome crea-tures, with very long hair, silky and of every variety of colour; black, white, dappled, and fawn being the most common. Their milk is plentiful and very good, though from the scarcity of water its price has of late been raised. The streets of Valetta are full of them, and it is the custom for the milkman to lead about his goats every morning and evening to serve his customers at their respective houses.

Horses, which are scarce, are of the Barbary breed : the mules and asses of Malta and Gozo are remarkable for their large size and their elegant shape, and are the chief vehicles employed for draught and burden; they are very numerous, especially the mules, which are generally used for riding.

The race of Maltese dogs, so renowned for their scarcity and singular appearance, is now nearly extinct, though they may still be obtained at an exceedingly high price. They are very small, with long glistening hair reaching down to the feet, and a turned-up nose. Buffon terms them "Bichon" in his Natural History. Her Majesty Queen Adelaide procured one of these little creatures during her residence in Malta. It was carried to England, where it was greatly admired as being the only one of its race in the whole country.

We returned home by the light of the moon, and in passing through the suburban streets of Floriana we were serenaded by the chirping of numberless crickets. The Maltese seem greatly attached to these insects; they capture them as we would a bird, and hang them up in little wicker cages, full of leaves, outside their windows.

CHAPTER IV.

THE KNIGHTS OF ST. JOHN OF JERUSALEM.

" Lo, I must tell a tale of chivalry !"

In speaking of the island of Malta, I should be guilty of an important omission if I neglected to mention the knightly order of St. John of Jerusalem, which occupied this spot for nearly 300 years, and with whose history the name of Malta must be ever associated. On the 23rd of March, 1530, Charles the Fifth, king of Sicily, gave over to the order of St. John of Jerusalem the islands of Malta, Gozo, and Comino, with Tripoli, in Africa, as a free and noble fief under certain conditions. The remains of the order, who had fled from the island of Rhodes, and were then in the Papal States, took possession of this grant in the autumn of the same year. The island, after having successively been under the dominion of the Phœnicians, Greeks, and Carthaginians, fell from the hands of the Romans during the middle ages under the precarious sway of the Arabs, and Sicilians, but now began to rise into importance under the military government of the knights. On their arrival they found the island in a state of great destitution, and exposed to continued attacks from the Turks and Barbary corsairs. The first act of the Grand Master was to refortify the old castle of St. Angelo, which was built by the Arabs ; and thus to secure a defence against the attacks of his enemies. In 1546, the famous corsair Dragut effected a landing, and sacked the village of Tarshien, but was compelled to retreat with great loss. After this, repeated attempts were made by the Turks to gain possession of the island, and they were as often repulsed, till under the reign of John de. la Valette, Malta underwent its severest assault from the hands of the same people. Solyman, enraged at the seizure of a Turkish galleon belonging to his chief eunuch, vowed the destruction of Malta, and for that purpose sent a formidable armament under Dragut, the admiral of the Algerine fleet, which appeared off the island, in May 1565.

They first attacked the fort of St. Elmo, but after a most desperate battle, and a loss of 3000 men, the Turks were obliged to suspend their operations. The assault was, however, soon afterwards renewed, and 300 knights perished on the occasion. The cruel Turk, who had now lost 8000 men, wishing to be revenged for the death of his troops, ordered a search to be made amongst the dead and wounded for the knights, whose hearts he ripped out, and after cutting their bosoms in the form of a cross, commanded them to be set afloat upon boards, intending that the tide should carry them across to St. Angelo, where the forces of La Valette were. By way of reprisal, the Grand Master ordered all the Turkish prisoners to be put to death, and loading his cannon with their still bleeding heads, he fired them into the enemy's camp !

In the following year, after the defeat of the Turks, the first stone of the city of Valetta was laid, and the fort of St. Elmo repaired and fortified. On the death of La Valette, the city was completed by Grand Master Pietro de Monté, and from that time it became the seat of government. The successive Grand Masters continued the fortifications which were begun under La Valette, raised numerous forts along the coast, and established various works and institutions.

During the Grand Mastership of Emmanuel de Pinto, the king of Sicily made pretensions to the kingdom of Malta, declaring that it had only been yielded up to the Order on condition that the supreme sovereignty should still be vested in the hands of the kings of Sicily. For this purpose he sent an embassy styled the "Monarchia," to desire the knights to resign the island at once into his hands. This proceeding the knights treated with contempt, and the result was, that all the ports of Sicily were closed against Maltese vessels. This was a terrible blow to Malta, as all her supplies were then derived from that quarter. The Grand Master, however, entered into a truce with the Turks, who gladly accepted his proposals, and the united powers soon made the king of Sicily feel that he had raised up against himself a formidable enemy ; and after losing many of his vessels, he sought for peace, and made all possible reparation to the Grand Master for the war which he had occasioned.

The bailiff Emmanuel de Rohan, of the lineage of France, succeeded Ximenes, the successor of Pinto, in the year 1775. He formed a regular battalion of infantry, improved the judicial courts, and facilitated public education. But this prosperity was not of long duration, for during the latter part of his reign the Order suffered various losses by the extinction of several of its commanderies, and the exhausted state of its resources. During the reign of his successor Hompesch, it was found necessary to melt the plate of the galleys and hospitals.

The French government, which for some time had manifested a spirit of hostility to the Order, now came forward to display it more openly. On the 6th of June, 1798, a division of the French fleet arrived before the port of Malta. Through the treachery of some of the knights, the French army gained possession of most of the important posts in the country with scarcely any resistance, and after a short time it was resolved to yield up the city into the hands of the besiegers. No sooner did the

French find themselves masters of the island, than they required all the knights to leave it within three days. About £10 was advanced to each knight for the expenses of his journey, but he was not allowed to depart till he had torn the cross from his breast, and mounted the tri-coloured cockade. Hompesch, the last Grand Master, embarked, accompanied by twelve knights, on board a merchant vessel bound to Trieste, and in 1804 this unfortunate man died at Montpelier, in the sixty-second year of his age. The knights who fared best in the general dispersion were those who took refuge in the Russian dominions. The Emperor Paul was solemnly inaugurated as the seventieth master of the Order in the year 1798. At the same time the standard of St. John was hoisted on the walls of St. Petersburgh, where it continues unfurled to this day.

CHAPTER V.

PALACE—ARMOURY—TAPESTRY AND PAINTINGS.

"The boast of heraldry, the pomp of power,
  And all that beauty, all that wealth e'er gave,
  Await alike th' inevitable hour—
  The paths of glory lead—but to the grave!"

I HAVE been this morning to see the palace, which is now the residence of the British Governor, who is absent on a visit to England. It was formerly the abode of the Grand Masters, and is situated on one side of the Strada Reale, having a spacious square in front, called Piazza St. Georgio. This square is the usual evening promenade of the fashionables of Malta; and every evening the military band perform here for their gratification. On the opposite side is situated the "Casino," or Exchange, where the merchants generally meet, either for business or conversation. The external appearance of the palace presents nothing striking, the whole forming a pile of massive building, about 300 feet square, surrounded on three sides by open balconies. It has two principal entrances in front, which open into a large central court. At the back of the palace is situated the market; and the stalls, which are fixed up against the whole length of the building, tend greatly to spoil the appearance of this part of the structure. The interior of the palace was beautified and adorned by Grand Master Emmanuel de Pinto. It consists of an upper and lower story, each containing a range of noble apartments, which run round the building. The interior court is surrounded with arches, and opposite the entrance is a fountain, ornamented with a bronze statue of Neptune, fixed in the wall behind it. In a smaller court adjoining the former is a racket ground, where I observed several military officers amusing themselves with this healthy exercise. On ascending the staircase to the upper suite of apartments, I found the person whose duty it is to conduct strangers through the palace. After proceeding through several spacious halls, embellished with old paintings of the battles of the "Order," executed by Matteo da Lacce, I passed into the waiting-room, the walls of which were hung with the productions of two modern Maltese artists of considerable merit—Caruana and Bussatil. The former of these is certainly the most pleasing master; and his painting of St. Michael is very good, both as regards composition and colouring. The other pictures which more particularly attracted my attention were, St. George and the Dragon, St. Peter, Mary Magdalen, and Eneas. Some of the works of art in the suite of apartments are by Caravaggio, Guisippe d'Arpino, and the Cavalier Favray. There is a full-length portrait of the Grand Master Wignacourt, clad in a splendid suit of steel armour chased with gold, by Caravaggio, and is one of the finest works of art in the palace. Several ancient scriptural paintings, the gift of the Grand Master Zondadari, adorn the walls.

In the corridor, leading to the armoury, I was shown a room entirely hung with very beautiful tapestry, each piece was about twelve feet high, and from six to eight feet in width, and represented an infinite variety of animals, birds, flowers, and insects, tastefully grouped together, of the size of life, and all exquisitely worked in their natural colours. These extraordinary specimens of needlework were brought from France about the year 1700 : yet even at the present day the colours look quite fresh and new. But by far the most interesting sight in this palace is the armoury, which occupies a large saloon at the end of the corridor, and into which I was shown after examining the tapestry. Here are preserved the armour, and many of the warlike instruments belonging to the Knights of Malta, together with trophies of their splendid victories over the Turks. There are ninety complete suits of armour for mounted knights, and 450 cutlasses, cuirasses, and gauntlets for the infantry. These latter arms are arranged around the upper part of the room, with their respective shields, on which are portrayed the white cross of the order on a red field. The suits of armour for the men at arms are placed upright on pedestals at equal distances from each other, and are posted along the rows of muskets, looking like so many sentinels placed to guard the whole. One of these suits of armour was pointed out to me as having been experimented upon to try its power of resistance against a musket-ball ; several of which were fired at it from sixty yards distance, and only produced a very slight impression upon the steel. At one end of the room was a gigantic suit of black armour, seven feet in height, and three feet and a half in width; it must have been impossible for any man of the present age to have worn it, and I should think it only fit for a Cyclops of Mount Etna. I lifted the helmet, which alone weighs thirty-seven pounds. Adjoining this grim armour figure, stands a case containing a large assortment of musketry, daggers, guns, and other arms, which were taken by the knights from the Turks in their various engagements. Amongst them the sword of the famous Dragut was shown to me as a valuable relic. The workmanship of some of these ancient weapons is very curious, when compared with the improvements made in modern warfare. My conductor pointed out to me a cannon made of tarred rope, bound around a thin lining of copper, and covered on the outside with a coating of plaster painted black ; this curious machine was captured from the hands of the Turks in one of their attacks upon the city of Rhodes. At the other end of the hall is the complete armour of the Grand Master Alofio Wignacourt, beautifully chased in gold. Above it is a painting of the same, copied from the original by Caravaggio. The regular arms for the use of the British troops are arranged in the middle of the room, and consist of

19,555 muskets and bayonets,
1,000 pistols,
30,000 boarding pikes,

and besides these there are numerous other curious weapons of warfare, arranged in various parts of the hall. There is something melancholy in witnessing these instruments of bloodshed and death, which were wielded by men in days of yore, who have long since finished their warfare, and now sleep silently in the grave; and one can but exclaim on viewing them, "How are the mighty fallen, and the weapons of war perished!"

E

CHAPTER VI.

AUBERGES OF THE KNIGHTS—HOSPITALS.

"They meet in mirth and wassail,
  Within their lighted halls;
  The red wine sparkles in the cup,
  The banners deck the walls.
  Each noble knight and courtly page,
  The gallant and the free,
  They meet in Malta's palaces
  With shouts of revelry!"

HAVING in my last chapter described the Palace of the Grand Master, I shall now speak of the various "Auberges," or "Inns," of the Knights. Each language of the order possessed one where they all assembled and met together for the various purposes of business and entertainment. The superior of every language was dignified with a distinctive title, and held some commanding post in the government.

The Auberge de Provence is situated in the Strada Reale, and is now occupied by the Malta Union Club.

The Auberge de Castile is the largest of the whole, and occupies a delightful situation, commanding an extensive view of the surrounding country. Over the principal entrance is a marble bust of the Grand Master Pinto; and in the interior is a magnificent pyramidal staircase. This Auberge is at present in the occupation of the officers belonging to the British garrison. The other Auberges are those of Auvergne, Italy, France, Germany, Arragon, and England. When the English Commanderies were confiscated by Henry VIII., this language was succeeded by the Anglo-Bavarian. Most of these languages, besides their respective churches, had small chapels in the cathedral of St. John where many of the Knights lie buried. The present military hospital was formerly used by the Knights of Malta for the reception of the sick. It is a large building, situated at the foot of the Strada Mercanti, not far from the castle of St. Elmo; in the interior is a spacious court with a fountain in the centre. During the existence of the order, this establishment was open to strangers, as well as to the citizens, for whom suitable accommodations were provided. The Knights constantly made a practice of attending to the sick in person, and provided them with all kinds of medicine and surgical assistance free of expense, and served up their food to them on vessels of solid silver. On the arrival of the French, in 1798, they seized upon all the plate belonging to this establishment, and used the building as a military hospital. On the inhabitants demanding another, the nuns of Santa Maddalena promptly yielded up their own convent for the purpose; some of them taking refuge in the monastery of Santa Catarina, and some returning to their own homes. Opposite to this hospital is the public one for men, and adjoining it is the public female hospital founded in 1646, by the Lady Catarina Scoppi Senese, who endowed it with all her wealth.

There is another large building called La Camarata, where many of the more pious Knights were accustomed to meet together for purposes of devotion; this is now occupied by private families.

CHAPTER VII.

WALLS AND FORTIFICATIONS—CASTLES OF ST. ELMO AND ST. ANGELO—FORTS RICASOLI,
TIGNE, AND MANOEL.

BOURBON.—"Look there!
PHILIBAT.—"I look upon
A lofty battlement."

THE walls and fortifications of Valetta, and the towns on the opposite side of the harbour, are very stupendous. They have been the scene of various engagements between
the Knights and their enemies, as well as of those of more recent times, connected
with the history of our country's warfare; and some short account of them may not
therefore prove uninteresting.

The fortifications which surround the town are of great height, and many of them
are partly formed out of the limestone rock. They were in some places excavated
and raised by the Turkish slaves during the reign of the Grand Masters; and
they have at various times been greatly increased and strengthened. The walls generally measure about fifteen feet in width, and are chiefly composed of the common
limestone of the island; their total circumference is two miles and a half. The ditch
which crosses the peninsula from the Quarantine to the Grand Harbour, thereby
cutting off all communication with the city, is about one thousand feet in length,
one hundred and twenty feet deep, and as many wide. This immense ditch is crossed
by five draw-bridges; one leading into Porta Reale, which forms the principal entrance to the city, and the others connected with the covered ways called St. John's
and St. James's Cavaliers. The first fort which I visited was the Castle of St. Elmo,
situated at the extremity of the peninsula, on which the city is built. This fort was
first erected on an occasion of an attack of the Turks, in 1488. In the year 1687, it
was almost entirely rebuilt under the directions of the Grand Master Carafa; and at
the commencement of the last century the bastions were added by Grand Master
Roccaful. The bastions, as well as the fort, are built of a very hard limestone, called
by the natives, "zoncar," and they are well supplied with bombs, cannon, and other
artillery. On the angles of the ramparts are two turrets, formerly used as places of
look out: at present, however, they are closed with two slabs, one bearing an inscrip-

tion to Sir A. Ball, formerly governor of Malta; and the other, a similar one, in memory of Sir Ralph Abercrombie, whose embalmed body is enclosed in a barrel within the turret, just as it was brought from the battle of Aboukir: hence, the bastions to the west are known by the name of Ball's, and those to the east by the name of Abercrombie's bastions.

In the centre of a small square, on the most elevated part of the fort, a beautiful Grecian monument has lately been erected to the memory of Governor Ball; it is built of the Malta stone, which in this fine climate retains its dazzling whiteness unsullied for many years. Around this monument is a row of shady pimento trees, and adjoining it is an arched way formerly used as a place of amusement by the Knights, from which the distant views of land and sea are delightful, varied, and extensive. The deep azure blue of the Mediterranean sea stretched out below, till it mingles with the distant horizon, contrasts well with the snowy whiteness of the various xebecs, galliots, and other boats, which appear like specks upon its surface. Far away to the north lay Capo Passaro, whence I could trace the shores of Sicily towards Palma and Alicata. On a very clear day at sunrise, Mount Etna, too, may be seen towering above the waters; but this is not, as many writers have supposed, an every-day occurrence. On the outermost angle of the fort stands the lighthouse, which has lately been much improved by the British Government. Leaving Fort St. Elmo, I crossed the Grand Harbour in a boat to Fort St. Angelo, on the opposite shore. This stupendous work of defence was begun by the Arabs in 870; on the arrival of the Knights it was greatly enlarged, and in 1690, under Adrian de Wignacourt, it finally assumed its present aspect. Towards the Grand Harbour it presents an imposing front composed of four batteries, one above another, and each mounting fifty-one guns. The only objects worthy of notice here are the extensive powder magazines, and a small chapel containing two sienite pillars brought by the Knights from the island of Rhodes.

Fort Ricasoli is built on the extreme point of the same side of the harbour as St. Angelo, and corresponds with St. Elmo, on the opposite shore. It was built by the Cavalier Gianfrancesco Ricasoli, and was called after his name by Grand Master Cottoneo, in 1670. On the 3rd of April 1807, this fort was the scene of an event as disgraceful as it was tragical. The account given of it by a resident here, is as follows :—

"During the war a French nobleman proposed to raise for the Mediterranean service a regiment composed wholly of Greeks. The bargain being struck, he gathered together a horde of various men from the Levant,—Sclavonians, Albanians, and others,—who were enrolled under the English banner, and denominated 'Froberg's regiment.' Soon afterwards they were transported to Malta, and appointed to occupy this fort. The officers placed over them acted with great severity and harshness, which was further aggravated by the promises of advancement which had been offered

to lure them into the service proving only a deception. The occasion of an officer striking a drummer on the face with a cane, led to an open revolt, in which several of them
were put to death, and finally they closed the gates of the fortress and declared themselves independent. Internal quarrels, however, soon lessened their numbers, and
after some of them had surrendered, only about 150 of the most resolute remained
in possession of the fort. An English officer resolved upon and effected its capture ;
and all but six of the rebels were taken. These six blockaded themselves in the
powder magazine, and then protested they would blow it up if any measures were
taken to seize them. Of those who were captured ten were hung, and fifteen were
musketted on the plain of Floriana. Pinioned and handcuffed, they were made to
kneel upon their coffins without being blindfolded, and after the first volley was fired
at them, several who were not mortally wounded rose up and ran about the plain pursued by the soldiers like so many hares. One of them in particular managed to reach
the bastions, from whence he cast himself headlong down a height of 150 feet." Indeed the account which I have heard of these barbarities is almost too shocking to be
remembered, and stands out as a foul blot on the characters of all connected with them.
" The six rebels who remained, after seeking in vain for pardon, threatened after six
days, in case of refusal, that they would blow up the fort as soon as the first vesper
bell tolled from the cathedral of St. John. All was still till the appointed hour, when
the fatal crash was heard, and the whole building was seen rising a mass of ruins into
the air ! Some time passed away, and the affair was almost forgotten, when one
lonely night a priest returning homewards on a donkey was terrified at the sight of
a man in the ' Froberg' uniform, pointing a musket at him over a wall. The affrighted
Father took to his heels, and on giving his information, an armed force was sent in
pursuit of the bandits. Pale and emaciated they were led into the town, and shortly
afterwards publicly executed. It appears that during the siege they carried out one
of the mines to the extremity of the fortifications, and left only a thin wall through
which to escape. When all was ready they laid the train, and at the moment of
firing, made their exit by this means, hoping that some vessel might appear on the
coast in which they might return to their native country, from whence they had been
so shamefully and cruelly decoyed away."

On the opposite side of the Quarantine Harbour, stands Fort Manoel, which is now
used as a lazaretto for persons arriving in vessels which are obliged to undergo
quarantine. The quarantine regulations of Malta are very strict, and all vessels
arriving from the eastward have to pass from ten to thirty days in the Quarantine
Harbour before they are allowed to hold any communication with the shore. For
passengers, especially, this proves a very great nuisance. They are allowed an apartment in the lazaretto, furnished with one table, two chairs, and a bed-board. If they
wish for any more furniture they can bespeak it of a person who supplies it, however,

at a very high rate. As to food, it is said that if a person has not means wherewith to pay for a breakfast or dinner, at the enormous rate charged by the " Trattoria," he stands a very good chance of being starved to death.

To the north-east of Fort Manoel stands Fort Tigné, on the point called Cape Dragut, where that famous corsair was slain in the great siege of Malta. It is intended to act in conjunction with Fort St. Elmo, for the defence of the Quarantine Harbour, and is strongly fortified.

The walls of the city measure about fifteen feet in width, and their entire circumference is about two miles and a half. The ditch is a stupendous work, one thousand feet in length, one hundred and twenty feet deep, and the same in width. The bottom of this ditch is cultivated, and on looking over the drawbridge of Porta Reale, I saw fig-trees and prickly pears growing in this gulf below me; whilst here and there a sportive summer butterfly could be seen wandering like some light creature of the element over the green leaves of the stunted trees.

I went through the two underground passages which lead out of the city, called St. John's and St. James's Cavaliers: they are cut out of the solid limestone, and the air strikes very cold on entering them from the sultry atmosphere without. There are many outworks and glacis of massive stone beyond these walls, and a second series of fortifications outside the suburbs of Floriana, which render the city of Valetta one of the best fortified in the whole world. I finished my survey by a walk along the walls overlooking the ditch. That part called the Baracca, commands a very fine view of the harbour and the surrounding country, which looks like a parched desert covered with walls and buildings, over which the eye wanders in vain in search of some spot of green to relieve and cheer the burning glare of this southern landscape. In the centre of this platform, within a grove of trees, stands the tomb of Sir Thomas Maitland, one of the late governors of Malta; and several other monuments are raised in various parts of this fortification.

CHAPTER VIII.

RAMBLE IN THE COUNTRY—PIETA—BATHS.

" Where the shrill chirp of the green lizard's love
Broke on the sultry silentness alone."

I ROSE in the morning before five o'clock, after a refreshing night's rest, undisturbed by the mosquitos, though numbers of them had entered in at the open window, and were buzzing around the room in search of a victim. My muslin curtains were closed, so I had nothing to fear. During the night the thermometer stood at 80°, though I did not feel the heat at all unpleasant. The bedrooms in Malta are paved with tiles, which greatly helps to keep them cool. After eating a few grapes I set out with Joseph Soler in search of insects. We passed through the Porta Reale, and soon found ourselves on the parched plain of Floriana. Almost the first objects that attracted my attention were the numberless lizards that darted in and out of every crevice among the stone walls, and turning their slender and graceful forms in every variety of attitude. Sometimes they would rest for a moment on the side of a projecting rock, and suddenly raising their heads, as if in the act of listening, would dart off again with the speed of thought, and disappear in the nearest crevice. I also saw a small species of locust with red wings; the natives call these " Farfetta." By and by I caught several of these, which had pale blue wings, and with the exception of a few ants, and some black beetles, were almost the only insects I met with on the plains of Floriana. After returning to breakfast at the café, I set out again alone, and took my way along a path which overlooked the harbour. Presently I came to an old fort where a soldier was keeping guard. A great variety of thistles and sharp prickly herbs grew around, and a very aromatic plant, on every tuft of which I found specimens of the crimson-speckled footman moth (Deiopeia pulchella.) These moths are the most numerous of the Maltese lepidoptera; and in St. Paul's Bay, and some other places, they are in such great abundance that one can scarcely tread without raising a whole troop of them. It is worthy of remark, that this species is found about this latitude, distributed over a tract of country forming a belt around the whole globe. In Great Britain this species is exceedingly rare, and in the West Indies its place is supplied by a species closely allied to it, but of a deeper colour. I found the caper plant growing in great abundance on walls and the sides of rocks; it bears a beautiful blossom of a lilac colour.   After spending some time around this fort, searching for land shells and minute insects, I observed a narrow path leading to the right.   This I followed for some distance until I arrived at the village of Pietà, situated on the western side of the Quarantine Harbour.   It is prettily placed, and commands an extensive view of the water.   Feeling very thirsty, and seeing a woman standing at the door of a cottage, I made signs to her to sell me some milk.   Unfortunately the goats were all dry, and the woman shook her head and said "Nix," a common Maltese term for a negation, said to be derived from the German, though "Li" is their general word for "No."—"Eva" signifies "Yes."   A little farther on I fell in with a respectable looking man who spoke English.   Observing that I was collecting insects, he very kindly gave me permission to visit his master's garden, which was situated a little higher up the hill.   This garden belongs to an English gentleman resident in Malta, and is one of the prettiest and best cultivated of any I have seen.   The walks are paved with flag-stones, and stone pillars extend along on each side, over which the vines are trailed so as to form a complete canopy, which is a delightful protection from the heat of the noon-day sun.   There is a well in the garden, and most of the orange and other fruit trees have a small reservoir around them, which is filled with water at stated times.   A variety of flowers and shrubs adorn the borders; amongst which the large blossoms of the white jessamine breathed a delicious perfume on the air, and from the feathery boughs of the drooping pimento the redstart and the nightingale poured forth their songs.   It seemed a little paradise in the desert, and reminded one of the oases in the sands of Lybia and Egypt.   The presence of several palm trees gave an oriental appearance to the spot, and the Papilio Machaon, and other brilliant butterflies, swept swiftly through the sultry atmosphere, whilst the beautiful violet bee sought for honey in the clustering petals of the Turkish rose.   The principal curiosity in this garden is a deep hole in the rock which was originally filled with rich clay, but which has since been taken out to form the present soil.   This hollow descends almost perpendicularly for fifty or sixty feet and has an underground communication with the sea.   The owner has erected a tasteful balcony of stone work around the upper opening, and another half way down, which is approached by steps, and forms a very cool and shady retreat from the sun.   The wild parsley, which is common in underground places in Malta, grows in this ravine.   When her Majesty Queen Adelaide visited Malta, she came to see this remarkable spot, which certainly presents a very curious geological phenomenon, and one not easily accounted for.   Leaving this delightful place, I returned towards Valetta by another road.   The heat was excessive, not a breath of wind fanned the atmosphere; at the bottom of the hill lay the Quarantine Harbour, and just as I was longing to plunge into its transparent waters, I observed the sign over the door of the bath house of Pietà.   I went in, and after getting perfectly cool, I enjoyed a most refreshing plunge, and amused myself with catching the hermit crabs and top-shells that crept amongst the sea-weed which lined the sides and floor of the bath. Bathing is one of the greatest luxuries which can be enjoyed in Malta, and seems almost indispensable to health. The bath house of Pietà is pleasant and commodious, but it is much to be regretted that larger buildings devoted to the same purpose have not been erected in the immediate vicinity of Valetta, for the accommodation of the English residents there.

CHAPTER IX.

COSTUME—DRESS OF THE COUNTRY PEOPLE.

"And such was she, the lady of the cave:
  Her dress was very different from the Spanish,
  Simpler, and yet of colours not so grave;
  For as you know the Spanish women banish
  Bright hues when out of doors, and yet while wave
  Around them (what I hope will never vanish,)
  The basquinah and the mantilla, they
  Seem at the same time mystical and gay."

THE costume of the upper classes among the male population in Valetta is generally French, but the native dress is still worn by many of the lower classes. Its chief peculiarity is the Phrygian cap, which resembles a long bag made of wool hanging down behind, or over the left shoulder. This cap is of various colours, but generally it is either blue, brown, or white. On Sundays and gala days they generally wear a better sort of cap, of a crimson colour, which is dyed with the kermes of Barbary, and much esteemed. This article often forms a receptacle for small things which the wearer may wish to carry about with him; and sometimes it serves also as a purse. A girdle is frequently worn by the lower orders; it is generally from three to four yards in length, and with it the pantaloons are confined around the waist; this portion of the dress is commonly made of blue plaid cotton, and is called a "terha;" it is sometimes composed of red or yellow silk, when it is denominated a "bushakka." Those who wear this dress do not commonly have a jacket, its place being supplied by a "sedria," or vest, which if the wearer can afford it, is often ornamented down the front with several rows of silver buttons as large as half-crowns. At other times, instead of these I have seen them wear quarter-dollar pieces, and sometimes shillings with metal shanks fastened to them. A Maltese thus equipped, or "in gala," as they term it, presents a very smart figure, with a long curl of hair hanging down on each side of his face, and his fingers ornamented with massive rings, to which the Maltese are extremely partial. After the death of a near relation the men suffer their hair to grow very long. This custom I observed in the country, but particularly in the island of

Gozo, where the ancient manners are more strictly preserved than in Malta. Sandals are now only worn by the country people, and the capuchin friars ; but they used formerly to constitute a necessary appendage to the native dress :—they consist of two oblong pieces of untanned bull's hide drawn round the foot by two strings of the same material, and are called " kork." Most of the men and boys of the working classes wear over their shoulder what they call a " khurg," in which they carry their provisions to town for the day, and on their return home it is filled with supplies for their families. It is about three yards long and two wide, open in the middle, and reminds one of a gigantic purse.

As to the costume of the ladies of Valetta, a Jesuit writer very justly observes, " leur démarche et leur habillement sont si modestes, qu'on les prendroit pour des religieuses." It is certainly to be regretted that so many of them have lately adopted the English costume, which is far from being as simple and as modest as their own. The walking dress consists of a skirt of black silk worn over a body of some light material ; this is called a half " onella." The upper part or head dress is called the " onella" or " faldetta," and is likewise made of black silk, part of which is bound with whalebone ; and, on being drawn over the head, forms an elegant arch, displaying the countenance of the wearer in the most favourable manner possible. The whole is extremely neat, but it requires a peculiar grace in walking to show it off to advantage, in which respect the Maltese ladies are by no means deficient. The head-dress of the country-women consists either of a " faldetta" made of barred cotton, or a simple white hand-kerchief thrown over the head. On particular occasions they put on a " gezwira," which is a petticoat of blue cotton drawn up into very thick folds around the waist, and open on the right side, where it is fastened with bows of coloured ribbon. Very few of the country people wear shoes, and even in Valetta all the lower orders go barefooted ; most of the women, however, like to possess a pair, which are reserved for very particular occasions. The following anecdote is current in Malta :—Not long since a Maltese overheard a countrywoman ask her companion while engaged at their outdoor toilet, beside the walls of the city, how long she had had her shoes ; the answer was, " Since the time of the plague," (1813.) " Oh," replied the other, " mine are much older than yours, for I have had them ever since the blockade of the French !" I do not vouch for the truth of this tale, but it certainly shows the economy of the Maltese countrywomen in the article of shoe leather.

CHAPTER X.

> " A rocky hill which overhung the ocean :—
> From that lone ruin, where the steed that panted
> Paused, might be heard the murmur of the motion
> Of waters, as in spots which are enchanted
> To music by the wand of Solitude !"

EARLY in the morning I set out on a pedestrian excursion, accompanied by my host,
M. Michael Fabreschi, whom I found to be a very kind, obliging, and intelligent young
man. We proposed visiting the harbour and village of Marsa Scirocco, which is
situated to the south of Valetta, on the opposite side of the island. As I had already
engaged to meet my friend, Mr. S., in the afternoon, with whom I intended to make
an excursion of some length, I found our time necessarily rather limited ; but, notwithstanding the heat and dust, we managed to return at the hour I had appointed,
allowing myself a sufficient period for rest before undertaking another trip. Walking under the burning sun of Malta is altogether a very different thing from strolling
in the green fields and flowery lanes of our more northern island. Here the eye has
nothing to rest upon but parched and barren rocks, walls and buildings, which from their
glaring whiteness only render the prospect most painful to the dazzled eyes ; whilst
every breath of wind raises a cloud of suffocating dust which covers the roads to the
depth of many inches. Many of the English on their arrival in Malta become ill if they
expose themselves to the effects of the sun, and very few of them ever venture on foot
to any distance from the city :—whether pride or incapacity is the cause, I cannot
say. During the whole of my stay in Malta I was constantly exposed to the sun,
and the heat at times was very great, but I never felt any further inconvenience
from it than a profuse perspiration, which generally continued night and day without any intermission. But I am wandering from my purpose, which was to give
some account of my morning's excursion. After following the road by the margin of
the Grand Harbour, we arrived at a salt water inlet, enclosed for the purpose of rearing shellfish, on which many of the poor partly subsist. I obtained some of these

shells; they consisted chiefly of the murex brandaris, Venus casina, and pullastra, and the Cardium rusticum, all of which species are very abundant. Around the margin of this water the samphire grows in great quantities; it appears to be the same kind that occurs in Devonshire, where it is used for making an excellent pickle. Even here, however, amongst this scanty herbage the crimson-speckled moth, I have before noticed, rose into the air at almost every footstep; and the sea eagle, perched upon a jutting rock, sat silent and alone, the undisturbed monarch of the scene. The fields are surrounded with high stone walls; the cotton plant is almost the only article cultivated in them; it does not, however, attain to any great perfection in Malta, owing to the long absence of rain. We saw a boy at work among a bed of cotton plants, and obtained some of the seeds from him; they were of a brownish colour, and filled with cotton of a snowy white hue. I soon afterwards had an opportunity of observing the method in which the natives prepare it for spinning. In a small room in one of the Casals through which we passed, sat two young men stript to the waist, and almost smothered with raw cotton. Suspended from the roof were two curious instruments greatly resembling large bows strung with catgut:—through these they passed the raw substance, at the same time causing the strings to vibrate with great violence, which separated the heads of cotton, and reduced them to a light downy material; this is afterwards spun by the women, and made into native cloth, which they generally dye blue. We wanted to procure some water, but the people were so exceedingly shy that they ran away at our approach. An old woman, however, who had more the appearance of a dried mummy than any thing possessing life and blood, at last offered us a small pitcher of water, and after we had satisfied our thirst we paid her three grains, which are equivalent to an English farthing, for its limpid contents. The prickly pear grows most abundantly all over Malta, and forms one of the chief articles of food among the lower classes. The mode of preparing this singular fruit is curious. In its natural state of growth it is covered with small prickles, as are also the leaves and blossoms, and as fast as we could eat them the poor woman cut off the tops and bottoms, and then pared off the surrounding skin in a very expert and dexterous manner, handing the pulpy interior to her stranger guests with as much politeness and expedition as a French waiter of the first order. The peasants of Malta and Gozo are said to be an honest and harmless set of people. They live principally upon fish, fruits, and black bread; and the best provisions that their cottages afford are always set before the stranger who pauses at their door. We left the old woman's hut where we had partaken of the prickly pears, and descended a hill by a winding and circuitous path, which brought us suddenly in sight of the harbour of Marsa Scirocco, which is a large inlet of the sea on the southern side of the Island, as its name imports. Here we entered a fisherman's cottage, and if it had been possible to have aroused the spirit of Wilkie, a most amusing picture might have been painted.

At a large table on one side of the house sat the hostess, an immoderately fat woman, busied in dressing small fish called "sweethearts." Opposite to her was a group of men, women, and children, extending to the third and even fourth generation. At the door sat the grandfather and grandmother, whose snowy locks and timeworn countenances carried the beholder's memory back to distant days when the shrivelled forms before him sported as gaily as the little grandchild who brought her tiny bag of shells to earn a few pence from the occasional stranger. The back ground melted away into an interminable maze of shelves, bottles, jars, and a thousand articles, the necessary appendages to a Maltese cottage; whilst the foreground was enlivened by a strange medley of dogs and cats, ravenous almost to starvation. A quantity of fishing baskets hung about the walls. I purchased a small one to bring over to England, as their construction is very singular. At one end they have an aperture, through which the fish enter but cannot get out, and when baited with small crabs are sunk by a stone to the bottom of the water, where they are allowed to remain all night. Close to the harbour is a tank where a number of Maltese women and maidens were busily employed in washing. They first place their garments which are to be operated upon in the water, and after treading them out with their feet, they afterwards beat them most violently with wooden spatulas on the edge of the tank. A statue of St. Rocco stands on the shore, and two or three cottages are scattered along the margin of the bay. Leaving this place we turned our steps homewards, in order to be at Valetta in time to join my friend in the afternoon. Passing by a number of parched carob trees we returned by a different route to Vittorioso, and crossing the Grand Harbour in a "barca del passo," we returned to Strada St. Dominico, where after having partaken of some refreshment, I waited the arrival of Mr. S. with the horses for our proposed trip to Macluba, and the ruins of Hajar Kïm. We set out at four o'clock P.M., and after a delightful ride of seven miles, we reached the village of Macluba; and leaving the horses in the care of a peasant, we went on to the grotto accompanied by some women and children who acted as our guides. The oldest woman was the proprietor of the place, and carried the key of the entrance gate. We descended a rude flight of steps cut out of the solid rock, which conducted us into an oval hollow in the earth, which sunk abruptly from the surface to the depth of 130 feet. At the bottom we found a pleasant garden abounding with various fruit trees. The length of this deep hollow is 330 feet, and its width about 200 feet. The appearance of the inner sides is very wild and craggy, the rocks around are broken and scattered about in every direction, and the entire surface of the adjacent land bears evident signs of having at some former period undergone a violent natural convulsion. The land around begins to slope gradually until it reaches this spot, when it sinks abruptly down into a deep hollow. The word "Macluba," signifies "overturned;" and there is a tradition current among the inhabitants of the neighbourhood, that this spot was once the site of an ancient village, the inhabitants of which, like those of Sodom and Gomorrah, so displeased the Almighty that he caused the earth to open and swallow them up, as was the case with the tents of Korah. My friend Mr. S., climbed a tree to pick some small white grapes which were extremely sweet; and whilst our guides regaled us with the crimson seeds of the pomegranates, one of them recounted a story of a woman having been blown over the precipice, who alighted in the fruit trees without sustaining any injury whatever. My companion, having been long resident in the Island, spoke the native language very fluently, and kindly acted as my interpreter on these occasions. Having seen all the wonders of this place we ascended the steep and rugged steps that led up to the surface of the earth, and re-mounting our horses we started off immediately to the ruins of Hajar Kïm. Upon leaving the village of Crendi, our road lay over a rocky path, which was in some places very abrupt, and more fitted for mules than for the slight and graceful barbs which bore us. When we reached the summit of the hill we had been ascending, I was agreeably surprised by a sudden view of the sea below us, which burst unexpect-edly upon our sight. It was blue—deep hazy blue—as far as the weary eye could reach towards the shores of Tripoli. In the distance the rock of Filfila arose darkly from the sapphire plain, for the shades of evening already began to blend the garish tints of day into a mellow and sombre hue. I shall never forget the refreshing sight of that deep blue sea, after a day's toil among the parched and arid rocks of Malta. We reached the first ruin of Hajar Kïm, (for there are two distinct spots where these singular remains have been discovered,) after crossing a scorched plain studded with golden rod and other bulbous roots. A peasant residing in an adjacent hut acted as our guide, and leaving our horses at the point we had reached, we proceeded on foot to examine the ruins. They consisted of two separate chambers of an oval form opening into each other by a doorway composed of two large upright stones, with a third placed crosswise on the top. Communicating with these chambers are several smaller ones, in one of which are the remains of a fire-place. There are also several curious, but rudely carved relics scattered around. One of these in the largest apart-ment seemed to have been an altar for religious purposes. The whole was in the rudest style of primitive architecture, and is supposed to have been the work of the Phœni-cians, who occupied this island many ages since. The second mass of ruins is situ-ated at some distance lower down the hill, and greatly resembles the former in the style of building employed. These ruins were brought back to the light of day some years since. They were found buried under mounds of earth; and among the second ruins five or six skeletons were discovered, lying arranged upon flat stones in various recesses raised above the ground in the sides of the several chambers. Whether these habitations had been formerly covered in, may be considered doubtful. I should suppose that in this dry climate the original inhabitants would have scarcely needed a protection from the weather, especially in the remote ages of antiquity, during which these places were built. It appeared to me that these temples were originally dedicated to some heathen deity, or were, perhaps, designed for the worhip of the sun. As the twilight was fast approaching we hastened up the hill to rejoin our horses, where they were waiting for us, at the first mass of ruins we had visited. Here and there we roused a solitary quail, the lone possessor of this silent and sterile spot. The peasant who held our horses had a number of them in a bag, which he wished to give me; but being unable to carry them home, I was reluctantly obliged to decline his offer. Before we regained the hut I felt much fatigue, and suffered greatly from excessive thirst. Indeed my mouth was so parched that I would have given any thing I possessed for a glass of water, but not one drop of it was to be obtained. It reminded me of the descriptions I had read of the horrors of thirst, experienced by the unfortunate traveller in the arid deserts of Africa, and the lingering death of many a feeble pilgrim whose bones whiten in the burning sun that darts down from an unclouded canopy of perpetual boundless blue. On leaving the ruins our path lay in many places over large and slippery rocks, whose smooth surface was very dangerous for the horses' feet. I proceeded in safety until I arrived at the last surface of rock, which was worn and glassy; on reaching the centre of it my horse's legs slipped from under him, and before I was able to extricate myself from the stirrups, the horse fell with his whole weight on my leg and foot. I managed, however, to keep my seat until the old Maltese, who was our guide, seeing my situation came running back uttering loud cries, and with the assistance of another man he succeeded in extricating my leg and foot. The poor animal was much frightened, and lay quite still; but I must confess that his heavy body pressing on the hard rock gave my limb a squeeze that I did not at all relish. At first they feared that my leg was broken, but I found, fortunately for myself, that it was only severely bruised, and my foot swollen. By this time a number of the natives had gathered around me; the old man laid me down upon the sand whilst Mr. S. rode off for some water. I became giddy and faint from the pain of the bruise, and the fatigue, but more especially from the dreadful thirst I was suffering. Some water was soon brought, and after drinking it I was assisted by the old man into his cottage, which stood but a few paces off. Here I lay down upon a small straw pallet, and as my friend had an engagement at Valetta at eight in the evening, he returned thither immediately, promising to send back a calise and a man to convey me home. I was now surrounded by the whole village, men, women, and children, who filled the cottage, all chattering to one another in their strange language, whilst the old man was unceasing in his attentions to me, every now and then examining my foot, and wrapping it up in a cloth with the greatest care, and all the while uttering the most mournful exclamations. After a time the chief of the village came in, and brought a small quantity of rum, with which they rubbed my foot, and he sat by my side until the calise arrived, which was at ten o'clock. I can truly say of these people that they retain until the present day that which St. Paul said of them when shipwrecked here, which was, that they "showed us no little kindness." On the arrival of the calise two men contested for the privilege of escorting me to Valetta, one of whom was my old and hospitable host. However, the man appointed by my friend Mr. S. had the prior claim, and the old man contented himself with running for a mile or two by the side of the conveyance. I made him a small present, and he came to the window of the calise to kiss my hand, which is the common custom among the natives on taking leave of a stranger. The lightning was very vivid as we proceeded homewards, and the air extremely sultry. We arrived at Valetta shortly before midnight, and on entering the Porta Bombe I met my friend Mr. S. who had sallied out in search of me. On reaching my lodgings I found my kind landlord awaiting my return, and on learning that I had met with an accident, he immediately showed me every possible kindness and attention. Thus ended the expedition to Hajar Kïm, which, fortunately for me, was attended with no worse effects than a sprained ankle; but as I found that it would be impossible for me to walk the next morning, I arranged a plan for visiting Mellieha and St. Paul's Bay, with Fabreschi, who agreed to order the boat and get provisions ready by sunrise.

CHAPTER XI.

> " The white clouds are driving merrily,
> And the stars we miss this morn will light
> More willingly our return to-night.
> List, my dear fellow, the breeze blows fair ;
> How it scatters Dominic's long black hair."

As usual, a lovely morning broke over Malta, and ere the sun was well up above the azure bosom of the Mediterranean, the boat was all ready for our voyage. Fabreschi had paid a visit to the market, where he laid in a stock of provisions for the day for ourselves and the boatmen. We hastened to the Marina, and soon found ourselves seated beneath a canopy of blue striped cotton in one of the native flat-bottomed boats. Two boys brought our provisions, which consisted of bread and goat's cheese, melons, and a large keg filled with black and white grapes, as well as some Sicilian wine, and an immense bundle of celery for the men. After a short delay caused by filling up our water jars, I desired the boatmen to pull across to the schooner "Prospero," sending an invitation to the captain and his wife to accompany us ; they were, however, prevented doing so, and we started at once on our excursion, calling for a pass at the Pratique office, which was easily obtained. As the wind was favourable we sailed first into San Julian's Bay, passing by Sliema, where most of the English inhabitants reside. This village is prettily situated close to the water's edge, and is considered to be one of the healthiest spots in Malta. The houses are light and cheerful, and some of them are painted green and washed with various colours, which give them a very gay appearance. The wind ceased to favour us on our entering St. Julian's Bay and the men took to the oars, which, however, they used in a very lazy kind of manner. We landed at the innermost part of the bay, where there was a small sandy beach. Here I found numbers of small beetles (Cicindela) ; they were in incessant motion. I managed, however, to secure several of them ; and whilst thus employed I desired the men to seek for shells among the sand. After digging for some time, they could find nothing ; but they gave me to understand that we should meet with some in Mellieha Bay. We again entered the boat, and made the best of our way to the next place of interest. St. Julian's is a pretty spot, very secluded, and more picturesque than most parts of Malta. A statue of the saint adorns the beach, near which rises a small spring of limped water, at which we quenched our thirst.

Passing by St. George's Bay, we arrived at the Bay of the salt works. As I was very desirous to see the method of preparing the salt from the sea water by evaporation in the sun, we landed on some sharp rocks, and soon found ourselves in the midst of the salt pans. Large heaps of crystallized salt of snowy whiteness lay sparkling in the sun, and several men and boys were collecting it into baskets for use. They seemed to care but little about clothing, and one lad had nothing on but a ragged shirt. After recrossing the rocks, and furnishing ourselves with a supply of these glittering salt crystals, we again got on board and steered for St. Paul's Bay. We arrived about noon, and rowing to the Fort, showed our pass to the soldier on guard, who hailed us on landing. After searching for a shaded spot where we could enjoy our noontide repast, sheltered from the heat, we found a small sandy bank protected by the ruined wall of a stone building. After mooring our boat in a clear deep pool carpeted with green feathery sea-weed, we carried up our stores and proceeded to our repast. I had scarcely eaten a mouthful of grapes before the sand on which we were reposing was actually darkened with flies. It was in vain to drive them off, for the troublesome tormentors only returned in greater numbers, and with more audacity than before, till at last they resembled the old plague of Egypt, and fairly drove us back again to the boat; leaving them to feed on the grape-skin relics of our repast. We desired the men to pull along the shore to meet us, whilst we walked over the sand to the chapel of St. Paul, which is said to be erected over the very spot where the natives kindled the fire when the apostle was shipwrecked on this island. The scanty shrubs that grew on the beach were spangled with the coloured moth I have before described as being so very abundant; and at every step we took they rose in rich-coloured clouds upon the air. On reaching the entrance of the chapel we paused, for instead of beholding St. Paul in the doorway, we encountered a burly Maltese officer sitting at his dinner in the outer chamber of the sacred edifice, and doing ample justice to an enormous dish of boiled maccaroni. I bowed, and the officer looking up for a moment from his interesting occupation, returned my salutation. We requested permission to inspect the chapel, which was immediately granted to us, and we were invited to walk in. The only remarkable object in this small edifice is a very old painting, or rather series of paintings, around the altar-piece, descriptive of the shipwreck of St. Paul, (Acts xxviii.) The walls were whitewashed, and against one side stood an affair which I was assured contained every article relating to the sufferings and death of Christ.

We left the chapel, and descending the sandy beach, took our seats once more in the boat, and steered across the bay to examine the caverns on the opposite side. We passed a narrow channel inside the little island of Selmone, so shallow that we could easily see the bottom, when the bay of Mellieha opened to view. The wind blew fresh as we rounded the cape, but before we had proceeded far into the bay, the land so sheltered it that it fell nearly a complete calm, and our boatmen had once more recourse to their oars. At the extreme end of the bay the water was shallow for a considerable way out, and floored with fine white sand. Here we landed, and I enjoyed a delightful bathe. We searched for shells but found very few. A number of small compact balls of sea-weed lay strewn along the sand, and at a little distance from the shore grew quantities of a bright yellow flower, somewhat resembling the camomile blossom. Our next object of search was the church and village of Mellieha, which are situated at the head of a deep and rugged ravine stretching from the shore. As the wind blew quite contrary for our returning to Valetta, and I did not wish to be all night tossing about off so dangerous a coast, I dismissed the boatmen, and ascended the ravine, hoping to find at the village a calise, or, perhaps, a cart. Half way up is a small tank filled with water, which filters out of the limestone rock, and falls down the ravine towards the sea. This little stream is embowered with canes, and other masses of luxuriant vegetation, as far as the salutary influence of its waters extends. The foliage around was rich and beautiful; the cicada sang long and loud from the dark green carob and fig trees, as we ascended the winding path that led to the village; the sun was low in the western horizon, the tired butterfly folded his wings on the stone wall, and the lizard hastened to its hole. Around the tank were grouped a number of tall dark-eyed girls, filling their earthen jars with water, and, poising them on their heads as the Arab and Hindoo maidens are wont to do, they wound up the hill towards their homes, forming picturesque objects as they wandered farther away from the spectator. On arriving at the village we found the sacristan who kept charge of the keys of the church, which we were desirous of visiting. Before the door was an enclosure containing some olive trees, and several statues were dispersed along the walls. On entering we were followed by one or two of the peasants, and a fat old man who took a vast deal of trouble to explain to me the various pictures, offerings, and relics in the church. He could speak a few words of broken English, and with such assistance of this sort as he could render me, he told me a long story about a number of bishops whose forms and portraits were painted on the ceiling; but I could make little of it. At first I took him for the village blacksmith, then I believed that he might be a priest in his dishabille; but at last I discovered that he was from the neighbourhood of Valetta, and that he had a calise in the village, in which he was about to return home. He kindly offered me a seat in it, which I accepted; but we informed him that ere we returned to Valetta, we must visit the Grotto of Calypso, a short distance off. He readily agreed to wait for us, but when we came back he was gone. We found a vast number of absurd pictures hung up in one part of the church. Upon inquiry, we learned that these were placed there by mariners and boatmen, who, when overtaken by a storm, invariably make a vow to the Virgin, that if saved they will hang up a painting at her shrine, in Mellieha church. The result of all this is, that the majority of these native offerings are of an exceedingly ludicrous nature; they consist chiefly of representations of a vessel nearly engulfed by the rising waves, with the Virgin and Child appearing in the sky in the left hand corner of the picture. The church contains many other relics reckoned precious, but which are, in reality, very absurd; such as silver and waxen limbs, pieces of old cable, chains and fetters, and various other incongruous articles. We were sadly disappointed at not being able to see an original painting of St. Paul, said to have been the work of St. Luke, and which these simple people assert is under the church! Having viewed all that was worth notice here we set off for the Grotto of Calypso. Three ragged boys volunteered their services as our guides, and after leading us over a very steep and rugged path, they brought us to a series of small caves in the side of a hill, which commanded an extensive view of the sea, and the places towards Marfa. The most distant of these holes they describe as being the Calypso; but what was my astonishment on finding, instead of the cave of the goddess so enchantingly sung by Homer, only a miserable hovel, a complete pigsty! To serve still further to dispel the poetical illusion, our approach was signalized by the exit of three or four pigs, and a black donkey. I managed, however, to get clear of the live stock, and with the aid of my pencil and sketch book, I endeavoured to make the best sketch of it I could; though I must confess to having suffered a terrible mortification in finding the sacred cave employed for so unpoetical a purpose. I made one of our youthful guides sit on a stone whilst I introduced him into my picture, a circumstance which was the cause of no little merriment to him. I rewarded this "sitter" with a penny, upon which the other two immediately came forward, and very civilly gave me to understand that they wished to have their portraits also taken in a similar manner. This was an honour which I respectfully declined; and the "douceur" of one penny each satisfied all their lingering scruples, and we returned to Mellieha, hoping to get a ride home in the calise. We found, however, that the fat man had started without us, and we therefore hired a cart, the only conveyance that was to be obtained. Whilst it was getting ready we visited the Grotto della Madonna, a small cavern just below the church, in which is a spring of water, in the centre of which stands a stone statue of the Virgin. There is a miraculous report respecting this said statue, to the effect that it has been frequently taken up and offered a more respectable asylum in the church; but that during the night she has again chosen to descend the forty steps to her old station in the cave. We carried a torch with us, by the light of which we discovered several other headless statues, supposed to be those of heathen gods and goddesses, arranged in niches around the sides of the cave. Ascending the forty steps, we left the Virgin the "sole possessor" of her favourite cavern; and after waiting some time for our rustic conveyance, we took our seats, or rather our positions, on this primitive vehicle. The carts of Malta have no sides, but consist of two immense wheels, between which is a sloping platform composed of bars of wood, over which is laid a piece of matting. On this uncomfortable foundation we stretched ourselves in a reclining posture, with a straw bolster placed at one end for our heads to rest upon, and our feet pressed against the lowest bars. Though the road was bad, yet I enjoyed this novel mode of travelling very much; it was perfectly eastern, and strongly reminded me of the manner in which the orientals recline at a feast. A beautiful moonlight ride over the plains of Naciar brought us to Valetta, soon after eight o'clock, much amused and pleased with our day's excursion.

CHAPTER XII.

VISIT TO THE GARDENS AND PALACE OF ST. ANTONIO, AND CIVITA VECCHIA, THE
ANCIENT CAPITAL OF MALTA.

> " Like childhood making mirth of age
> In its unthinking hour,
> So on those ruined walls the sun
> Spends his meridian power."

To-day I have paid a visit to the old city, which is situated nearly in the centre of the island. After taking a hasty lunch at Valetta, I joined my friend Mr. S., who had ordered a calise to be in readiness for us, and we started about noon to Civita Vecchia, calling, on our way, at the palace of St. Antonio, where the Emir of Bey-root is at present residing with all his family and suite, under the protection of the British Government. The sun shone bright in the heavens, and the noontide heat was great. Our road lay by the side of the aqueduct built by the Grand Master Alofio Wignacourt, in the year 1610. This great work is in time of drought almost the only means of supplying water to the inhabitants of Valetta. It extends to a distance of nine and a half English miles, commencing at a plain called Diar Chandal, two miles west of Civita Vecchia. As far as Casal Attard this aqueduct runs under ground, and its course is afterwards above and below the earth, owing to the unevenness of the surface of the ground, until it reaches the city of Valetta. Every gentle breath of wind stirred up the dust, which arose in clouds, and compelled us to close the windows of the calise. As this vehicle differs considerably in its form and fashion from an English carriage, a brief description of it may not be uninterest-ing to my readers.

They have no wheels in front, but are furnished instead with a species of prop for a support, which is let down when the calise is at rest, and is fastened beneath the body of the carriage when travelling. They are constructed somewhat in the Spanish fashion, and those used in Valetta are, many of them, very neat, though it occa-sionally happens that they are to be met with in the villages of the most outlandish form and structure conceivable. They are drawn along by one horse or mule, the driver running along by the side, and with a small piece of wood called a " niggieza," in which two short nails are fixed, he pricks the animal in order to urge him forward. These calise-men will run for many miles in the sun and dust, yet they never seem tired. Indeed they take a delight in travelling as fast as possible; and should another calise appear in sight in the distance, the passenger has only to point it out to the driver, and away he starts to overtake it. When the other calise-man sees his rival he starts off likewise, and both gallop away, neither choosing to give in till they arrive at their ultimate destination. We found this plan succeed admirably when we wished to get back to Valetta in time for any particular engagement.

Turning out of the main road we arrived at the palace of St. Antonio; the approach leading to it was shaded by some of the largest trees I had seen any where in Malta. At first we doubted whether we should be able to gain admittance; but as it was the time when the ladies were taking their siesta, we obtained permission to walk about the gardens by making a present to the gardener. The ladies belonging to the Emir's suite are numerous, including his own and his son's wives. Being Arabians, they are kept in a state of great seclusion; and when they do show themselves, a long white veil covers their faces, disclosing only a pair of large black eyes of uncommon beauty. We rambled through these gardens which were once the summer residence of the Grand Masters, and were much pleased with the tasteful and picturesque manner in which they are laid out. They are certainly the most extensive gardens in Malta, and contain numerous tall cypresses, with a variety of orange, lemon, cedar, vine, rose, and palm trees. Some of the flowers growing on the margin of the paved terrace in front of the palace were very beautiful. The walks are all raised, and formed of slabs of stone, whilst at the various intersections of the principal ones there are broad fountains and ponds covered with white and yellow water-lilies, which form a cool and pleasing variety to the scene. Around these fountains resort myriads of dragon-flies of every variety of colour; the blue and crimson bodied ones were the most numerous, and as they darted about in the sunbeams they shone like winged jewels in the air. We walked along many of the terraces, which were bordered with vines; but unfortunately we could not find a single grape though the stalks hung very thick, and we were therefore led to conclude that the Arab ladies of the Emir's harem amused themselves by plucking off the grapes one by one, during their evening walks, as they must have but little to do in their monotonous and secluded situation. In a shady balcony above a little grove of orange and mimosa trees, looking into the garden, we saw one of the Emir's grandchildren, a beautiful little girl about eight years of age, playing with some toys and attended by an Egyptian slave. Her dark eyes were shadowed by a long fringe of ebon lashes, and her slight form attired in the rich and elegant costume of Eastern magnificence. Her hair was braided, and hung down nearly to her feet. She appeared

H

to take no notice of us, but continued playing with her toys, and listening to the nightingales that sung among the pimento trees. She was occupied with her own childish and happy thoughts, mingled, perhaps, with recollections of her distant Syrian home. She reminded me strongly of Moore's beautiful line,

"'Twas she—that Emir's blooming child."

Leaving St. Antonio, a ride of about five miles brought us to Civita Vecchia, which is situated on an eminence overlooking almost the whole of Malta. It is surrounded with walls, and fenced with bastions and other modern fortifications, which render it very strong, considering the elevated situation on which it stands.

Brydone, who visited Malta some sixty or seventy years since, mentions a park which formerly stood here, but I certainly saw no vestige of it, nor does it seem likely ever to have consisted of more than two or three trees scattered about, here and there. In early times this city bore the same name with the rest of the island, and was called Melita, according to Ptolemy the geographer. Upon the authority of Cicero and Diodorus Siculus, we learn that the capital of Malta formerly contained many stately buildings, and was very rich in the style of its architecture. This I can easily conceive to have been the case from several remains which are still to be seen scattered about the city, and by the vestiges of ancient baths and temples which have been discovered during the progress of the excavations, both within the walls, as well as without the suburbs. We first visited the Cathedral, which is built, according to tradition, on the site of the residence of Publius, who was governor of the island at the time of St. Paul's shipwreck. It is built in the Corinthian style of architecture, and contains an altar composed of rich marbles. The view from the terrace towards Valetta is very beautiful, and takes in nearly the whole extent of the island. We went into the library, where we saw a few antiques, and then visited the College of Priests, where the young abbots are instructed in the Catholic religion. Among the boys, Mr. S. recognized one with whom he was well acquainted. He had formerly been at a Protestant school in Valetta, but was removed here on his friends determining that he should become a priest. He appeared to be a lad of fine mind and good understanding, but he will probably lose all that he had acquired previously, as he is only taught the doctrines of the Popish faith with a little Hebrew. One of the priests belonging to the establishment showed us the sleeping apartments of the scholars, consisting of several long airy rooms, with a number of small beds arranged on each side. Every boy provides his own bedding, so that the furniture of the apartments is very various. Over most of the bedsteads was affixed either a small picture of the Virgin, or some favourite saint, to which they attach great importance. Several had Latin inscriptions upon them, and some were got up with a certain degree of childish taste, and were ornamented with small bows of ribbon. On leaving the college we proceeded to view what are termed the Catacombs of St. Paul. They are situated a short distance from the church, the sacristan of which accompanied us, and carried a supply of tapers for our use. The descent to the entrance is about nine feet in depth, by a staircase leading to a gallery dug under ground, with a great number of others branching off in various directions. The sacristan lighted our tapers, and we entered this dismal abode of the ancient dead. The sides of the various passages contain many niches cut in the walls to receive the bodies. They are mostly arranged without any order; some are entirely uncovered, whilst others are in two stories, and partly closed up with a layer of mortar raised up in a circular form. These sepulchres are of various dimensions, some are of a proportionately small size for infants; these generally occupy the sides, whilst in many of the larger ones the presence of two circular holes of a sufficient size to receive the head, attests that they were intended for two full-grown persons. There are several halls among these galleries. The roof of one of these is supported by a group of rough fluted columns; and on the floor are two circular blocks, about four feet in diameter, flat on the top, with a low edge running round the circumference. Some persons are of opinion that these latter were used for the purpose of washing the bodies before burial. Several of these passages have been walled up, as parties whose inquisitiveness has led them too far in, have lost their way, and never afterwards been heard of. A schoolmaster is said to have entered the catacombs with all his pupils, who proceeded along the winding paths till they missed their way, and all perished in these avenues of death. A wall has since been built up against the path which these unfortunates took, where their bones now mingle with those of the men of days long gone by, without a line to reveal the facts of their mysterious death, and the agonizing manner in which they must have perished. Some have ascribed the construction of these catacombs to the early Christians, who, during times of persecution, lived and buried the bodies of their martyrs and confessors in them. This is the opinion which obtains at Rome; but it seems much more probable that they are of Phœnician, or early Roman origin, whose custom it was to bury in caves. But when the Romans derived from the Greeks the method of burning their dead, this mode of sepulture came into general use, and the catacombs were at length perfectly neglected. From the catacombs the sacristan led us to St. Paul's cave, a spot which has been very celebrated in Malta for ages past. It stands underneath the small chapel of San Paolo, and according to tradition is the identical spot where St. Paul, accompanied by St. Luke the apostle, and Trophonius, resided for the space of three months, the time of their stay in the island. The veneration for this cave increased very much about the year 1600, when a citizen of Cordova, named Fra Giovanni, left his native country and came to Malta in order to tenant this cave as an anchorite. We carried a large torch with us, and descending several steps we entered the cave by an iron gate. It is about twelve yards in diameter and eight feet in height. A fine marble statue of St. Paul occupies the centre of the cave, and beneath it is a Latin inscription. The stone of which the sides of this noted cavern are composed, is a soft white magnesian limestone, which for centuries has been very celebrated as a cure for various kinds of diseases. Large quantities of it have been exported to Italy, and other Catholic countries, where it is greatly valued. The general belief is, that the more the limestone is removed the faster it re-accumulates, and a pickaxe is constantly kept in the cave for the use of strangers, who are allowed to carry away a piece of this precious remedy. I knocked off several small portions which I preserved, not as a febrifuge, but as a relic of the place; for though many may disdain the idea, yet I confess to being very fond of mementos of this kind:—they have a voice, a memory in themselves, which when one looks upon them, may serve to bear him back through the region of thought till he stands in the long-forgotten spot from whence they came; and every association gathers from the shade of oblivion as vividly as when he first gazed in rapture upon the mouldering ruin, or the moss-covered trophy of past ages.

Returning from St. Paul's cave, we partook of some refreshment; and after a quiet ride home reached Valetta about six o'clock, when we immediately set about making preparations to visit the island of Gozo, intending to start that evening at eight o'clock, or soon after midnight.

CHAPTER XIII.

> " What think you, as she lies in her green cove,
> Our little sleeping boat is dreaming of?
> If morning dreams are true, why I should guess
> That she was dreaming of our idleness,
> And of the miles of watery way
> We should have led her by this time of day."

City of Rabbato, Gozo, Sept. 29, 1841.

WE left Valetta soon after eight o'clock last night in a boat with four men, which we
hired for the occasion, and steered towards the Island of Gozo. The wind was
favourable at starting, but afterwards it died away, and the men were obliged to
take to their oars. As we were both much tired by our trip to Civita Vecchia, in
the morning, and were in expectation of a great deal of fatigue on the next day,
we laid ourselves down in the bottom of the boat, and after the men had covered us
with a sail to keep off the ill effects of the moon and the dew, we managed, despite
the mosquitoes, to get a few hours' sleep. At half past one in the morning we arrived
at Gozo quay, in the little bay of Migarro. It was, however, quite useless to attempt
to proceed into the interior of the island until four or five o'clock, we therefore
moored the boat to the shore, and whilst one man acted as sentinel we lay down
again to sleep, a rest, however, which was soon broken by loud and long continued
shouting from the shore. We were quickly aroused, and found that we had slipped
from our moorings and were fast drifting out from the shore into the bay. Our
men, however, took to their oars, and we soon reached our original situation, where
we moored ourselves more securely. We did not feel disposed again to tempt the
god of sleep, and we therefore left our boat, and taking two of the men with us, we
walked up the beach to a small fisherman's cottage. It was still quite dark, but we
went in and obtained some coffee, which was served to us in cups very little bigger
than a thimble. Here we refreshed ourselves and prepared for our walk to Rabbato,

the chief city of the island, which was three miles distant.   I now discovered that
the mosquitoes had been annoying me in good earnest, for my face and hands were
covered with the effects of their bites.   We left orders with our men that we should
return to the boat before sunset, and we forthwith proceeded on our trip to Rabbato.
Mr. S. had provided himself with a pair of pistols, in case of any dispute with the
natives ; but fortunately we had no occasion to use them.   Passing Fort Chambray,
we ascended the steep hill that leads down to the shore, and on gaining the high
ground we looked back and enjoyed a most enchanting prospect.   The dark and
rugged shores of Gozo lay beneath us, with the island of Commino to the right.
Farther on, to the eastward, Malta bounded our view, and the strait of Fregi wound
between like a vast river of the deepest azure.   The first golden streaks of morning
lightened the top of the Maltese hills, and gleamed over rocks and seas till they
gilded the spot whereon we stood.   By-and-by the round red sun rose up, defining
with the brightness of his beams countless objects that were before gloaming in the
twilight.   We reached Rabbato about six o'clock, and after examining the old
castle and fortifications, and enjoying the beautiful panorama of the island, we
breakfasted at a small albergo kept by Signor Lippo, where we found tolerable
accommodation.

The island of Gozo was called Gaulos by the Greeks, and Gaulum by the Romans.
From its vicinity to Malta, it has generally shared the fate of the latter island.
During the time of the " Order," its government was committed to one knight and
four Giurati, or magistrates, appointed by the Grand Master.   At present it is included under the jurisdiction of the Govenor of Malta, and the administration of its
affairs is carried on by persons invested by him with civil power.   Like Malta, all
the accessible spots on the island are secured by fortifications ; but the whole of the
southern and western coast is guarded by inaccessible cliffs.   The face of the country
is more fertile than that of Malta, and produces wheat, barley, and cotton, though
it has suffered in part from the long drought.   Occasional showers have fallen in
Gozo, and I saw it raining heavily over the sea whilst at Rabbato.   This, I am
informed, is a common occurrence at no great distance from the shore, though the
rain seems very loth to fall upon the land.   The interior of the island is broken up
into rugged hills ; some of these are of a conical shape, and are supposed by many
to be extinct volcanoes; but this, I believe, is an error.   The mules and asses of Gozo
are of a very large size, and are far superior to those of Malta in strength and beauty.
The dialect of the inhabitants is a much nearer approach to the pure Arabic than
the Maltese, and I was informed that the natives are able to converse with the Arabs
so as to be easily understood.   The inhabitants are a very fine race of people, both
hardy and industrious.   Several of the ancient customs of the Maltese are still preserved in Gozo, particularly their ceremony of burying the dead, which is conducted

From Nature & on Stone by George French Angas.

Day & Haghe, Lith'rs to the Queen.

GENERAL'S ROCK; GOZO.

by mourners termed " newieha," who smite their breasts and commence singing in a low dismal voice, till at length they grow more affected and begin to howl and tear their hair. This tragic action they generally accompany with some sentence like the following " Alas! my brother! he was lovely but he is gone! Will you not think of us hereafter? Remember us to those who have gone before! Why, oh! why, didst thou abandon all who loved you?"

The population of Gozo amounts to about 17,000 souls. Besides the city of Rabbato there are several casals, or villages, scattered over the country. The stone found on the island is softer than that of Malta, and the houses are not generally such well-built dwellings as those of the sister island. The situation of the city is imposing and romantic, but there is nothing within its walls that is worthy of notice. After breakfast we inquired for a calise to visit the " Hagra tal Girnal," or General's Rock. For some time we were not able to find such a thing as a calise, but at last they procured one for us, which certainly surpassed every thing of the kind I had previously seen. Mr. S. was afraid lest the bottom should come out, whilst I, more amazed than alarmed, ascribed its manufacture to the Phœnicians, for it looked as though it had been dug up from the earth. We both came to the conclusion that it would prove a most valuable affair in the hands of an antiquary; for it was so very ancient, all over of a rusty brown colour, and patched up here and there with bits of leather. Still, with all this evident antiquarianism about it, it was the only calise to be met with, and we had no alternative; we therefore got in, and after tying up the door (for, wonderful to say, it had one) with a piece of string, we underwent a complete and thorough shaking over a terrible path, till we reached the hill that overhangs the small bay of Duejra, where stands the General's Rock, at the western extremity of the island of Gozo. Here we left our antique conveyance, and proceeded on foot down a steep path, over limestone rocks abounding in fossil echinæ, and other sea shells. We had not gone far before six women came running down the hill after us, with various curiosities for sale on their heads. These they faithfully assured us were the identical teeth and tongues of the serpents which St. Paul cast out when he was shipwrecked in Malta! We purchased a number of these valuables, and the women all followed us to the rock, pretending to be our guides. A young man and two or three boys augmented our party, which by this time had increased to a respectable force. Our picturesque group halted at the extremity of the point, between which and the General's Rock ran an arm of the sea, which we had to cross in a small box, moved along by a rope and pulleys. When the machinery was adjusted, one man crossed the chasm first, which was 150 feet wide. On the return of the box I got in, and holding firmly by the rope, I soon reached the opposite side also. The journey over this arm of the sea was any thing but pleasant, as it consisted of a series of jerks, and the landing on the rock was very steep and dangerous. The famous "Fungus Melitensis" grows here, and the fruit called "cynomorium coccinium," which is not known in any other part of the country. The summit of the rock is covered with bushes, wild stocks, and golden rod. After wandering about and searching for a fungus, which I succeeded in finding, I returned in the same manner, and rejoined Mr. S. and our numerous convoy on the mainland. Some time since the cables of this novel aërial conveyance gave way, and precipitated the passenger into the gulf below.

On ascending the hill, I sat down for a few moments upon a stone to make a sketch of the rock, whilst Mr. S. descended to the beach to enjoy a bathe. At first the simple natives could not understand what I was doing, but they soon divined my purpose; and on seeing the representation on the paper, they screamed with delight. I made signs to one of the women to sit on a rock in the foreground, and introduced her into the sketch I was taking. I very soon had candidates sufficiently numerous to fill up the canvass of an historical picture, and by the time Mr. S. arrived, I had so fully gained their good feelings that they were very unwilling for me to leave them. Rejoining our calise we again arrived at Rabbato, when we dined off some fine maccaroni and peaches, and immediately afterwards set off in an opposite direction to visit the " Torre tal Gigant" or Giant's Tower. This is one of the most interesting Phœnician remains in the island. It consists of an enclosure surrounded by enormous masses of rock piled one upon another, somewhat similar to those at Hajar Kim.

It seems probable that these gigantic masses were the remains of a temple to some deity. The entrance faces the east, and the interior consists of two separate chambers. Many of the slabs of stone exhibit marks of rude chiselling, and in the doorposts there are several large holes, probably intended for the introduction of bolts. From all the information that I could collect, it would seem to have been a " Puratheion," or one of those open edifices in which the rites of fire were celebrated; the element under which the Phœnicians, who are supposed to have been the first settlers on this island, worshipped the sun. Here then exists one of these deserted temples of the earliest ages, almost as perfect as when the first pale flame rose from its altar, and the hundred worshipers of the element bowed down before the spirit they conceived to be enshrined in its tapering fires. The sun was fast sinking in the west by the time we reached Fort Chambray, where we dismissed our roguish boy, and his ancient chariot. A little lad, who conducted us to the Giant's Tower, spoke of having had the honour of acting as guide to Queen Adelaide, who paid it a visit when she was at Malta; though I doubt not but that all the neighbourhood had enrolled themselves in the list of guides, and that her train was in consequence as numerous as a Celtic chief's in the olden time. An Italian sonnet written and put up in honour of Her Majesty's visit, still remains on the wall of one of the chambers of the

Giant's Tower. The wind blew strongly from the eastward, and on reaching the Bay of Migarro, we refreshed ourselves with a delightful bathe in the surf; and then getting into our boat, bade farewell to the Island of Gozo. As we approached the middle of the channel the waves ran very high, and we were in some danger of being upset. The boatmen, however, carefully watched for every wave, and dexterously avoided it with their oars. We soon got under the shores of the island of Commino, where we found a partial shelter. This small island is only five miles in circumference. and consists chiefly of barren rocks. It abounds in rabbits, which afford the occasional sport of a day's chase to the Governor and his officers. The steep perpendicular cliffs along the north side of this island are bold and picturesque, broken into a variety of grotesque caverns and isolated rocks. In one place I traced an exact resemblance to a sheep lying down, and in another, a little imagination might have converted a huge mass of rock into the headless trunk of a Cyclopean giant. Several of the caves are full of deep water, but so clear that their carpets of green and purple seaweed were distinctly visible, seeming appropriate residences for Neptune and his sportive train of Naiads and Tritons. But the days of mythology have passed away from her once cherished shores, and the lonely heron now reigns in these caves undisturbed, nor is he changed into a water god by the creative fancies of southern nations. After passing the shores of Commino, we again launched out into the open straits, and underwent a second tossing, which wetted us through and through with the spray. On rounding the promontory called Dahlet e Scilep, the men commenced crossing themselves, and praying to a figure of the Virgin which stood on the summit of the rock. We succeeded in crossing the mouth of Mellieha Bay; but as the wind blew more violently, and the boatmen assured us that if we reached Valetta in safety, it would not be until two or three o'clock on the ensuing morning, I determined not to risk it, and ordered them to put in at Mellieha, where I depended on the cart that I had before made use of to convey us on to Valetta. After getting some distance into the bay the water was nearly calm, owing to the lee of the high land just above us. We landed at Mellieha and dismissed the boat, leaving the men to pass the night there, where they would probably stay until the weather proved more favourable. We ascended the hill towards the village, taking with us a little Gozzitan boy, apparently about nine years old, who was under the care of the boatmen, to be conveyed to his father, then at Valetta with his speronaro. I proposed the plan of taking this little fellow with us to my friend, who thought it much better than letting him be exposed to the risk which he must necessarily run, if left with the boatmen. After a delay of about three quarters of an hour, we were fortunate enough to obtain the identical cart on which I had built my only hope of reaching Valetta that night; and reclining backwards after the eastern fashion, I took my little protegé under my care, who soon fell fast asleep in my lap. He was a fine little fellow, with a very

I

intelligent countenance, and what is sometimes met with in Gozo—blue eyes. It is
a very curious fact, that although the Maltese are proverbial for large black eyes,
there is a village called **Casal Zehbug** (olive) where all the inhabitants have them of
a blue colour. This little lad was rendered more interesting by being dressed out
in a smart blue shirt with a braided collar, such as the boys wear on board a man-of-
war. After a lovely moonlight ride, enhanced by the feeling that we were not exposed to the mercy of the waves, whose distant murmur broke on our ears, we arrived
at Valetta about half-past eleven o'clock.

In passing through Casal Nasciar, the circumstance of the church being lighted up
attracted our attention, and we looked in. Several tapers were dimly burning around
the altar, and all the rest of the building was shrouded in gloom. An aged and
venerable man was bending before the altar, apparently engaged in earnest prayer,
and several women and a lad were kneeling at a short distance off. On inquiry I
learnt that they were praying for a dying man, that he might have an easy entrance
into purgatory ! Arriving at Valetta, and reaching the Strada Reale, to my infinite
surprise my little charge darted off all of a sudden in the direction of the quay. On
the next day, as I was walking along the Marina, he came running up to me quite
delighted, and shook my hand most cordially. I made him a present of a few cop-
pers, and he returned to his father in the boat : after this I never saw him again.

CHAPTER XIV.

CONVENT OF THE CAPUCHIN FRIARS.

" Within the twilight chamber spreads apace
The shadow of white death; and, at the door,
Invisible corruption waits to trace
His extreme way to her dim dwelling-place."

At sunrise I paid a visit to the convent of the Capuchins. It is situated on an eminence in the suburbs of Floriana, and commands a superb view of the harbours and surrounding country. I had on a previous day applied for admission, but as it happened to be the time when the brotherhood were taking their siesta, I was refused, and told that if I particularly wished to see it, the Superior should be duly informed, and I must come at six o'clock in the morning. The approach to the building is marked by a cross of black wood, erected on a mound of stones, and a broad road cleanly swept; the pathway bordered with tapering cypress trees, leads the traveller to the porch of the convent, underneath which a number of beggars are continually thronging, who are fed daily by the hospitality of the monks, who prepare a dinner expressly for the poor. In the centre of the square in front of the convent stands a large statue of a Capuchin saint, arrayed in the garb of the order, with a gilt glory surrounding his head. In all their statues of the saints, the Catholics have a clever method of fixing the glory (which generally consists of a gilt or brazen circle) in such a manner, by means of a thin wire behind the head, that it has the appearance of resting in the air. The door of the convent was opened to us by a very old Capuchin servant; and after proceeding along a narrow passage, we entered the chapel, where a mass was being performed. The walls were covered with several pictures, which chiefly represented saints and their miraculous achievements. In one of the ante-chambers a waxen model of our Saviour, as large as life, was exhibited, enclosed in a glass case; and in another were several pictures; one of them, of the Virgin, was very good. The floor of a little silver shrine through which we passed, was composed of green and white mosaic. After going through the lower apartments we ascended a wide stone staircase hung

I 2

with small paintings, and entered the corridors, which extend through the entire length of the building, and are lined on each side with the cells of the monks, who are about fifty or sixty in number. The walls of these passages are hung with pictures representing the astounding miracles performed by friars of the order. Over each cell is a small Latin inscription taken from the Holy Scriptures. This convent is very much frequented by the inhabitants of Valetta on holidays, when it is thrown open, and great numbers of persons come here to pass an hour in traversing the corridors, examining the pictures, or chatting with some of the fraternity, and enjoying the fine air and beautiful prospect which surrounds the convent.

From the balcony of the corridor we overlooked the garden, which contains orange and pomegranate trees, with various culinary vegetables, and a few flowers; the whole of which are kept in very neat order by the servants of the brotherhood. We observed one of the servants very busy at work amongst some egg plants, and though he appeared upwards of eighty years of age, with a long beard of snowy whiteness, yet he seemed as hale and as hearty as if he had reached but half that amount of years. The long life to which these ascetics attain, may partly be ascribed to their very simple mode of living, and the primitive habits which they follow, unalloyed by anxiety, or any of the numerous troubles resulting from an intercourse and connexion with the outer world, which so often destroy the health and happiness of those who are engaged in the active pursuits of life. In this convent the four giraffes, sent by the Pacha of Egypt to Great Britain, were located during their stay at Malta; and many are the absurd pictures and descriptions given of them by the natives, who had never seen or heard of such creatures before; for the spirit of discovery does not proceed here with such rapid strides as it does in our own favoured island. Descending the staircase from the corridors, I expressed a wish to see their " carneria," or charnel-house, as it is termed, which occupies an extensive vault below the convent. By the permission of the Superior we gained admittance; and, descending a narrow staircase, and passing a grated doorway, the monk who conducted us turned the great key of a heavy portal, when this modern Golgotha burst at once upon our view, horrid and disgusting in the extreme. The dim light of morning stole unwillingly through a small aperture above, admitting just enough light to assure us that we were in the abodes of the dead. Here it is that the monks who die in the convent, after being disembowelled, well dried, and baked, are dressed up in their original clothes, and fixed in niches in the walls, where they remain till time reduces them to decay; the bones of each are then taken up and nailed upon the walls, interspersed with small branches of evergreens, so as to form a kind of sepulchral decoration. The skulls, likewise, are arranged along the ceiling, looking like so many grim spectators of the mockery and indignity offered to their remains. In one of the sides of this vault are two enclosed coffins, containing the bodies of two friars who, they say, performed miracles during their lifetime. At one end of the vault stands a small altar, above which is a figure of our Saviour. There is a mass annually performed here, which is called the " festival of the dead ;" at which time the whole vault is illuminated, and each of these ghastly remains of human frailty is decked and adorned with flowers. This is a mockery, indeed, of the lowest kind, to make use of Nature's brightest and sweetest ornaments, the lovely flowers, to decorate with their glowing petals the filthy and decaying body of an old monk. I love flowers, but I love to see them wreathe the sunny brow, and meet the starlike smile of childhood; and I would inhale their fragrance not in a charnel-house, but in the mossy slopes and undisturbed solitude of a forest glen.

Of the various aspects of these rotten mortals, some tall, some short, and several sunk from their original position against the walls, I could give a sickening description ; but they have even now destroyed my appetite for breakfast, and I gladly leave them to decay in their cells, quite unambitious ever to have the pleasure of seeing them any more.

CHAPTER XV.

PUBLIC LIBRARY—CATHEDRAL OF ST. JOHN—CHURCHES AND NUNNERIES.

> Gleam, marble and mosaic,
> From gilded shrines around,
> So many are the monuments,
> They cover all the ground;
> Giall, and verde-antique
> From every tomb shine bright,
> And the precious lapis lazuli
> Sends forth its azure light.

THE public library of Valetta, which is a handsome building, adjoining the Governor's palace, is worthy of some notice. I visited it before proceeding to the church of St. John of Jerusalem. The books are arranged around a lofty and spacious apartment, with considerable taste and order, and they amount to nearly 40,000 volumes; though I am informed that for so large a collection they contain very little that is really useful. In the same room is a small collection of antiquities, found at different times in Malta and Gozo; they consist chiefly of earthen vases and lachrymatories, and other relics of Phœnician origin. Besides these, there is a statue of Hercules, in Grecian marble; a Syracusan altar, dedicated to Proserpine; a marble slab, on which is a basso relievo of Tullia and Claudia; the former the daughter of Cicero, and the latter the wife of Cecilius Metellus, who lived at Rome, at the same time; a square marble with a basso-relievo bust of Zenobia, Queen of Palmyra, and a small brass figure found in Gozo, representing a young beggar seated in a basket. A very trifling collection of stuffed birds, a wolf, and a wild cat, occupy the window recesses, and an enormous snake, said to have been taken in Gozo, is stretched out at full length upon a board; the loss of its natural head being amply supplied by an enormous one of wood, armed with sharp teeth, and a long red tongue, which give it all the ferocious and awe-inspiring appearance of a dragon.

Having thus visited the Library, St. John's Church next claimed my attention. This building is rendered famous by having been the grand cathedral of the knights, and now holds the first rank in Malta, as the duomo, or mother church.   It was built in the reign of the Grand Master, La Cassiera, about the year 1576, and was afterwards greatly enriched by the frequent presents of the succeeding Grand Masters. The entrance is flanked by two square towers, surmounted by small spires, and the whole extent of building that stretches out on either side, exhibits nothing but a monotonous and uniform façade of stone-work.   The interior of the building is, however, gorgeously magnificent ; being entirely covered with carvings, gilt, tapestry, and numerous paintings.   A row of separate chapels, belonging to each of the various languages, extend along both sides of the nave.   The arched semicircular roof, which covers this part of the church, is adorned with a series of paintings illustrative of the life of St. John, painted by the Calabrese artist, Preti, who executed many of the paintings in the other parts of the edifice.   During the short occupation of Malta by the French, most of the treasures amassed here were seized and taken away.   The pavement is composed of sepulchral slabs of various kinds, of coloured marble, inlaid with lapis lazuli, verde-antique, jaspars, agates, and other precious stones.   These are beautifully worked in mosaic, and cover the graves of the knights. The Grand Masters are chiefly buried in the chapels of their respective languages. The grand altar is very sumptuous, and is beautifully inlaid with gems and marbles. On a raised pavement around it stand two chairs, covered with crimson velvet : one being occupied by the Bishop Caramana, and the other intended for the sovereign of the island, above which is placed the arms of Great Britian.   The various chapels are splendidly decorated, and form the two aisles.   They are profusely carved in alto relievo, and in many parts are a complete mass of gilding.   In the oratory, or chapel of the crucifixion, is a fine painting representing the beheading of St. John, by Michael Angelo Caravaggio.   Several of the mausoleums of the Grand Masters in these chapels are very superb.   The following are among the finest :—In the chapel of the Portuguese Knights, that of Emanuel de Pinto, with his portrait in mosaic, and a large statue of Fame ; that of Manuel de Vilhena is still more costly ; it is of bronze, supported by two lions, and beneath his bust is an alto relievo group, representing the Grand Master giving directions concerning the erection of Fort Manuel. In the Spanish Chapel those of Perillos e Roccaful, and Nicholas Cottoner.   The former is surmounted by a large copper bust, having the figures of Justice and Charity on each side ; the latter is sustained by a Turk and an African, and is adorned with variously coloured marbles.   The splendid copper mausoleum of the Grand Master Zondadari, flanked with marble columns, is very imposing ; and several more of the monuments that adorn the building are well worthy of notice.

After leaving St. John's Church, I paid a visit to the other principal religious edifices in Valetta.   The churches are numerous, but a description of one of them will give an idea of the whole.   They are all more or less ornamented with numerous altars, painting, and carving, and are paved with marble or tiles. It is said that the priests and friars in the islands of Malta and Gozo, exceed one thousand in number. There are, also, th   thousand abbati, or boys, preparing for ordination, who are likewise supported by the ecclesiastical establishment. In Valetta, the principal churches are St. Giovanni, St. Paolo, St. Francis, St. Dominic, St. Maria di Gesu, St. Barbara, St. Giacomo, St. Rocco, St. Catarina, and the church of the Jesuits. There are, also, the nunneries of St. Ursula and St. Catarina, though their inmates are fast decreasing in number. The chief convents are those of the Capuchins, Zoccalanti, Carmelitans, Franciscans, Dominicans, Tariasini, and Augustine Friars. After this I need not say that Malta is a place where the Romish church is all powerful : yet amid this pomp and glitter of the ceremonial religion, I must not forget to notice the Cathedral Church of St. Paul, erected mainly by the benevolent means placed at the disposal of the British residents in Malta, by her Majesty the Queen Dowager, and dedicated to the worship of the pure Protestant faith. Whilst writing these lines, I have received a letter from Malta informing me that this building is ready to be consecrated. Surrounded by the gaudier edifices dedicated to the Catholic worship, this single Protestant church may be the beacon-light to many a wandering heart, who now and hereafter, as he may enter that temple of prayer, will ever remember that he bends in worship before an altar raised to the sacred religion of his forefathers, by the virtue and piety of a British Queen.

From Nature & on Stone by George French Angas.

CHIESA SAN PUBLIO AND PROTESTANT CHAPEL, FLORIANA.

(Looking towards Valetta.)

Day & Haghe Lith. to the Queen

CHAPTER XVI.

FLORIANA GARDENS—IL GROTTO—NATURALISTS.

> " The plumed insects swift and free,
>   Like golden boats on a sunny sea,
>   Laden with light and odour which pass
>   Over the gleam of the living grass;
>   And the jessamine faint, and the sweet tuberose,
>   The sweetest flower for scent that blows;
>   And all rare blossoms from every clime
>   Grew in that garden in perfect prime."

IN the centre of the plain intervening between the city of Valetta, and the suburbs of Floriana, is a long narrow garden, enclosed by a high wall, with gates opening at each end. This is termed the botanical garden; and it is open to the public, to whom it affords a pleasant morning's walk before the heat of the day, or a cool place of retirement in the afternoon, for recreation or conversation, as stone seats are ranged along on both sides between the pillars that border the paved walks. On entering the garden from Valetta, the stranger comes upon an open space covered with flag-stones with a small summer-house at the end, and in the midst is a pond containing gold and silver fish. Around this pond I noticed that beautiful flower the marvel of Peru, covered with blossoms of every shade of crimson, pink, and white; and the dragon flies, attracted by the water, darted about in all directions, displaying their richly coloured bodies and gauze-like wings, impaled for one moment, as it were, on the edge of the stone basin, and the next dividing the air like an arrow, with the swiftness and rapidity of their flight. The rest of the garden is divided into three parts, each of them under the superintendance of a different gardener. Two parallel walks extend along the whole length of the garden, bordered with carobs, palm, and pimento trees, and a variety of solanos, and other shrubs. The spaces between the walks are ornamented by rich flower-beds; whilst around the stone pillars are twined numerous creepers and climbing plants, which grow so rich and luxuriantly in the spring, as to throw a deep shade of green over the pathways beside them. Owing to the long continuance of the drought, this garden is watered by artificial means,

K

and small channels convey the water to every part of it from a tank, situated near the gates. The flowers are, many of them, very familiar to an English eye, and a number of annual plants grow along the borders, and attain to a large size; whilst at the same time the delicate plants which in our northern clime are raised in hot-houses, may here be seen flourishing and blooming in all their beauty in the open sunshine, and unfolding their gay and gorgeous petals to the warm and sparkling atmosphere of a southern clime. The harmless lizards, (called by the natives "Gremsicola,") dart across the pavement at every step, and are so extremely shy that it requires no common degree of dexterity to catch them. Wherever flowers abound, there the insect tribes resort in great numbers; and this green spot is one of the few haunts of the butterflies of Malta. The violet bee, skimming over the sweet marigolds; the rich vanessæ, sweeping down the vistas, till, in the aërial distance, they dwindle to a mere speck, and are not completely lost to sight as they would be in England, in the density of the atmosphere; the bird-like hawk-moths, fluttering and hovering, with trunks uncurled, around the sweetest and most mellifluous blossoms; and the full-grown larva of the death's-head, reposing at ease among the solano leaves; these, and many others, are among the sights that meet the eye of the entomologist in most gardens in this rocky island. I have frequently rambled through this garden at the hottest period of the day, for the purpose of collecting insects, and have constantly met with the lovely papiliones machaon, and podalirius. The Maltese boys often catch these little spirit-like beings, and fastening a fine piece of cotton around their bodies, with a long end attached to it, they follow their fairy coursers from flower to flower, sometimes tying them up on a particular bush. These children are seldom cruel, for they generally let the insects go free when they have done playing with them. One little lad, whose bright sharp eye made me set him about catching lizards, seemed very particular and careful not to hurt them.

Near these gardens there are others belonging to the English chaplain of the Governor; they are very beautiful, and kept in excellent order. Most of the plants are arranged in stone vases around the borders, and in a small pond in the centre grows the papyrus. Adjoining to this garden is a little chapel, or rather room, which is the only Protestant place of worship in the suburbs. The gardener was very obliging in giving me free and liberal access to these beautiful grounds; for I had only to knock at the door, and I might wander through the garden for hours. A third garden, called "Il Grotto," the residence of Miss Hamilton, is also well worthy of a visit; it contains several grottos of beautiful shell-work, and strongly reminded me of the ruins of some eastern abode. This lady very kindly gave me permission to make free use and enjoyment of her garden, but my time would only allow me to pay it one short visit. On the same day, I had the opportunity of calling on a Maltese naturalist residing in Floriana. He was by profession a physician, but has a strong predilection for the natural sciences. I found him sitting in his "sanctum sanctorum," stuffing a Tethys redstart, surrounded by numerous and various curiosities. At the sight of strangers he arose, and, putting aside his spectacles, proceeded to show me all his treasures. Amongst them I was greatly amused by a nondescript bird, composed of the body of a parroquet, with the tail of a bird of paradise, and a flaming crest of flamingo's feathers! These were all very artfully joined together by some lover of nature, who, no doubt, thought to turn this "rara avis" to good account. Such a monster might dare to show itself in a country where science seldom smiles; but could it be tolerated in the presence of a French or German naturalist? However, I must not altogether condemn my poor friend, for doubtless his was the "pursuit of knowledge under difficulties;" and though not so skilful as many of his contemporaries, yet he was very kind and obliging, and I gained some information from him on various topics connected with the natural productions of the island.

CHAPTER XVII.

" ULYSSES.—Would you first taste of the unmingled wine?
SILENUS.—'Tis just—tasting invites the purchaser.
CYCLOPS.—   And is
The new cheese pressed into the bulrush baskets?"

THE market of Valetta, though small, is well supplied with fruit and fish. Very little
animal food is used by the natives, and owing to the heat of the climate, it is obliged
to be eaten on the same day that it is killed. On going through the market to
purchase some fruit, I had occasion to pass by one of the butchers' stalls. The
Maltese are a very shrewd people and love a joke with the English. "Any beef,
John," said the butcher, with an arch smile:—this he intended, no doubt, as a hit
at our national character, though it was said with that naïveté and good humour
which it was impossible to be offended at. The greatest portion of the fruit sold
in the market is brought over in boats from Sicily, and some also from Gozo. At
the time of my visit the finest fruits were nearly over; grapes sold at 1$d.$ per rotolo,
(1¾ lb.), and a superior kind, called "ladies' fingers," of a long pod-like shape, for
1½$d.$ per pound. The prickly pears were sold at four grains per rotolo; pomegranates, one halfpenny each; apricots, 1$d.$ and 2$d.$ per rotolo; peaches 4$d.$ per ditto;
figs, of two or three kinds, 1$d.$ per rotolo; melons, one farthing per pound; of
these the musk, water and winter melons were in considerable abundance. The
oranges I saw were those of the last year's growth; they were very scarce, owing to
the want of rain. Fish are in great abundance; they consist chiefly of mullet,
whitings, tunny, sword-fish, turtles, eels, and various species of crustacea, such
as lobsters, crabs, prawns, &c. Shell-fish are much eaten by the lower classes.
The men who gather them expose them for sale in the markets in small dishes upon
the ground. I used frequently to examine them on account of the good shells that
are often found amongst them. I obtained the spondylus, two species of the murex,
the arca-noæ, the sea-date, the haliotis and three or four kinds of Venus, in this
manner. The little fish called sea-horses are common on the Maltese shores.

The hotels of Valetta are good; Morell's is the first, where the English may find excellent accommodation; but the Minerva, where a table d'hôte is daily kept, I found to be very comfortable, and the charges moderate. A person in this manner may live very cheaply in Malta. The finest Marsala wine is 10*d.* per bottle, and the common Sicilian, 2*d.* The best beef is 4*d.* per pound, maccaroni soup, 4*d.* per basin, and a person may dine sumptuously for 1*s.* 6*d.* per diem. Breakfast is best obtained at the cafés, which are open at a very early hour. Travellers passing only a short time in Malta will find these places extremely convenient, as they can drop in at any hour of the day and take coffee or ice, which latter article is consumed in Malta to a very great extent. It is obtained from Mount Etna in the form of snow, and boats are constantly arriving from Catania laden with this useful and cooling substance. In the cafés it is no uncommon thing to see them grinding up whole vats full of frozen snow, which, at first sight, appears very singular to a stranger in so warm a climate. Most of the cafés are situated in the Strada Reale, opposite the Library. I found the best attention at "Saits," and some of the prices are as follows:—Cup of coffee, 1½*d.*; breakfast, 5*d.*; ice cream, 2½*d.* lemonata ice, 1½*d.*; Rogiata ditto, 1½*d.*; other ices, including chocolate, coffee, cherry, strawberry, and pine-apple, 2½*d.* or 3*d.* The Mediterranean Hotel is French, and the Albergo del Sole, Italian. Foreigners of these nations find good accommodation at these hotels. Liqueurs, particularly Rosolia, and many rich cordials, may be obtained in Malta at very low prices. Owing to its being a free port, cigars may be had at the rate of ten for a penny, and sugar from 2*d.* to 4*d.* per pound. The butter is bad, and is chiefly imported from England. The native cheeses are made of goats' and sheep's milk, pressed into small rush baskets: these, when fresh, are very pleasant, but are obliged to be eaten a very few hours after they are made. Tea is rarely used as a meal, except by the English. Eggs are very good, at 4*d.* or 6*d.* per dozen. Poultry is plentiful, consisting of turkeys, fowls and ducks; quails are also very abundant in April and September; and in the market I have seen rails, larks, and wheatears. The yellow wagtail, (papa-muscæ,) are sold by the natives at from ¼*d.* to 1*d.* each, in the market, for the purpose of catching the flies in the houses, where they will live for several weeks, and answer this purpose as effectually as the chameleons do in Malaga. Olives are very much eaten by the Maltese, and oil enters largely into their cookery. The egg plant is considered a good vegetable by them, and when stuffed and roasted, it makes a palatable dish. It is the custom here, when you go to market, to be followed by a number of little boys with empty baskets; they are called market-boys, and get their living by carrying home purchased articles. You choose one, and he will follow you wherever your business leads, making his basket the general receptacle for fish, fruit, bread, and, in fact, of every thing you buy. I have always found these boys honest; and after emptying the contents of the basket at my lodgings, at the end of half an hour's service, they considered one halfpenny, or at the utmost three farthings, an ample remuneration : one poor little lad was trotting off without any thing, after carrying an earthen jar all round the city, until I called him back, and gladdened his heart with a twopenny piece. A number of beggars generally throng around the cafés, who are extremely importunate ; a single grain will however satisfy them, or if you do not feel disposed to relieve them, " Allein," (or " God help you,") will answer the same purpose. One dumb boy, in particular, was always to be seen at the café door, and though unable to tell his wants by articulation, yet his gestures were so significant, no one could misunderstand him. " Nix mangé, seigneur," is the constant language of the Maltese beggars, which signifies, " Nothing to eat, sir." Sometimes they will make little nosegays of mimosa, tied up with a rosebud, at the end of a small stick, which they sell to the people as they pass from the cafés. Numbers even of the labouring classes sleep in the streets, and on going along the Strada Levante, after dark, whole rows of men and boys may be seen reposing on their little mats on that side of the street which is shaded from the full light of the moon. I have often been in danger of stumbling over some of these sleepers, and once or twice just looked down in time to discover a little boy lying curled up at my feet on the bare stones.

The bread in Valetta is good, and like that of the south of Europe, unleavened. It is the custom to cover the top with small seeds, which are cultivated on purpose, called " Girginella." The honey is highly esteemed ; that made by the bees of Mellieha is reckoned the best ; its price is 8d. per pound. The " carubæ," or beans of the locust tree, are, when baked, a very common article of food amongst the poor ; and in passing through the villages, travellers are often annoyed by children holding out their hands, and begging for " Habba, harroob," or a grain to buy locusts with.

Besides the current money of Great Britain, and the additional small coins called grains, which are one-twelfth of a penny, accounts are also kept in taris and scudis.

$$20 \text{ Grains (Sicilian)} \quad . \quad . \quad . \quad 1 \text{ Tari,}$$
$$12 \text{ Taris} \quad . \quad . \quad . \quad . \quad 1 \text{ Scudi,}$$
$$1 \text{ Scudi, equal to } 1s. \; 8d. \text{ English.}$$

There is a small police force in Valetta composed of native officers, but they do not seem to be at all popular with the inhabitants.

The few following words will give my readers some idea of the Maltese language :—

Gremsicola . .	Lizard	Zimal . . .	Horse	Mosa	Goat
Farfetto . . .	Locust	Baal	Mule(*male*)	Kelpé	Dog
Asfur	Bird	Bacra	Cow	Himar	Ass
Hut	Fish	Naga	Sheep	Baala	Mule(*fem.*)

CHAPTER XVIII.

DEPARTURE FROM MALTA.

"Adieu! the joys of La Valette!"

EARLY to-day I received a message from the Marchioness of Testaferrata, a noble Italian lady, for a copy of my sketch of the General's Rock, a request with which I complied. I afterwards walked out with my host, Signor Fabreschi, to make several purchases, and went to see the "Manderagio," or lower part of the town, which is quite a curiosity. The streets are composed of winding stairs only a few feet wide, forming a complete labyrinth; and the houses on each side are so high, that the light of day is almost entirely excluded. Many of the poorer classes in this part of the town are employed in platting straw hats, and making cigars. On returning home to my lodgings, I was introduced to the Baroness Philomena de Saian, a little Messinese girl, whose father was a desperate gamester, and had squandered away his whole estate. This little girl lived in Malta with her mother, who was acquainted with Fabreschi's family. The articles which are chiefly worth purchasing in Valetta are, black silk mits, fine embroidered linen, various articles of gold and silver filigree work, with vases, costumes, and other figures, beautifully chiselled out of the white stone of the island; and these latter may be best obtained of James Soler, 78, Strada Forni, opposite Morell's Hotel. Lovers of natural history may occasionally meet with gazelles here, which are brought over in the market boats from Africa. I purchased a pair of young ones which I intended taking with me on my return to England. Canaries, and little French dogs, may be also obtained at very moderate prices. The "Bichons," or native dogs, as I have before observed, are very scarce, and fetch a high price.

My kind host had prepared a light supper of bread and cheese, fruit, and maccaroni, which he requested me to partake of before retiring to rest. He had on a former occasion invited me to dine with him; these, and numerous other little attentions, which insensibly win a stranger's heart, and are the result of genuine hospitality, contributed to raise this amiable family in my estimation. The father is a Leghornese, and seems a pleasant man; but unfortunately I could only converse with him through the medium of Michael, who acted as my interpreter to the rest of the family. The mother and the three daughters, Maria, Carolina, and Rosina, were unceasing in their attentions. The latter, Rosina, intends becoming a nun; she has a tame parrot which she calls "Papa-gar," and to which she is very fondly attached. I understood that Grand Cairo is the place where she intends taking the veil. Giovanni, the youngest, is a fine boy about thirteen years of age, and of a very affectionate disposition. After I left Malta I happened to find the following inscription inserted in my pocket book which had lain upon my table:—

> "John Fabreschi, he right yo in
> That book to not forgete him."

Besides the kindness I received from this family, I must also notice that of my friends, Mr. S., and Josef Soler, the Spanish lad. On the next morning I rose very early to pack up my things, and get all in readiness for my voyage to Sicily, having taken a passage in a speronaro to Syracuse, which was to sail at six in the evening, should the wind prove favourable. After getting my money exchanged for Sicilian dollars, I went to the market with Michael Fabreschi to purchase a supply of provisions for my voyage, as it was uncertain how long it might last. I laid in a stock for three days. My bill may amuse; it was as follows:—bread, 7d.; cheese, 2d.; eggs, 6d.; sausages, 4d.; grapes, 7d.; melons, pomegranates, &c. 5d.; sugar, 2d.; figs, 1d.; lemons, 1d.; amounting in the whole to 2s. 11d. This ample supply filled a large hamper basket, which, with my other luggage, I sent on board the speronaro. A passport was the next thing to be obtained, and this I procured from the Neapolitan consul's office, after a short delay. As I had every thing in readiness for my departure full two hours before the time, I crossed over with Fabreschi to Sliema, on the opposite side of the Quarantine Harbour; the fare is only one farthing each in the ferry boat. After searching for shells among the rocks, and watching the numerous bathers who resort here, the declining sun warned us to return again to Valetta, and we recrossed in the boat with a number of priests, who had been to bathe on the opposite side of the water. I was not long in taking leave of my kind friends, several of whom accompanied me to the quay, where I found the speronaro in readiness. As we were on the point of starting, the steamer from Alexandria arrived, bringing the news of the taking of Canton by the English. Another farewell look at Malta, and we were lightly skimming over the moonlit waves for another and a greener isle!

CHAPTER XIX.

VOYAGE FROM MALTA TO SYRACUSE.

> " The day was fair and sunny, sea and sky
> Drank its inspiring radiance, and the wind
> Swept strongly from the shore, blackening the wave

OUR speronaro sailed soon after sunset, from the quay of Valetta; and as the wind blew favourably for crossing the channel, we were soon out of sight of Malta. The rocky shores of that impregnable island melted away in the soft hazy light of a full autumnal moon; and as the graceful bark glided onwards over the waves, the silvery light shining on her snow-white sails, and the gentle murmur of the breaking waves that divided as she passed, echoing pleasantly, I had an opportunity of looking around me, having busied myself when I first went on board in arranging my boxes, and in getting every thing in order for my little voyage. Though the distance from Malta to Syracuse is only 120 miles, yet the passage sometimes occupies four or five days; for the wind in the Mediterranean is so very variable that it often happens that these small vessels are obliged to put back again, and wait for a day or two, until the wind favours them. When becalmed, the sailors have recourse to their oars, reminding one of the bygone days of chivalry, when the proud galleys of the knights of Rhodes traversed these very seas, and struck terror into the breasts of surrounding nations. Our speronaro had ten oars; and, like the generality of the Sicilian boats, the prow was adorned with an upright post four feet high, on the top of which was a shaggy fleece, apparently a goat's skin, dyed blue. This post is an invariable appendage to all the speronaros, and other Sicilian boats, which I have seen. In some places the fleece is superseded by a round knob of black wood, and in others by a bird, or fish, carved and painted. The outsides of these boats are generally adorned with various strange paintings of nymphs, goddesses, and swans, and other grotesque representations. The figure of an eye, seems a favourite sign, underneath which is often placed the name of the vessel. Ours was the " Concetzione," or " conception," belonging to Syracuse; her crew consisted of the Captain, nine men, and a lad, all Sicilians; none of them understood a single word of English, or indeed of any other language than their own " patois," in which they chattered with all the vivacity and liveliness so characteristic of the people of the south.

I was quite alone with these mariners, unable alike to understand or be understood by them, but I found them very friendly, and exceedingly anxious to make me as comfortable as their small vessel would allow. An arched cover at one end of the deck served as my cabin, underneath which they provided me with a mattress on which I slept at night; the owner's son, a handsome young Sicilian, kindly gave up this cabin for my use. Here I gathered together all my boxes, and setting my supply of provisions before me, commenced my supper. A picture of St. Lucian, the guardian saint of Syracuse, and another of the Virgin, were pasted upon my humble bedboard; an earthen lamp shed sufficient light to illuminate my little abode, but the extreme heat soon drove me outside the door, and I sat upon the deck in a flood of moonlight, where I finished my repast with some delicious pomegranates which the young Sicilian presented to me. All of a sudden the whole crew commenced singing, and continued to do so with great spirit for a considerable time. The effect was novel and unexpected, but until long after midnight they made such a noise that I found it impossible to get any sleep; however, at length they grew tired, and wrapping themselves up in their huge Sicilian cloaks and drawing the hoods over their heads, one after another lay down to sleep, and all was again still save the rippling of the waves on the moonlit sea. Behind my cabin was a recess like the back seat of a coach, in which the helmsman sat, and steered the vessel; a small window opened into it, through which I supplied him with some supper of bread and hard eggs, with a few figs. The only means of getting into this recess was by climbing over the roof of my little domicile; for the genius of invention is not so much patronized among the Sicilians, as it is in our own country, of which I afterwards met with several ludicrous examples.

The morning brought a calm;—the clear sunlight shone over the glossy sea, and the breeze during the night had speeded our progress, so that the shores of Sicily were now in sight, though almost shrouded by the warm haze of morning. This soon cleared away, and the island of Passaro, with a long line of coast, shone brightly beneath the deep blue sky of noon. Our men now took to their oars, not pulling them as we do, but standing up and pushing them forward, singing all the while, and modulating their voices to every stoke. Feeling hungry, I went to my basket, and got out some sausages which I wished to have cooked. I held them up to the Captain, and said, " Rosto, Capitano ; " he took them away, as I supposed, to fry them on a square fire place resembling a small altar, which stood on the deck at the other end of the boat. Presently I heard a frizzling sound, and the little boy laid me a clean cloth on the top of a box, and brought me a plate, and some wine with a tremendous glass tumbler of water, nearly a foot high. This completed, I began to look anxiously for my sausages, when, to my surprise, the plate came back filled with salt fish, swimming in olive oil. I conjectured of course that they had made an honest exchange, and quietly sat down to eat the fish, which was not over and above palatable;—when I had finished, the sausages were brought in, hot and smoking, to my great astonishment, as I had concluded that they were all devoured. I sent them back again to the generous folks at the other end of the boat, from whom I received a profound " Grazie, Seigneur," which I answered by an equal sincere " Padrone." The salt and pepper box amused me exceedingly; at first I thought it was an antiqué, and fell into a train of meditations which carried me back to the days of Hiero and Dionysius; but I afterwards discovered that it was the manufacture of the present age, though certainly as worthy of a place in the British Museum as the club of a Fejee savage, or the war-triton of a South Sea islander. The dress of the Sicilian mariners consists of white native cotton, the trowsers are full, something like those of the Greeks, and turned up at the knees; their feet are bare, and they seldom wear any covering on the head. Capo Passaro, the south-eastern promontory of Sicily, is a low rocky island, and not in reality a cape. When viewed from the sea, it has a barren appearance, with a few shrubby plants growing here and there upon it; and, like Malta, it seemed quite parched up beneath the burning sky. The heat at noon was excessive, and I was obliged to retire under the shade of my cabin roof, where I lay down and attempted to sleep, but the extreme liveliness of a number of young cockroaches running in all directions over the cabin, totally defeated my purpose. At sunset it was calm and cool, and I resumed my box and tablecloth outside the cabin, to make an evening meal of fruit. My little barefooted page waited on me with the greatest attention, for which I rewarded him with the remainder of my stock of provisions, reserving only a few branches of grapes for a " dejeuner" in the morning. The sun set over the Sicilian mountains, bathing that lovely country in its warm and glowing light; and, nearly at the same moment, up rose the full moon, pale and cold, from the deep blue eastern sea. The town of Noto presented a picturesque appearance on the rising hills, and several scattered villages were sprinkled about near the shore. Along this coast is a tunny fishery, famous for the excellency of the fish, and the large size to which they attain. The flesh of the tunny is much used as an article of food by the inhabitants, and when salted greatly resembles in flavour the Gorgona anchovies. Very far distant, and but just distinguishable in the haze of the evening atmosphere, the mighty Etna, now called Mongibello, rose proudly to the sky, forming an eternal beacon by which the mariner may steer his way through the halcyon seas that wash its widely-spread base. Some time afterthe last red streak died away in the west, I continued sitting on the top of my little cabin, till the dew warned me to retire beneath it; and I exchanged the pensive light of the moon, and the refreshing air of the evening breeze, for the close atmosphere, and the rustic lamp of my night-quarters, where I again lay down to sleep. The Sicilians were sitting around a lage dish on the deck, out of which they were eating their supper very quietly with wooden spoons, when suddenly they all jumped up, and throwing aside their heavy cloaks, took to the oars, and began to sing with all their might. This chorus, as before, continued with some intervals during the night; but, as I was more reconciled to their noises, it did not prevent my sleeping. Their mode of singing is peculiar ; one of the party makes a kind of sharp hissing noise, modulating his voice to the music, whilst the rest roar out with the most stentorian lungs imaginable ; and it is not unusual for them to complete the effect with a shrill scream. Several commenced dancing at the same time, and altogether they seemed as light of heart as their Greek ancestors at the Olympian games, though probably their music has rather degenerated since the days of classic story. At early daybreak, Syracuse was in sight before us. The modern town of Siragusa, on the island of Ortygia, is now all that remains of its ancient glory ; but the noble harbour, the spacious plains, the gently swelling hills, the towering mountains, they are still the same ; and it only requires a slight effort of the imagination to bring back its hundred marble palaces, its magnificent temples, fanes, and statues, and to repeople the silent wastes with the teeming population of ancient Greece. It must, indeed, have been a splendid city ; but its ashes sleep amidst the wrecks of time, and the sun of its glory is set for ever ; though its climate is such that, in nature, Cicero's remark still holds good, " that there never was a day at Syracuse, on some portion of which the sun did not shine."

As we approached the entrance of the harbour we met several boats piled up with immense tunny nets, made of wicker work, on their way out to the fishery. The singular appearance of these boats added to the picturesque character of the scene ; and on passing the southern promontory of the bay, I observed a number of the natives busily employed upon the rocks in pursuit of shell-fish. Presently our fairy bark was at anchor, where the fleets of the Romans had anchored before us, and the mighty inventions of Archimedes had been called into practice to defeat the common enemy of the world. A beautiful panorama was stretched around us, canopied beneath the azure heavens ; and the sleeping waters of the Grand Harbour were so clear and still, that its bed of long green sea-weed was distinctly visible beneath the spot where we lay. The owner's son, after securing a number of letters inside his stockings, exchanged his mariner's dress for the costume of a Sicilian gentleman ; and when I had got my things in readiness we stepped into the boat, and the whole company rowed ashore to the custom-house, where we had to undergo the scrutiny of the pratique officers. After a delay of about an hour, during which time my passport was inspected by the various authorities, we returned again to the speronaro, guarded by two dogans, or Neapolitan soldiers, with an officer of the custom-house, to examine my baggage. Whilst this operation was going forward the gleam of a small pin that I wore in my handkerchief attracted the attention of the officer, and seemed to take his fancy amazingly. He pointed to it with his finger, exclaiming "bellissimo! bellissimo;" and, at the same moment, drew from his own cravat an enormous gold brooch, containing dark-coloured crystals. These he intimated to me were from Mongibello, (Mount Etna,) and after putting it into my hand endeavoured to explain to me that he wished for an exchange. I did not understand him at first; but afterwards, by the aid of an Italian phrase-book, I managed to decline his offer, and retain my bauble, without in any way offending the officer, who bowed politely, and replaced the crystal brooch in his bosom. The custom-house is situated close to the water's edge, leading down to which is a broad flight of steps covered with carpet, on which we landed. To the right is a cluster of fig-trees, and on the left, towards the entrance of the town, is a level promenade, planted with weeping willows and shady pimento-trees, beneath which are several seats interspersed with flowers. The famous fountain of Arethusa empties itself into the sea about half a dozen yards from the custom-house, in the form of an insignificant channel, running underground, and falling from a stone trough which serves as a tank, where a solitary washerwoman was rinsing her linen. The original site of the fountain, however, is a little higher up, within the walls of the town, from whence this stream issues to flow into the harbour. Here I paused, and involuntarily exclaimed, " O Syracuse, how art thou fallen!"

CHAPTER XX.

RIVERS ANAPUS AND PAPYRUS—TEMPLE OF JUPITER OLYMPUS, AND THE FONTE CIANE.

> " And nearer to the river's trembling edge,
>   There grew broad flag-flowers, purple prankt with white,
>   And starry river-buds among the sedge,
>   And floating water-lilies, broad and bright,
>   Which lit the oak that overhung the hedge
>   With moonlight beams of their own watery light;
>   And bulrushes, and reeds of such deep green
>   As soothed the dazzled eye with sober sheen."

I HAD no sooner landed than one of the " dogans," or soldiers, led me to the autho-rities of the Neapolitan Government, and gave me to understand that I must pay them my "devoirs" for the services which it was supposed they had rendered me. This I accordingly did, and after a number of formal bows and bends on both sides, I was most graciously dismissed, and permitted to enter the town with my luggage. I now found myself in a strange country, just entering a city, every street of which was unknown to me; and what was worse, without a single person who could speak even a few words of English. I was possessed of a letter of introduction to the British Consul, who is a Maltese by birth, and after a short delay I proceeded to his residence, accompanied by the young Sicilian who had been my friend on board the speronaro. I found the Consul at home, but could get very little information from him; and as my chief desire was to visit as many of the antiquities in the neighbour-hood as possible, I declined his invitation to call upon him on the following morning. My next object was to procure an intelligent guide; and as I had been recommended to Signor Polité, by my friend, Dr. H., of London, I set off in quest of him. At first I could not make myself understood, but afterwards a sailor was brought to me who had been many years ago in England, having served on board a man-of-war, and with his assistance as interpreter I explained my purposed errand. Passing through a number of narrow miserable looking streets, we arrived at last before the domicile of the Polités. The person recommended to me by Dr. H. was by profes-sion an artist, and one well acquainted with all the antique treasures around Syracuse;

he had a brother at Girgenti who followed the same profession there, and likewise acted as a guide to all the numerous antiquities of that place. On inquiring for Signor P., I found that he was deceased, or as they beautifully expressed it, "that he was above," pointing to the blue sky overhead. His son, however, an obliging young man, now takes his place, both as an artist, and also as a guide to strangers visiting the neighbourhood. On making myself known, he immediately prepared to accompany me to the temple of Jupiter Olympus, and the Papyrus river, and ordered a boat to be in waiting at the quay for that purpose. As is the custom in Sicily, he laid before me a box full of the cards and addresses of all the parties who had employed his father, and himself, as guides, for many years past; and I was agreeably surprised at finding amongst them that of my friend Dr. H., dated 1824, an undeniable proof that my chosen guide was no impostor. We lost no time in getting down to the boat, and soon found ourselves again crossing the pellucid waters of that noble harbour. Our boat was protected from the sun by a canopy of blue striped cotton; and I found that they had laid in a stock of bread and tunny-fish, presuming, no doubt, on my English appetite, for unfortunately we Britons are proverbial for our roast beef and plum pudding propensities. The day was sultry, and the sky, as usual, without a cloud; we soon reached the opposite side of the harbour, at the mouth of the river Anapus. Here the sand had so choaked up the bed of the river, that our men were obliged to jump out of the boat, and by main force drag it across the bar; the water was as clear as crystal, rippling over the white pebbles, and so extremely shallow that a child might have forded it. After crossing the bar, the water became considerably deeper, and our men pushed us on by means of the oars; for the breadth of the Anapus is so inconsiderable, that there is scarcely room for two boats to pass one another in some places. The margin is bordered with luxuriant vegetation, backed with canes fifteen or twenty feet high. Amongst the reeds, I observed the false papyrus growing here and there, but it was much smaller, and in less abundance than the true kind, which is only met with on the banks of the Papyrus river. Myriads of dragon-flies darted around us in every direction, and the butterflies were also very plentiful, particularly the papilio, "machaon," and P. "podalirius." We had not proceeded far, before we were completely embowered in the canes, among which the nightingale and sedge warbler were singing most melodiously; our unceremonious intrusion amid these quiet haunts roused a purple gallinule, or coot, that was feeding amongst the rushes. The bird was evidently taken by surprise, and flew forwards in the direction of the river. Signor Polité, the two men, and the boy, all simultaneously jumped out of the boat, and ran along the shore, in pursuit of the bird, leaving me alone on the stream; they chased it a long way, making a desperate hunt; and after one or two very narrow escapes, the terrified fowl at last found a secure retreat under a bed of matted reeds, and its pursuers returned to the boat. Whilst they were running after the bird, I got on shore also, and looked about for insects. I found several of the "mantis" tribe, and an innumerable quantity of grasshoppers; but as my time was necessarily so very limited, I had but few opportunities of making any search for them. I may merely state, with regard to the insects of Sicily, that I should imagine that country to be a rich field of enterprize for the industrious entomologist, particularly in the early part of the summer, when the lepidoptera are the most abundant. The next creature we fell in with was a large viper, swimming down the stream, and afterwards a multitude of frogs peeping up from the leaves of the water-sedge, like the picture in Æsop's Fables, where they are praying to Jupiter for a king. We now arrived at the junction of the river Papyrus with the Anapus, where we landed for the purpose of visiting the ruins of the temple of Jupiter Olympus, leaving the boat to await our return. The first object I saw on getting clear of the canes, was a beautiful hoopoe feeding upon the ground; the moment it saw us, however, it erected its crest, and spreading its wings, flew away before I had time to admire it. A walk of a few minutes across some parched fields brought us to the ruins. Only two pillars of this once magnificent temple now remain standing; they are at some little distance from each other, and have a fluted appearance. The accompanying sketch, which I made on the spot, will convey some idea of it. Near this my guide showed me an oblong pit, about twenty-three feet deep, and of considerable width; it was probably an ancient receptacle for retaining water. The lizards I found to be of a larger size, and of a much brighter colour than those of Malta, but not quite so numerous. On crossing one of the fields on our way back to the boat, I was charmed with the quantity of large spreading olive-trees that grew on all sides, imparting a *classical* air to the scene that harmonized well with the fallen fragments of mighty Greece.

Re-embarking in our boat, we ascended the river Papyrus to its source, at the Fonte Cianè; amongst the rank exuberance of vegetation on the sides of this stream, were placed a number of fishing baskets of wicker-work, which are used to ensnare the various fish with which the Papyrus abounds:—the water is very deep, but so clear and transparent, that every snail shell at the bottom is distinctly visible. It was now the hottest part of the day, and the evaporation arising from the fierce rays of the sun pouring down upon the water, rendered the atmosphere like a vapour-bath. As we proceeded, the vegetation increased; in many places we were obliged to push aside the canes to form a passage, and it required considerable power to urge the boat onwards through the tangled mass of white and yellow water lillies, and other river plants that impeded our progress. Almost every leaf was the resting place of a dragon-fly; and as we moved along those brilliant creatures thronged the air, fluttering from one spray to another. I counted no less than nine varieties; some were immensely large, and of a bright blue colour; others crimson, and others again

From Nature & on Stone by George French Angas.

Day & Haghe Lith.rs to the Queen.

RUINS OF THE TEMPLE OF JUPITER OLYMPUS, SYRACUSE.

were entirely of a dark purple hue. But the most interesting production of this
river is the plant from which it derives its name—the Papyrus, or "paper-rush" of
the ancients. Here it grows in unbounded luxuriance, forming one of the prettiest
sights imaginable; immense groups of this singular plant rise to the height of
eight, ten, and even twelve feet, completely covering the margin of the river, and
forming a rich canopy of its feathery clusters. For some distance both sides of
the stream were entirely composed of papyri, growing up from the bottom of the
water. We pulled up several to examine the lower part of the stem, which is the
portion of which the paper is made; it is about as thick as a person's wrist, and
of a snowy whiteness for twelve or fifteen inches from the bottom. After a great
deal of time lost in contending with the matted water weeds, we arrived at last at the
Fonte Cianè, a large and capacious basin, from whence the river takes its rise. The
water is extremely limpid, and though twenty-two feet deep, every object at the
bottom is clearly discernible; the whole Fonte is surrounded by tufts of tall papyrus,
backed by rushes, amongst which a number of those beautiful and picturesque creatures, the Sicilian oxen, were quietly browsing. The chief attraction to this place
is the opportunity afforded by the extreme clearness of the water, for observing the
fish swimming about at the bottom of the pool. For this purpose we remained till
the boat was perfectly steady; and on looking over the side, we saw hundreds of blue
mullet roving amongst the beds of aquatic moss below, as distinctly as though they
had been gold fishes in a globe of crystal. After quenching our thirst by several
very copious draughts of the pellucid water, we returned again to the spot where we
were to disembark. At this place we found mules in waiting for us, and another
cicerone, or attendant. Here I dismissed the boat, and Polité and myself mounting
the mules, we set off at once for the ruins of Tychæ and Neapolis.

M

CHAPTER XXI.

TYCHÆ—NEAPOLIS—FORT LABDALUS—THE QUARRIES OF THE PHILOSOPHERS—STRADA
DEL TOMBE—SUBTERRANEAN PASSAGE—TEMPLE OF CERES.

> "I stood alone on Tychæ's ruined height—
> The noble harbour as a lake below,
> And the broad plains—but all was desolate—
> The lizard and the grasshopper alone had life,
> And as I stood, strange melancholy thoughts—
> The shadows of the past—they haunted me!"

OUR ride lay through an extremely rich country, (once the classic soil of Theocritus,) the path being bordered in many places by hedgerows of prickly pears, enclosing vineyards and hemp fields. We crossed a small bridge where I observed quantities of the castor-oil plant, (palma christi,) growing spontaneously on the margin of the stream bed. My guide picked me a handful of fine blackberries, and had it not been for the southern air of the aloe and Indian fig beside me, I could for the moment have fancied myself once more in a Devonshire lane, wandering as I was wont to do, with my schoolmates, in the merry hours of childhood.

I observed a small tree frog, of a light green colour, upon the leaf of a cactus, which I pointed out to my guide to procure for me. The old man was quite horror-struck at the idea of my wishing for such a creature; and it was with some difficulty I could prevail upon him to pluck the leaf on which the little animal was reposing; despite, however, the old man's fears, I got him safely to Syracuse, where he found an asylum in a phial of alcohol, without having spit either fire or poison in my face! We next ascended a steep rocky path, overhung with several very fine weeping willows, beneath one of which we halted to pick up some bunches of immense white grapes, which a man was gathering from a vine that spread itself completely over the topmost boughs of a tall mulberry tree. These grapes are used for wine, and owing to their shady situation they had not attained that degree of sweetness usually met with in the grapes of Sicily; nevertheless, as we were uncommonly thirsty, they suited our purpose all the better. A little farther on we reached a small tank where

From Nature, & Stone by Geo. French Angas.   Day & Haghe. Lith.rs to the Queen

EAR OF DIONYSIUS,

In the Latomie—Syracuse.

we watered our mules, and soon afterwards found ourselves among the walls of ancient Tychæ, and the scattered ruins of that part of the city called Neapolis. Heaps of stones confusedly piled up, interspersed with creeping briars and bulbous plants, are the only present remains of the once formidable walls of Tychæ. My guides, (for old Alosco the muleteer proved a very good one, and showed evident signs of having filled that office long before young Polité's time,) next pointed out to me the site of a gateway, through which Marcellus entered when the Romans made themselves masters of Syracuse. Near this place a small naumachia, and the remains of a diminutive amphitheatre, were also pointed out. Ancient wheel-tracks are distinctly visible in several places; some of which I traced for a considerable distance, worn in the bare rock. Passing the Quarries of the Philosophers,—so called from the circumstance of this place having been the prison in which Dionysius confined the poet Philoxenes, and several philosophers, for refusing to praise his poetical compositions,—my guides next showed me the ruins of Fort Labdalus, which form a conspicuous object at the extremity of the table-land over which these scattered vestiges of antiquity are spread. The wall facing Epipholæ is still discernible; my guides informed me that it was erected in twenty days at a sudden notice. The view from this place is enchanting; it consists of an extensive panorama, including the modern town of Syracuse, with the harbour, and beyond it the sparkling waters of the Mediterranean Sea; to the north the Campo Romano, and the country towards Catania, with the promontory of Magnesia stretching out into the sea, backed by crowded mountains half lost in the distance; beyond which, at the extremity of the vast plain near the sea coast, the mighty Mongibello towers far above them all, mingling his sulphurous crest with the clouds. On the south and west the sluggish waters of the Anapus, winding through a marshy valley luxurious to excess, while still further to the westward the eye rests on the verdant slopes of the lesser Hybla. After contemplating for some minutes this delightful panorama, we descended a rugged hollow, at the foot of the ruins of Fort Esapilo, and prepared to enter the subterranean passages, which have only lately been excavated. At the time of Mrs. Starke's visit to Sicily they were but very partially exposed, and my old guide told me that "Madame Starkey," as he called her, crept in as far as she could on her hands and knees to explore this subterranean abode, where the bat and the scorpion have dwelt for ages past. Now, however, the passages are so cleared, that by the light of our torches we penetrated for a considerable way in various directions. These passages are so lofty as to admit cavalry, and are generally supposed to have been formed for the purpose of transmitting troops and provisions from one part of the city to another, in times of warfare and attack.

Several openings to these underground ways are pointed out from above; and as we proceeded in our subterranean march, we were here and there cheered by a

M 2

peep of sunlight streaming through the aperture overhead. Evident marks still remain in these passages of their having been the abode of men and horses, and holes for rings in the wall at equal distances, are pointed out by the guides, as the places where the cavalry tied up their horses when awaiting some onset.

Returning by the Strada del Tombe, in the quarter of Acradina, my old cicerone, Guiseppi Alosco, pointed out a number of small tombs cut in the rock on both sides, interspersed with marks of marble slabs, originally having Greek inscriptions. Amongst these I was particularly called to observe one which the guides assured me was the tomb of Archimedes; though differing considerably from the description given of it by Cicero, when he was quæstor of Sicily. He describes it as " a small column rising but slightly above the brambles, on which were graven the figures of a sphere and a cylinder." The one which I saw consisted of two fluted Doric columns, much broken, supporting an architrave and frieze, above which was a pediment, all hewn out of the solid rock. The interior contains niches for urns, and the remains of a sarcophagus. This, therefore, cannot be the true sepulchre of the philosopher, according to the ancient accounts, which tell us that Archimedes had it inscribed at his own desire with the figures of a sphere and a cylinder, and that even before the time of Cicero it had been lost and wholly neglected by his ungrateful countrymen. The pleasure and triumph of the illustrious orator, on once more discovering this relic, is too well known to be repeated.

Just before arriving at the gates of the city of modern Siragusa, we passed the remains of a temple dedicated to Ceres and Proserpine, only *one* pillar of which is now standing. Two others of variegated marble have lately been removed from their original position, and are now lying in the town close to the cathedral, which is formed partly by the columns of the Greek temple of Minerva. Here they appear totally useless, and I fear, if no one has sufficient reverence for the remains of antiquity to replace them again where they formerly stood, that they will, like most precious relics, be broken to pieces by order of the King of Sicily, either to mend the roads, or to pave his Majesty's kitchen. By this time we arrived at the Albergo del Sole. It was nearly seven o'clock, and I found my landlord anxiously awaiting my return, afraid no doubt that as I had ordered dinner at five o'clock, it would all be spoiled before I came in. I ascended the interminable flight of stone steps that led to the corridor of the Albergo, followed by Polité and old Alosco, and there I found the boatmen I had employed in the morning waiting for payment. After concluding our bargains, in which my landlord acted as interpreter, I dismissed the whole train, and entered the saloon, where I found a good dinner laid out for me. As I had arranged with Polité to act as my guide on the following day, and promised Alosco that he should escort me on the day afterwards to Catania, I sat down to partake of my host's liberal repast after the adventures of the day, first presenting him with half-a-dozen gigantic papyri, which we had brought from the Fonte Cianè, as an ornament for one corner of the room. My landlord waited upon me in person, bringing in course after course of macaroni, fish, ragouts, pastry, &c., with excellent Syracusan wine. The water here, as in Malta, is all iced before it is brought to table, which renders it exceedingly refreshing in so hot a climate. The desert was copious, consisting of fresh grapes, figs, walnuts, apples, and almonds. A large mastiff was my only companion for the remainder of the evening, and after I had dined I threw myself on one of the four couches that adorned the room, and rested myself before proceeding upstairs to note down in my journal, and pack up the antiquities and other curiosities which I had collected during the day. The walls of this inimitable saloon were decorated by six very ancient-looking mirrors, carved all over with images of Venus, Bacchus, and a host of other divinities, so that their original utility as mirrors was totally set aside. It was certainly a grotesque example of combining the useful and the ornamental; for I had not the least idea, on approaching these glasses, to find a bevy of gods and goddesses, instead of my own reflected image. After amusing myself with these mirrors, and various other remarkable articles of furniture belonging to the apartment, I ascended several more flights of stone steps, and reached my bedroom, which my landlord had kept locked all day for the safety of my luggage. After the interchange of " buona sera," I secured the door with a couple of chairs, and putting the window wide open to admit a breath of air, I lay down to sleep, and to dream of Syracuse and its former glory, after the day's ramble amongst its ruins— the first I had spent in pleasant Sicily.

CHAPTER XXII.

> " Arethusa arose from her couch of snows
>   In the Acroceraunian mountains,
>   From cloud and from crag, with many a jag,
>   Shepherding her bright fountains,
>   And under the water, the earth's white daughter
>   Fled like a sunny beam ;
>   Behind her descended, her billows unblended,
>   With the brackish Dorian stream."

No sooner had the morning dawned, than my faithful Polité was in waiting at
the doorway of the Albergo, to act as my guide through the city, to the numerous
places of interest and antiquity which still remained for me to visit. I soon despatched a cup of coffee, and joining my guide we set off on foot, intending to make a
pedestrian excursion, as most of the spots we had to visit, lay either in the suburbs
of the city, or at a short distance from it. The museum, which is situated near the
cathedral, first claimed our attention. It consists chiefly, indeed I may almost say
exclusively, of antiquities discovered in and about the neighbourhood of the ancient
Syracuse. A marble statue of Venus, without the head, which was found buried
beneath a fig-tree in the quarter of Acradina, is by far the finest piece of sculpture.
The other objects most worthy of notice, are a Greek head of Esculapius, some very
curious ancient pictures in fresco, lamps, and other articles of household furniture,
two glass cups finely coloured, inscriptions taken from the street of the tombs, of
white marble, some of which are very legible, rings, vases, ladies' hair-pins, lachrymatories, and coins. There is also a fine headless drapery exquisitely sculptured in
marble, a basso-relievo of Timoleon, found in the amphitheatre, a leaden sarcophagus
excavated from the Scala Græca, Campo Romano, containing portions of a skeleton
with an amazingly thick skull ; another large sarcophagus, and, lastly, a curious relic
consisting of a quantity of earthen pots and cups, one inside another, which appear
to have belonged to a pottery manufactory, and to have been suddenly crushed by

some violent concussion. These were dug up along with a number of Græco-Sicilian antiquities in the vicinity. The usual charge made to visitors at the museum is four taris, but the guardian finds it more profitable to leave it to the generosity of the visitors, (a common practice on the Continent,) which often imposes an unpleasant tax upon strangers. Near the cathedral I observed the two pillars belonging to the temple of Ceres in Acradina, which have been purloined from the fane of the goddess to serve some miserable purpose in repairing the modern city.

The cathedral, which I before noticed, is an erection of the 7th century, and dedicated to the Virgin. It is built in the temple of Minerva, or rather, the remains of that edifice have been cruelly mutilated and disfigured by being transformed into the walls of this building. Some idea, however, of the simple beauty and grandeur of this Doric temple may still be formed by a survey of those portions which now remain. It formerly displayed forty columns, fluted, without a base, erected on a raised quadrilateral platform. The Cella was enclosed by walls, formed of large stones neatly joined without cement: these walls were cut through to form communicating arches with the sides when it became a church. Eleven of the columns on the north side of the edifice are built into the wall, where they may still be traced. Those on the south side are in better preservation, and at the western end two more are visible.

The Monastery of St. Lucian, the guardian saint of Siragusa, is one of the finest religious establishments in the city. I peeped into the chapel during mass, and was much struck with the remarkably light and pretty appearance of a vast number of suspended lamps hanging at various distances above the altar-piece, and reaching quite up to the ceiling of the church. The cords by which these lamps are hung are so fine as to be almost imperceptible, and give one the idea of their resting in the air. Santa Lucian is to the Syracusans what St. Michael is to the inhabitants of Malta—their favourite guardian saint and patroness—and in almost every cottage, and even in the speronaro and fishing-boat, a rude picture of this idolized being is constantly to be found. In more wealthy families, the pictures of the saints are oftentimes elaborately painted, and finely executed, though the character of the individual represented is preserved the same in these as in more humble editions. After visiting the Collegiate Church, where there are several tolerably good paintings, my guide proceeded to show me the far-famed fountain of Arethusa, which still wells up from the ground, broad and bubbling, though its shoals of sacred fishes, and the translucent purity of its waters, are fled for ever. It is now converted into a tank for washerwomen, and is the receptacle for the purification of all the dirty linen in Siragusa. Never again could a poet sit down and sing of Arethusa, if he had once witnessed the sight which I was favoured to behold on looking down from the wall which commands a view of the fountain and its rocky source. My guide wittily said to me on reaching the spot,

" These are the nymphæ modernæ," pointing at the same time to nearly half-a-hundred women with their clothes tucked up above their knees, standing in rows in the water, and all busily engaged in washing and beating their dirty garments with wooden spatulas, forming the most grotesque " coup d'œil" imaginable. This was unexpected, for I did not conceive of nymphs in the year 1841, and so great a number of them too. Such a scene was hardly " comme il faut," and reminded me of the surprise I experienced on first discovering the grotto of the goddess Calypso in the island of Malta. It is said that this is the identical river Arethusa which sinks under ground near Olympia in the Peloponnesus, and that, continuing its course for five or six hundred miles below the ocean, it rises again in this place. Many of the old Sicilian authors state that the golden cup won at the Olympic Games was thrown into the Grecian Arethusa, and was soon afterwards cast up again by the Ortygian one. They also state that after the great sacrifices at the former place, the waters of the fountain rose for several days tinged with the blood of the victims. Near to Arethusa, in the grand harbour, bubbles up another spring, called the " Occhi di Zillica," through the sea, and rises to the surface almost unimpregnated with the salt water. This is Alphæus, who, according to the poets, pursued Arethusa all the way to Sicily, and was by Diana converted into this fountain, just as he was approaching to seize the terrified nymph, who was at the same moment transformed into the spring, which still bears her name. Thus much for Arethusa. I certainly *was* disappointed in finding it so degraded and debased, but I consoled myself by the feeling that I *had* seen Arethusa, and that it was the *very same* of whose " sweet waters" Cicero speaks as containing an incredible number of fishes, &c. Had he said " washerwomen," the description would have better suited its appearance at the present day! Oh! the miserable sordid taste of these modern times. There is *no* regard paid to many of the precious relics of antiquity, which are the only speaking monuments of ages that once were—of ages when the eloquence of a Demosthenes—when the courage of a Leonidas or a Miltiades—the chisel of a Praxiteles, and the pencil of a Zeuxis—when a brilliant phalanx of warriors and statesmen, and philosophers and poets, *all* contributed to render Greece the wonder of her time, and the glory of the world. As Ali Pacha wilfully and maliciously pulled to pieces the venerable temples in Upper Egypt, so in many other countries, ignorant and avaricious men destroy the crumbling edifice that bids them do reverence to a long line of forgotten ancestry. Nor are these instances of a savage and destructive mind few and far between; look at England, our own country, and let the guilty blush at home! For many a fair baronial castle, and many a precious relic of the chivalry and feudal spirit of the middle ages, is sacrificed to the cursed love of gold by the wretched worshippers at the shrine of mammon.

But to return to my subject :—having by this time completed my survey of all that was most interesting within the limits of the modern city of Siragusa, we next pro-

From Nature & on Stone by George Frenicodoyes

By High Lith: Wd 76: Street.

VIEW FROM THE RUINS OF TYCHA, LOOKING TOWARDS ETNA.

ceeded to the quarters formerly called Acradina and Neapolis, where by far the greater part of the existing remains of ancient Syracuse are to be found. The celebrated Ear of Dionysius is situated in one of the numerous "latomies," or quarries, from which it is generally supposed that a great portion of the stone used in building the ancient cities was formerly excavated. This latomie is extensive, and is filled with a luxuriant garden of fig trees, prickly pears, and other fruits. A winding descent leads the traveller into this garden, to the left of which stands the Ear of Dionysius, hewn out of the perpendicular limestone rock. This lasting memento of the crafty and cruel tyrant, is cut in the form of an ass's ear, being fifty-eight feet in height at the entrance, seventeen feet wide, and 210 feet long. The sides converge gradually towards the top, and terminate in a small channel, which conveyed every sound in the cave, however trifling, to an aperture near the entrance. Hence all the sounds in this prison were directed to one common tympanum, which communicated with a small private apartment, where Dionysius spent his leisure time in listening to the conversation of his prisoners. This chamber, as pointed out by the guides, is merely a small square recess, situated almost at the top of the cavern; the only present mode of access being by means of a rope and pulley, the adventurer hazarding his life in a little crazy chair. The apparatus was duly prepared, and they, no doubt, expected to give me a ride to enable me to stand where Dionysius stood. Not feeling inclined to venture my bones on so uncertain a foundation, I contented myself with a view of the chamber from below, and pacified the pecuniary desires of the owner of the latomie, by having a small cannon fired off in the Ear, which produced a succession of thundering echoes, resembling a whole volley of artillery discharging at the same time. A piece of paper torn at the same spot, is also heard distinctly throughout the whole cave. After purchasing several ancient coins, which had been dug up in the latomie, and making a sketch of the Ear of Dionysius, we proceeded to the contiguous quarries, or grottos, out of which an enormous quantity of the stone appears to have been excavated, but which are now converted into rope-walks. These quarries having been dug underneath the rock, and portions of the stone left as supporters for the roof, they present a picturesque and not unpleasing appearance.

The most remarkable circumstance is, that the ancients appear to have hewn out the blocks of stone, (with some tool of peculiar construction,) from the solid rock, at once in the shape and size required. This is evident from the marks on the roof and sides of the quarries, which appear indicated in geometrical quantities, and show the neatness with which the blocks must have been cut out. In the walls are still visible the holes to which prisoners were chained, and the general opinion is, that after the stone had been excavated, it was used as a state prison by Dionysius the tyrant. The great latomie, or Garden of Paradise, as the Sicilians term it, is situated at a short distance from the former, and consists of a similar, but larger

N

and more precipitate quarry, which is converted into a most picturesque and
luxuriant garden, and belongs to a nobleman of Syracuse. As we walked on, my
guide, Polité, pointed out to me at almost every step, spots where either he or his
father had dug up coins, vases, or lachrymatories; so numerous are the scattered
vestiges of this once magnificent and powerful city. We entered the garden by a
number of steps; and as it was the hottest time of the day, and we were fatigued
and thirsty, we gladly availed ourselves of the opportunity of rest afforded by a small
room erected as a retreat for visitors, by the owner of the latomie. Here we found
an old woman and her son, who had the care of the garden. The lad was just
recovering from a violent fever, and presented one of the most sickly and emaciated
countenances I ever beheld. The woman quickly set before us some grapes, walnuts,
figs, and locusts, with a quantity of good Sicilian wine, and bread; the latter commonly eaten by the peasants of the country, but so black and sour, that were it to
appear at an English table it would meet with very few customers. But habit renders all things tolerable, and in time I was able to eat the black bread with considerable relish. After writing my name in a small visitor's book, gaily adorned with
ribbons, and ornamented on the outside with a picture of Queen Victoria, I wandered
through the walks of this subterranean garden amongst cypresses, sorbs, orange,
lemon, and bergamot trees, interspersed with a variety of flowers, nearly similar to
those in our English gardens, particularly China-asters, and pinks. I had the pleasure
of tasting some of the last year's lemons, which had remained all the winter upon
the trees, and were very sweet, and not unlike an orange in flavour. I would here
remark that the oranges of Sicily are, in general, inferior both to those of Spain and
the Western Islands. Lemons form a much more important article here; and in
the Val di Demone, particularly for many miles around Messina, they grow in such
abundance as to form a considerable article of export from that city, and also from
many of the other towns on that part of the coast. But I am again wandering.
Communicating with this garden by a long subterranean passage, just high enough
for a person to stand upright in, is another and much smaller latomie, now used
partly as a farm-yard, and containing an orchard of orange and lemon-trees. There
is in this latomie another " Ear," smaller, but exactly corresponding in form and
intention with that of Dionysius, which I have not heard mentioned in any traveller's
account of Syracuse.

From the Garden of Paradise, we next visited the aqueduct and nymphæum,
situated on an eminence overlooking the remains of the theatre. Beneath a cave,
in which rises a spring of water, the tripod of Apollo formerly stood; and even at
the present time it requires but a slight stretch of the imagination to restore the
tripod, and all the mystic things that pertained to the oracle of the divinity; to call
back the golden cauldron, and the trembling inquirers of the mysterious Pythia—

the white-robed priestess, crowned with a wreath of laurel, frantic in her incantations, and filled with the divine afflatus, "who knew things past, and present, and to come." Such an oracle, placed as this was, and overlooking one of the most charming and delicious prospects in Sicily, must, when all the cities shone in their marble splendour, and the blue waters of the Mediterranean were covered with the fleets of the triumphant Greeks, have excited a wonderful influence over a nation whose religion was of the wildest and most imaginative nature possible; when every stream had its presiding nymph, and every grove its company of fauns and satyrs. Close to the site of the Pythian oracle is the Strada Sepulchrale, or street of the tombs. I have already mentioned a similar street under the denomination of the "Strada del Tombe," which is situated in Acradina. This, however, in Neapolis, is much more perfect, and is of a semicircular form, cut in the rock. The tracks of ancient carriage wheels, worn in the stones, are very evident; and the whole way, on both sides, is bordered with a number of sepulchral chambers, containing recesses of various sizes for families, or single individuals; some appeared very small, and were cut in the exterior wall; these were probably for very young children, and were afterwards sealed with a marble tablet having an inscription.

The following lines, suggested by my excursions amongst all that now remains of ancient Syracuse, may not be out of place here:—

I.

Spirit of Greece! awake thy song once more,
And from the ruin-mantled deserts rise;
Send forth thy numbers on th' Ortygian shore
And bid them live—as when the bird that dies
Bursts from its ashes with a wild surprise.
Return again! for thou hast slumbering been—
Thy sun went down beneath the wintry skies
Of long dark ages, and its ray serene
Forsook thy cherished fanes as though it ne'er had been.

II.

Return again! to that loved spot of thine,
For the dark olive shades thy temples o'er;
Round many a column wreathes the tangled vine
And silence triumphs on thy wave-washed shore!
Spirit! thy mystic grandeur I adore.
Speed thy white wings across the ocean foam—
Nor let the sunset streak thy path once more
As a bright weary bird that 's born to roam,
But fold thy placid wings and seek thy Grecian home

III.

Hast thou forgotten every snow white fane?
Shall pensive maiden fling her lyre aside?
Shall never minstrel boy breathe song again,
As swells his bosom with romantic pride?
O Spirit of the Greeks! thou dost abide
Somewhere, though hovering in the star-lit air;
And every lily at the waterside,
And every tall papyrus waving there,
Call on thy magic aid their sweetest song to bear!

From Nature & on Stone by George French Angas

Day & Haghe lith.^{rs} to the Queen.

THE GREEK THEATRE, SYRACUSE .

CHAPTER XXIII.

> "I marked the beauties of the land and main,
> Alone and friendless on the magic shore
> Whose arts and arms but live in poets' lore;
> The past returned, the present seemed to cease,
> And glory knew no clime beyond her Greece.
> And yet unwearied still my footsteps trod
> O'er the vain shrine of many a vanished god."

THE theatre, hewn out of a rock on the shelving side of the hill, beneath the nymphæum, and commanding a view of the fertile valley of the Anapus, with the mountain of Hybla in the distance, is still in tolerable preservation, though in parts entirely overgrown with brushwood and wild flowers, over which innumerable butterflies
were chasing each other in the sultry sunshine of a Sicilian afternoon. Cicero called
this theatre "Maximum;" and Diodorus thought it the most beautiful edifice of the
kind in the whole island. But little remains of the Scena; most of the materials
of which it was composed were used by Charles the Fifth, of Spain, in building
his fortifications around the modern city on the island of Ortygia. The shape of
this immense theatre is nearly a semicircle, the seats arranged one above another in
rows. A contrivance is visible in some parts for preventing the feet of one person
from interfering with the comfort of those in front, by the back of each tier of seats
being slightly raised above the rest of the stone; the diameter is nearly 120 feet,
and persons have computed it to have held 40,000 spectators. It is generally considered to be the most ancient Greek theatre now in existence, and is built of white
marble. The positions where poles for the support of an awning were fixed, are still
evident; and among the seats of the upper corridor is one having a Greek inscription
graven on the back, portions of which I perceived were easily legible. After climbing
among the seats of the theatre, and searching out every cranny and corner, I picked up

and brought away with me a bit of the marble—the pure and white Parian—that by it I might still remember the great theatre of the Greeks. I would not have my readers here condemn me for sacrilege, for there is no one deprecates the barbarian, yet too frequent, custom of mutilating antique remains, more than myself: still I considered the *loose* and *scattered* fragments of the theatre to be like the ears after harvest—common property. Not far from this spot is the amphitheatre, considered to be the work of the Romans, and to have been constructed when the cities of Sicily were under the yoke of that nation. Until the commencement of the last year, this vast building was almost entirely overgrown with trees and a great part of it covered with earth. It has, however, been lately excavated, and many perfect remains of antiquity have been brought to light. In the centre is a naumachia, where probably the water fights were exhibited. The corridors are covered, and almost entire. The low covered ways for the beasts are also remaining; from these are several openings into the arena, from whence the animals were let loose to the combat. The grand entrance by a flight of steps, which we descended, is to the north, and we found ourselves in the centre of the amphitheatre, which sloped up gradually on all sides. At each end is an arch, formerly covering the entrance to the arena, which together with portions of the columns and mouldings of the ornamented parts of the building, are in good preservation; the aqueduct runs beneath one side of the walls towards the south. The next object claiming our attention was the catacombs, or "Le Grotti di S. Giovanni," situated near the little chapel of St. John, and not far from the amphitheatre. On regaining our footpath, my guide accosted a primitive looking monk, who was slowly wandering along on a donkey. The beast appeared as much a recluse as its master, and now and then stopped to crop the herbage, unchecked by the monk, who sat with arms folded, leaving the donkey to pursue its own way homewards to the convent. He saluted us as we approached, and I presently discovered that he had the charge of the catacombs, towards which we bent our steps with some degree of alacrity, which was also imparted to the beast by a good cudgel from the holy father. On reaching the entrance to the catacombs we halted, and the monk having prepared an earthen lamp with four wicks, lighted it and went forward, followed by Signor Polité and myself. The antechamber is an oblong room cut out of the solid rock, from whence many passages branch off in various directions; these again terminating in other chambers, and sepulchres for whole families. At several intervals in the main street, or passage, are holes communicating with the air above, probably cut to admit light, and also to purify these abodes of the dead. Many of the sepulchres consist of hollow coffins scooped out of the rock, and lying in rows parallel to one another, of various sizes; those intended for very young infants are mostly cut in the sides of the walls at some height from the ground. In one of these chambers I particularly noticed a

From Nature & en.... by George French Angas.

Daub'g the Light'd to the Queen.

THE ROMAN AMPHITHEATRE, SYRACUSE.

rude painting of doves, which I should consider of great antiquity ; it much resembled many of the Egyptian paintings in hieroglyphics, which are met with in the tombs of that nation.   I afterwards discovered several other remains of paintings on various portions of the walls, rudely daubed on the smooth rock.   One of these represented a plain black cross, which is said to mark the burial-place of some of the early Christians of Syracuse.   These catacombs are amazingly extensive, and must have been a prodigious work whenever they were excavated ; but history throws little light on their origin.   In many of the hollow coffins I met with bones of various parts of the human body, mingled with heaps of mouldering dust that once, no doubt, thronged the busy streets of the mighty city ; but now both city and people are laid low.   Many of these bones crumbled to dust on my exposing them to the light of day when I regained the mouth of the catacombs, whilst others remained more per- fect ; and I added these precious fragments of the ancients to my store of relics. The rib-bone of a Grecian baby, and the skull and finger joint of one who lived in the days of mythology and renown, can awaken reflections more pleasing to me than all the tawdry pageantry of a city carnival, or a modern rareeshow.   A large sar- cophagus standing in the centre of one of these underground chambers is worthy of notice, and, no doubt, many more curious remains might be unfolded by a minute examination of these singular subterranean dwellings.

On once more gaining the bright sunshine of a Sicilian sky, our eyes were so dazzled that we could for some little time see nothing ; and the cold damp chill of the cavernous abode was exchanged for the sultry glow of the atmosphere above.

The chapel of St. John is a very old Gothic building, nearly in ruins, situated close by the catacombs.   Beneath it I was shown the underground chapel of the primitive Christians.   This spot was, no doubt, chosen in times of persecution from the Pagans.   The descent into it is by a narrow and retired staircase, and the whole place has the appearance of great simplicity.   The cornices of the pillars supporting the roof bear the forms of the four Evangelists ; and a very old painting, and a de- cayed wooden cross, constitute the altar-piece.   In one corner are the remains of a large baptismal font, I should suppose for adults, but the place was so dark I could scarcely distinguish it sufficiently to judge.   But by far the most precious relic in this chapel, in the opinion of the inhabitants, is the tomb of St. Marcian, the first Christian bishop of Syracuse, whose remains lie in a small crypt covered by a stone. These ruins when viewed from a little distance are very picturesque, and the richly fretted gothic window frame adjoining the western wall of the building, peeping out amongst the silvery foliage of the olive, and the dark green leaves of the fig-tree, would alone make a charming vignette.

The convent of the Capuchins, beautifully situated on the brink of one of the most romantic of the Latomies, next claimed our attention.   It is a lovely spot, and the view from the windows is delightful; overlooking a barrier of dark rocks at whose base the blue waves of the Mediterranean are ever murmuring their gentle and melancholy music.   Farther on is the Portus Minor, and the island of Ortygia, crowned with the domes and churches of modern Siragusa; to the right stretches out the classic ground we had just returned from exploring, and if the happy and retired inmates desire a change of the view, they have only to turn to those windows that overlook the Latomie, which they have converted into a garden, and they will then have a rich grove of orange, pomegranate, and mulberry-trees, clothing the steep sides of this romantic subterranean garden; and up above the margin of the descending cliffs, like a dim and misty thing, but vast and grand, the mighty Etna bounds the distant landscape.   Such a scene under the blue and sunny skies of the south is, indeed, charming; and after I had enjoyed it as long as my time would admit of, we proceeded to pay a visit to the inmates of the convent, and a very nice set of monks we found them.   These Capuchins are principally the sons of respectable families, who, after attaining to a certain mature age, renounce the world, and giving their money to the convent, spend the remainder of their lives in religious duties, and the various offices of the brotherhood.   We first requested permission to visit the Garden of the Latomie, which was immediately granted, and two of the monks accompanied us thither.   It is a wild and romantic place, and the hermit-like garb of the Capuchins seemed to accord admirably with the character of the scene.   On the summit of a vast isolated mass of rock, which projects nearly into the centre of the garden, are a number of steps cut in the side, which must have been done before the excavations were made around it, as there is now no possibility of ascending to the top.   I remained in the garden a short time to make a sketch of this charming spot, and I then expressed a wish to see the interior of the convent.   Before leaving, the good-natured monks feasted me on delicious pomegranates, which they plucked from the trees. They were not contented with my eating them only, but insisted on my carrying some away with me.   One of these, which was the largest pomegranate I ever saw, I preserved among my baggage until I reached England, when it was perfectly good.

I was disappointed in not seeing their cemetery, (where the dead bodies of the monks in an embalmed state are dressed up and arranged in niches around the walls,) as the party who had the charge of the key of this place was gone to Siragusa, and I was unable to gain access to it; but having seen something of the same kind in the Floriana Convent at Malta, I was less anxious to view it than I should otherwise have been.   These Capuchin brethren treated me with the greatest kindness and hospitality.   I had no sooner entered the convent than I was met by the guardian, who conducted me to one of their little cells, a small apartment furnished with a

From Nature & on Sone by George French Angas.

Day & Haghe, Lith.rs to the Queen.

GIBRALTAR FROM THE MEDITERRANEAN.

Bearing W.N.W.

table, chairs, book-shelves, maps, and various articles for culinary and medicinal uses. Here I was quickly surrounded by about a dozen of the monks, who insisted on installing me in a huge arm chair at the head of the table, and set before me a repast of cakes, walnuts, and figs, with wine from the grapes of the Latomie. I pointed out to them on the map of the world, my route from England, by the way of Gibraltar, which they seemed much pleased with, and they wanted me to come again to Sicily at some future time. As I could not in courtesy take leave of these kind people, (who crowded around me in their coarse garments, and hooded cowls, with their long patriarchal beards, rosary, and miniature skull,) without returning in some way their hospitality, I made a present to the guardian, who acts as treasurer of the common property, and bade them all farewell at the outer gate of the convent.

Our way to Siragusa lay along the sea-shore by the Porta Minor. A little lad, who had been visiting at the convent, accompanied us back to the city, and made himself useful in assisting us to search for antiquities among the rubbish that is continually washed down from the bank by the murmuring waves of the sea beneath. We found many broken pieces of pottery, some of which bore ornamented patterns upon them, exactly resembling the Græco-Sicilian vases I had seen in the museum in the morning.

We spent so much time in groping amongst the crumbling remains of the once splendid Acradina, that the sun had set almost before we were aware of it, and the dark purple of the eastern sky began to assume the shades of twilight. A warm and mellow glow still rested on the Hyblean mount, and the far-distant hills stretching away toward

> " That fair field of Enna,
> Where Proserpine gathering flowers, herself a fairer flower,
> By gloomy Dis was gathered."

That long ridge of ground, once covered with the temples and towers of the five proud cities, now rose in dark and bold relief against the western sky, all still, and silent, and desolate. Fort Labdalus rising at the extremity like a cenotaph, to remind the beholder of past realities that are now but as a tale that is told. Sweetly and harmoniously sang the nightingales from the leafy shade of every spreading fig-tree, as we passed along the road that leads by the solitary pillar of the temple of Ceres. We soon reached the fortifications of modern Siragusa, which connect the island of Ortygia to the main land. These immense walls, with ditches and draw-bridges, are the work of Charles the Fifth, king of Spain. I passed through six separate fortifications, each connected by a drawbridge across a wide moat, and under as many stately arched gateways. We were now within the precincts of the city, and the many peasants returning homewards with their mules and asses, the women wearing over their heads bright scarlet and yellow shawls, so characteristic of the female Siragusan peasants, made a gay and picturesque appearance as they moved along, merry and lighthearted, enjoying the cool air of the evening. After dining at the Albergo del Sole, I rejoined my young guide, Salvador Polité, at his own house, to see his collection of drawings and antiquities, from which I had promised to make some purchases. Here I found his mother and two sisters, slight gentle creatures, with brilliant dark eyes, and that ease and suavity of manners which is common to the women of the south. Finding that I had been much stung by the ants and mosquitoes during the day, they kindly procured me some oil to allay the irritation, which I found of great service and comfort. I spent the remainder of the evening in examining the antiquities and drawings, several of which my good-natured friend presented to me, and which I treasure as graphic curiosities, as well as on account of the donor. Some of his late father's sketches exhibited considerable talent; and a painting by him of a smiling Sicilian boy with curly hair, I thought remarkably good. Having engaged Polité to procure passports for myself and old Alosco, previous to our journey to Catania, on the following morning, I took leave of the family and returned to my quarters for the night. The streets of modern Siragusa are narrow and dirty, and the lower orders of the population exhibit a sickly and impoverished appearance. As in most of the cities of southern Europe, there is in Siragusa an incongruous mixture of poverty and wealth, which, to the eye of an Englishman, is strikingly evident. Under a government approaching to despotism, and in a climate so luxurious as Sicily, the inhabitants have sunk into a careless indifference for any thing beyond their own immediate wants, having no stimulus to enterprise or scientific discovery. This is the character of the general mass; but there are here and there men who are deeply versed in classic lore, and who possess no common share of intellect and intelligence. The Sicilians, if they had the advantages and opportunity, might become famous in the arts and sciences, for there is a natural liveliness and penetration in their character quite opposed to the sluggish perceptions of John Bull, and which is often united to considerable talent, and a fervid imagination. The costume of the gentlemen in Siragusa is French, but that of the ladies is peculiar and pleasing. It consists of a mantle of black silk thrown over the head, and flowing completely down to the feet, which envelopes the whole figure, and is confined by one hand in a graceful manner at the waist. This simple and becoming garb I even prefer to the modest "faldetta" of the ladies of Malta. In Catania and Messina it does not appear to be worn at all. The Syracusans, generally, are not so handsome as the inhabitants of the north of Sicily; but the tall figures and dignified costume of the ladies give them an imposing and elegant appearance. In some of the people

I fancied I could trace the remains of the Greek countenance, and the profiles of many of the young persons are quite Grecian.

Before retiring to rest, I threw open the window of my bed-chamber, and went into the balcony to enjoy the calm loveliness of a still moonlight night; the pale beams sparkling on the breathless, waveless surface of the broad harbour, and the surrounding shores pensive, silent, and forsaken. A magic spell bound me to the spot as I gazed on those dim and classic shores, and it was with great reluctance I quitted the scene to obtain a repose sufficient to prepare me for the fatiguing journey of the next morning.

CHAPTER XXIV.

JOURNEY ON MULES TO CATANIA.

" The blue
Bared its eternal bosom, and the dew
Of summer night collected still to make
The morning precious—Beauty was awake !"

On retiring to bed I had, as usual, put the windows wide open to render the room sufficiently cool and airy; but here I was unprovided, as in Malta, with mosquito curtains, and I soon heard those nightly intruders come sallying in through the open window, with their well known and much dreaded humming sound, and in another moment they found me out and were commencing their unmerciful attacks. It was totally useless to bury my head completely underneath the clothes, for they knew where I was, and follow me they would, until being neither inclined to bear the suffocation nor the bites, I jumped up and began to drive them out in good earnest; when I imagined that I had got entirely clear of them, I closed the windows and returning to bed managed to go to sleep, but all my attempts had been in vain, and when I awoke in the morning my whole forehead was covered, and my eyes nearly blinded, with their venomous bites. I would advise every one who may happen to go to Siragusa, not to think of sleeping without mosquito curtains closely drawn, particularly in the autumnal season.

Before sunrise old Giuseppe Alosco was at the door of the Albergo del Sole, waiting with the mules, ready to accompany me to Catania. It was not long before we were again passing the solitary pillar of the temple of Ceres, in the outskirts of the city, with my baggage slung on Alosco's mule, and enjoying the fresh and balmy air of early day. The gold and crimson clouds soon began to gather in the east, and the bright beams of the morning sun shone along the waters of the Mediterranean Sea, bathing our path in its glory, as we bade farewell to Siragusa.

Our road for the first ten miles was tolerably good, commanding fine views of the sea, the Scala Græca, and the Campo Romano, with the promontory of Tapsos, (Magnesia,) stretching out before us, and the town of Augusta, (pronounced Aousta,) in the distance. Etna, like a beacon, far beyond, pointed out the place of our destination; for the city of Catania lies at the foot of the mountain, close to the sea-shore, at the end of the broad plain over which we were to travel for many miles. About six miles from Siragusa, on the left hand side of the road, stand two pillars, which I understood from my guide, mark the spot where some robbers were formerly executed. To the right, and farther on, are the remains of a trophy erected in honour of the Roman general Marcellus. It consists of a ruin sixteen palmi high, on the top of which is a fragment of a fluted column. By-and-by, we arrived at a new village, consisting of a number of detached cottages on both sides of the way, and presenting a neater appearance than Sicilian villages do in general. At this place we halted for a few moments to purchase some black grapes; and as the road terminated soon afterwards, we struck off into a narrow mule-track that led across a barren country, scattered with olive and locust trees. Here we met an armed courier mounted on horseback, bearing the Government letters to Siragusa. He accosted us with the usual salutation of " Buon giorno," and passed on. In the days of Brydone, travellers thought it not safe to pass along this road without an armed escort of guards, to protect them from the attacks of the numerous banditti, who infested the woods and mountain-passes of this picturesque land. But now it is only the couriers, who travel alone, and by night, having important despatches, that make use of the sword and pistol; and to speak from my own observation, I should imagine it *safer* for a traveller to stroll among the hills and valleys of Sicily, and lie down to sleep at night with his baggage unsecured by lock or key, as was the case with myself, than it would be for him to do the same under similar circumstances in this country. I placed the utmost confidence in the people; and though quite alone, and oftentimes at their entire mercy, a single fear either for person or property, never once entered my mind for a moment. Their vivacity and quick perception immediately discovered my feeling towards them, and instead of abusing the confidence I placed in their kindness and protection, they every where treated me with the greatest attention and hospitality. Perhaps my being so young, and quite alone, might, in some measure, engage their good feelings; and I also attribute my reception, in a great measure, to always taking notice of them, and treating them in a free and friendly manner, which has oftentimes won for me the hospitality of these warm-hearted and sensitive people. I also found it necessary to remember the adage, " He who goes to Rome must do as Rome does;" which I am sorry to say is little attended to by many of our countrymen who visit distant lands, and who, instead of making friends of the people, excite their dislike and contempt by their haughty and overbearing carriage: this, of course, subjects them to frequent insult, pillage, and opposition; and hence they return with a very unfavourable account of the inhabitants of a country, who, if they had altered their own conduct towards them, they would have described under very different feelings and impressions.

After watering our mules at a purling stream, over which was thrown a rustic wooden bridge, shaded by gigantic and spreading walnut trees, we travelled on through vineyards, and fields of pulse, and cotton, until we reached a wide barren track of rugged lava, which appears to have issued from the mountain in some dreadful eruption of past ages. We travelled over the rocky beds of this volcanic matter for some miles, and at length reached the summit of an extensive sandy common which commanded a fine view. The soil was covered with various prickly and aromatic shrubs; and in the centre of this heath rose a solitary palm tree, that had, apparently, borne the blasts and winds for centuries. At every step of our mules, a little flock of grasshoppers rose into the air, and spreading their green and crimson wings, settled down again as soon as the alarm had passed by. Beneath a flowery bank I saw basking in the sun a very large and brilliantly-coloured lizard; it was about seven inches long, and of the most exquisite shades of golden green imaginable. I tried to catch it, but the bright-eyed lacerta was too quick for me, and his shining and slender form shrank silently beneath the brambles with the rapidity of lightning. Shortly after, we crossed another stream, bounded with rose-coloured oleanders in full blossom, that grew luxuriantly as far as the vivifying influence of the moisture extended. The dark green dragon-flies were darting around every leaf, and the little birds had come down to drink of the cooling stream, where we also halted to slake our thirst.

In one of the tanks where we previously rested, I found a number of leeches, and some curious aquatic beetles; but as Alosco appeared shocked at my desire to catch them, I for once yielded to his feelings, and we went on without either the beetles or the leeches, although the latter would have proved serviceable to me afterwards when at Giardini. About noon we passed a lettiga, which is the national travelling carriage in the more rugged and mountainous parts of Sicily; it is made to convey two persons, and is in shape like the body of a vis-a-vis. It is also provided with strong poles, which are carried between two mules; a third mule goes before accompanied by a muleteer on foot, armed with a stick ten feet long to guide the mules, and another muleteer mounted and riding at the head of the cavalcade to pioneer the way. It is gaily lined, and painted outside with a variety of gaudy colours, often the representation of some favourite saint. It goes up and down over every hill, however steep, and makes the whole neighbourhood resound with the tinkling of thirty-two bells, which are fixed to the harness and trappings of the mules. I should imagine the motion to be very unpleasant and fatiguing, and the jingling of the numerous bells prevents the muleteers from hearing when called to, and of course renders conversation very difficult.

We had now proceeded twenty-four miles on our journey, and a steep and winding descent through an olive wood brought us to the little village of Scaro d' Agnuni, consisting of six or seven fishermen's huts, near the sea-shore, at the southern extremity of the vast plain over which the remainder of our journey lay, and which stretches northward beyond the river Giaretta, to the hills that skirt the base of Etna. The olive trees that formed this straggling wood were large and branching, and the myrtle bushes were as abundant as the blackberry and hawthorn in more northern climates. Beneath the trees the bright autumnal crocus lifted its starlike and leafless form, bordering our path with its lilac petals.

We halted at the village, and my guide, who seemed well acquainted with the place, entered one of the miserable looking huts, and presently came out again smiling, and significantly pointing to his mouth, said to me, " Mangé Seigneur,—mangé you, mangé me, mangé moolos," in his broken English. Now old Alosco felt very proud of his English, and it would have offended him highly to have appeared unable to comprehend the whimsical jargon he used to address to me during the whole of our journey ;—nevertheless he was a quiet and good-natured man, so I let him have his own way, and assented to all he said by a very gracious " Ce," repeated two or three times in a quick conversational manner, which satisfied him admirably. This, accompanied with an occasional smile, and a nod of assent, was sufficient to ensure the esteem of old Alosco ; and he would go on chattering about every place and every thing in a language intelligible only to himself, whilst I was mechanically uttering the C note, and giving a nod every three minutes. When he came out of the cottage, he appeared in high spirits, and I conjectured he had met with something excellent to provide me with for my dinner.

Imagine my astonishment when I found that they were beans—horse-beans—that had so raised the old man's pleasant sensations respecting the meal ; a large plateful of them, swimming in oil, was presently brought outside the cottage door, and two

broken chairs, one of which served as a table, were set down under the shady side
of the wall.   Alosco was mightily surprised to find that I could not eat the beans ;
and after they had ransacked the cottage a second time, I made a tolerable repast
on some little anchovies, which, like the beans, were swimming in oil, and out of
which I was compelled to drag them with my fingers.   Besides these, there was
black bread, and lastly eggs, broken and beaten up in a plate, which I ate with
a wooden fork.   This reminded me of the Devonshire proverb of "eating whitepot
with a knitting needle," and was certainly no easy matter.   But this was the
least annoying part of the feast, for the bees and mosquitoes swarmed around me
so numerously, that I was every instant in dread of being stung by some of them.
Good Syracusan wine was next measured out and brought to me in one of the
strangest jugs I ever saw.   Old Alosco drank my health, and I poured out a cupful,
and offered it to the host, who was standing by, according to the custom of the
peasantry.   Before my worthy guide had finished his beans, a smart lettiga arrived
with two gentlemen of Siragusa, and their muleteers, bound on the same road as
ourselves.   Observing that I was a foreigner, they bowed politely to me, invited me
to partake of some refreshments which they had brought with them, and offered
me a seat in the lettiga.   This latter favour I declined, but I accepted a piece of
goat's cheese and some sweet fennel, which the Sicilians use as we do celery.   I
soon became acquainted with the new comers.   When the mules had rested for
a sufficient time, the lettiga was suspended, and by mutual consent we agreed to
travel together to Catania.

We were now a rather formidable cavalcade.   A muleteer rode before, carrying a
long stick as pioneer ; then came the two mules with their thirty-two bells jingling their
music till its echo died away among the distant hills ; the lettiga with its gay
colouring, and the two gentlemen vis-a-vis ; and lastly, old Alosco and myself on
our brave mules.   We occasionally made slight deviations from the road to pluck
some attractive blossom, and then galloped back to join the equipage and to present
the flower to the occupants of the lettiga.   It was a bright and lovely afternoon ;
all the broad plain seemed bathed in sunlight.   Etna was before us.   The
Saracenic domes of the fair city of Catania, glittered like white specks at its feet,
and the blue waves of the sea, gently met the yellow sandy bank that lay to our
right, along which I occasionally strayed away from the party to gather the purple
shells that strewed its surface.   And far away to the left were the hills of Enna,
(now Castro Giovanni,) and the slowly flowing Giaretta winding its way through
flowery meads, and intersecting the broad plain till its waters mingled with the sea.
In many places among the sands, I noticed a prickly species of Solano, bearing
round seeds of a bright golden colour.   These, my guide informed me, were the
"pomo del' amo," and pointing to the projecting knob in his throat, commenced

giving me an incoherent story about Adam and Eve, which, as I understood it, runs thus—that these fruits were so called from their supposed resemblance to the apples of Paradise eaten by our first parents, that Eve swallowed hers, but that the portion which Adam ate stuck in his throat, which caused that small projection in the windpipe of men to this day, and which is a memorial of the disobedience of Adam, that is entailed on his descendants to the end of time. Many fine bulbous plants also grow on the plain, and myrtles, canes, and aloes spring spontaneously from the soil.

We had now to cross the river Giaretta, (anciently the Simetus,) in a flat-bottomed ferry-boat, almost resembling a raft, into which mules, lettiga, and passengers all entered, and we were soon towed to the other side by means of a rope suspended from poles across the river. The stream was not very wide, but of considerable depth, and bordered with sedge and rushes. It is remarkable for its amber, which is collected in considerable quantities at its mouth, where it is cast up on the sandy beach that runs between it and the sea. This amber is said to be the finest in the world, and fetches a very high price. Quantities of it are taken to Catania, where it is manufactured into a variety of beautiful trinkets. Saints, crosses, necklaces, rings, smelling-bottles, and brooches, all exquisitely wrought, are from thence exported to Messina, Palermo, and various other parts of Sicily, and form a considerable article of traffic amongst the ingenious artificers of Catania. One reason of the superior beauty of the Catanese amber is owing to the bright iridescent reflections which give it oftentimes a beauty little inferior to that of the opal. I have seen specimens of a deep blood red, olive green, black, and also rose colour, but these are very rare, and are sold at enormous prices. As we drew nearer to Catania, the mule track was exchanged for a tolerable road, and here we encountered upwards of 200 workmen, men and boys, all engaged in forming the new road to Lentini, which will hereafter form the line of communication between Catania and Siragusa. It is to be constructed of lava, and huge heaps of that substance in good sized blocks, are laid at equal distances to form the basis of the road. This is afterwards to be filled up and covered with earth and gravel, so that it will have the appearance of a raised tram-road extending across the plain. We now had a fine view of the numerous domes of Catania, which presented a novel and imposing appearance. After crossing a track of black lava, the production of the melancholy eruption of the mountain in 1669, we entered the city through a magnificent gateway built of marble and lava.

CHAPTER XXV.

CITY OF CATANIA—FERDINAND AND ISABELLA—ILLUMINATIONS—ABBATE'S HOTEL.

'Skirting the midnight ocean's glimmering flow,
The city's moonlit spires and myriad lamps,
Like stars in a sub-lunar sky did glow."

WE had no sooner entered the gate of the city, than we encountered a vast concourse of people. Indeed, the whole population seemed to be abroad upon some occasion of rejoicing, and as we proceeded along the principal street towards the Piazza del Duomo, we met numbers of carriages and other equipages driving about rapidly in all directions. Not being able to account for so bustling and animated a scene, I made inquiries as soon as we reached the hotel, and found that the king and queen of the Two Sicilies, Ferdinand and Isabella, had arrived during the day from Messina, and that there was a general holiday on their account. Moreover, my new landlord, to whom I bore a letter of introduction from Polité, (who is his nephew,) also informed me that a grand illumination was to take place on the same night, and a display of fireworks in honour of their majesties. "Abbate," for that was my landlord's name, gave me to understand that his hotel was unusually full of Sicilian noblemen and gentlemen, and that some prince had just arrived, to whom he must pay extraordinary attention, but that there was a room vacant at the very top of the building which I might occupy, and ordered an attendant to show me (the Seigneur Inglese) every possible attention. After a journey of about half a dozen flights of stone steps, I reached my night's quarters, followed by old Alosco bearing my luggage. My first business was to pay the old man, and dismiss the mules, as he intended travelling back by moonlight as far as Scaro d' Agnuni. The old man stooped to kiss my hand, and, after beseeching a blessing from the saints to rest upon me, bade me a reluctant farewell. The Sicilians are a grateful people when kindly treated; but, naturally sensitive and proud of what their country once was, they cannot brook insult and hauteur. After taking a meal in my apartments, I sallied forth to see the illuminations that starred the long vistas of this beautiful and extensive city with myriads of sparkling lamps that covered even the domes of the convents and churches. The effect was so novel, so different from any thing in this country, that at first I almost felt bewildered as I strolled along street after street, admiring the tasteful display of lamps hung beneath the serene sky of a southern climate, which rendered their effect far more charming. Carriages filled with elegantly dressed ladies rolled along the streets, and the people crowded the foot-paths, and sat in groups outside the doors of their shops and dwellings, smoking, and chattering to each other very merrily. As I passed one of these groups, I heard some one calling, " Seigneur Inglese," and on looking round I discovered one of my two friends, with whom I had travelled in the lettiga ; he seemed much pleased at seeing me again, and, setting a chair for me, insisted on my forming one of the group assembled around the door. As I was, however, anxious to make the best of my time, I soon took leave of my new acquaintance, and seeing a number of persons pouring out of one of the largest churches, I went in, just in time to see the illuminations of the interior before they were extinguished. A mass had just been performed, at which the king and queen had been present, and the effect of the hanging lamps before the high altar was very fine. Instead of the vehicles of every description that traverse the streets of London on similar occasions, the only equipages I saw were open carriages with two or three horses abreast ; most of them were too shabby to appear in this country, but were probably considered very grand by the Sicilians. The grotesque appearance of the footmen, and the awkward look and clumsy " tout ensemble" of the equipages, amused me not a little as they drove rapidly by, following each other in quick succession. They were mostly filled with ladies elegantly dressed in the Frank costume, without bonnets, and having their arms only covered by delicate silk mittens. There were many very handsome women amongst them, much handsomer than any I had seen at Siragusa. Catania is the chief residence of the nobility of Sicily, being much preferred by them on account of its fine climate, and its proximity to Etna. Around the public statues coloured glass lamps, richly painted, were hung at regular intervals, and flowers were garlanded in festoons about them. The most general mode of illumination appeared to be by tumblers filled with red and green water, behind which were placed small oil lamps.

In the Square of the Elephant, I observed several stalls not unlike the ginger-beer and soda-water carts in London. The people were drinking what appeared to me to be water, which was obtained from barrels which men swung backwards and forwards all the time, like the rocking of a cradle. I was curious to know what this liquor could be, when laying down a small copper coin, I was immediately attended to. The barrels were swung round again, and a glass of the decoction handed to me, when to my surprise I found it to consist only of iced water, strongly flavoured with fennel juice. This, as I afterwards understood, is a favourite beverage of the Sicilians, particularly on holiday occasions; and though not very palatable to us, yet I have no doubt that it is of use in allaying thirst.

One of the most striking objects in the Piazza del Duomo, is the obelisk of red Egyptian granite, placed on the back of an elephant, sculptured in black lava, which ornaments the centre of the square.

The elephant is said to be the work of the middle ages, and the obelisk to have been sculptured by the ancient inhabitants of Catania, in imitation of those of the Egyptians. Both are in good preservation, and form a striking object on entering the square; the base of the pedestal on which they are mounted bears a date of 1736, with an Italian inscription. On my return from the illuminations, I witnessed a display of fireworks and sky-rockets from the Strada del Corso, and afterwards returned to my hotel, the "Corona d' Oro," where I was conducted to my apartment, and throwing open the window, I went out into the balcony, which was at a giddy height and only protected by a slight iron railing. I had a fine moonlight view of the bay, and the fearful promontory formed by the overwhelming eruption of lava, in 1669, which destroyed a great portion of the city. It rises black and rugged, and descends abruptly into the sea. Nature in this instance has done for the inhabitants of Catania what their art was unable to accomplish. Formerly they were destitute of a harbour, till the lava of 1669, running into the sea, produced the enormous mole which at present renders the port secure and capacious enough for small vessels. Despite the mosquitoes, I lay down on my humble bed, and soon fell into a profound sleep.

From Nature & on Stone by George French Angas.

ETNA. FROM CATANIA.

Day & Haghe Lith:rs to the Queen.

CHAPTER XXVI.

CATANIA—PRINCE BISCARI'S MUSEUM—CATHEDRAL—GREEK THEATRE—SUBTERRANEAN
AMPHITHEATRE—ANCIENT BATHS, ETC.

"I stood within the city disinterred,
   And heard the autumnal leaves like light footfalls
   Of spirits passing through the streets; and heard
   The mountain's slumbering voice at intervals,
   Thrill through those roofless halls."

CATANIA, it is said, was anciently called Catætna, or the town of Etna, and is reported
by the early historians to have been founded by the Cyclops, who were the fabled
inhabitants of the mountain. Others inform us that it was founded by a colony from
Chalcis, 753 years before Christ. Had I not been better instructed, I should have
concluded that it derived its name from the numberless cats that nightly peram-
bulate the walls and terraces of this extensive city. It was moonlight, and the
pale beams shone into my open window as I awoke from my sound and refreshing sleep, serenaded by the most dismal and hideous caterwaulings imaginable.
I lay still, hoping it might cease, but the chorus grew louder; and, as it showed
no signs of abatement, I jumped up, and going out into the balcony, sent the whole
multitude of tabbies, toms, tortoiseshells, and grimalkins, scampering over the roof
tops, by a volley of such small missiles as my bedroom afforded. Away they went,
and the distant crash of falling tiles, and the faint echo of renewed music elsewhere,
gave me the cheering assurance of their departure from the chosen spot beneath my
window. I arose early on the following morning, and sallied out along the Strada
del Corso, the principal street to the north-east of the city, towards Giarra, for the
purpose of making a sketch of Mount Etna, which I took from the open square that
terminates the street. The lava is again visible here descending abruptly to the
sea, and the view of the distant mountain, and the belted zones of vegetation that
clothe its base, form a charming and magnificent feature in the landscape. I returned to the hotel, where I made a hasty breakfast, and after purchasing some specimens of amber and lava from the artisans, who found their way into my bedroom

uninvited, and who most politely entertained me during my meal with a sight of their ingenious trinkets, I engaged a guide, and started at once for Prince Biscari's museum, which I understood contained many objects worthy of notice. The collection was formed by the Principi Ignazio Biscari, an enlightened and patriotic nobleman, who took great interest in the welfare and antiquities of his country. In the entrance court is a fine column of the Greek theatre, and an ancient obelisk of granite, somewhat similar to that upon the elephant in the Piazza del Duomo—sarcophagi of lava—a vase ornamented with bassi relievi, also of lava, and an immense pair of antique jars of coarse Sicilian pottery. Under the middle entrance is a statue of Biscari himself, and several other Sicilian worthies. One of them representing a doctor, whose face is dreadfully distorted by having received a kick from a mule, is very ludicrous, but uncommonly well managed. Among the collection of antiques in the long gallery, are two Bacchi, a beautiful sleeping female in variegated marble, portions of the tesselated pavements found in the ancient baths, tables inlaid with Sicilian and African marble, three sarcophagi of terra cotta, and a basso relievo of St. Nicholas, modelled in clay, from Caltagirone, a market town in the interior, long and justly celebrated for its manufactory of figures in terra cotta. A large collection of Roman penates, a curious harlequin with moving limbs ; also a fine fragment of the head of Medusa, and upwards of 400 Græco-Sicilian vases, some of them of vast size, and all beautifully shaped, and tastefully painted and decorated. One of them in particular is very highly prized for having a white ground, a circumstance which is seldom met with amongst these antique vases. In the other apartments there is a good collection of lavas from Etna and Lipari, a number of shells and corals from the Mediterranean ; a great variety of lavas and marbles finely inlaid in birds, flowers, &c.; a large piece of variegated brown and green wood opal from Palermo ; impressions of leaves in sulphur, from the crater of Etna, and a collection of calculi from Trapani. In one case there is a most remarkable variety of lusus naturæ, some of which I noted down. There is a calf with one eye, (probably an Ætnean Cyclops !) and an enormous tongue ; calves with two heads ; an exact mermaid, and a variety of children whose monstrous and unnatural appearances are not to be described. Returning by another gallery of antiques I was principally struck with the following articles of curiosity. A marble bust of Scipio Africanus, and another of Seneca ; a beautiful cupid ; a Venus similar to the one at Syracuse, but having a head ; another fine Venus ; some beautiful busts, with drapery of coloured marble ; an infant lying on a cushion of lava ! (modern ;) a collection of very old drawings, and a basso relievo of the battle of Constantine, A. D. 312. There is also a room filled with curious bronzes, and a philosophical cabinet which contains two exquisite ancient lachrymatories of iridescent coloured glass. I was much disappointed in not being able to see the coins, of which there is a very valuable collection. The entire museum indicates considerable taste and neatness in its arrangement, and certainly reflects great credit and honour on its enlightened founder.

My next visit was to the cathedral. It was originally built, and the see founded, by Ruggiero, A.D. 1193. The present edifice is one of the most chaste and beautiful I have ever seen. Twelve apostles of gold stand on the high altar. Along the facades are several columns taken from the scena of the ancient theatre. The cupola is very fine; the frescos on the ceiling are from scripture subjects, and to the left of the altar-piece is a very good painting of St. Agatha by Paladino. The arabesque work on the doors of the grand entrance is by the celebrated Gagini. In a chapel to the north of the choir there are some fine specimens of alabaster and lava. One piece of red lava is equally beautiful with the "rosso antico," though somewhat paler in colour. In a little capella stands the shrine and tomb of St. Agatha; a small lamp burns night and day before it, and many are the genuflexions that are made to this their favourite saint by the deluded inhabitants. In the same chapel is the tomb of the King of Spain, who was buried here in 1495. This monumental tomb is built of marble, and represents him as a boy of about eleven years of age, in a kneeling attitude, and attended by a pretty page some years younger. The monument of Petrus Galetti, Bishop of Catania in 1757, is inlaid with coloured marble, and deserves attention on account of the beauty of the materials, and the tasteful design of the whole composition. The tomb of Conrado Deodata, a priest, who died in 1828, is a very beautiful modern erection; it is of lava, inlaid with red figures, and supported by two bronze sphinxes. In the sacristy adjoining the cathedral is an old painting which represents the dreadful eruption of 1669, when the lava ran from Monte Rossi, just above Nicolosi, and overwhelmed the city of Catania.

The monastery of the Benedictines deserves especial notice, on account of having escaped the lava of 1669 in an almost miraculous manner, the stream of molten fire having appeared within five yards of the edifice, and then turned off to the left, and thus preserved it and its inmates from certain and irreparable destruction. The chapel of the monastery contains a fine organ, some paintings by Cavalucci, and a large and valuable museum, all of which I was disappointed in seeing, as the king had taken up his abode at the convent during the few days of his stay in Catania. The Greek theatre is approached by a descent of steps of lava, which, with the remains of the edifice itself, have been excavated from the soil and ashes that so long covered them. On arriving at the entrance to the theatre, I was accosted by a Maltese priest, a stout old gentleman, who had been puffing and blowing for some time in endeavouring to overtake me. Despite his canonicals, I thought he looked like a very jolly fellow, and finding that he could speak a little English, I accepted his offer to join him in his perambulation, as his visit to Catania was, like mine, one of pleasure. I told him that I had recently been at Malta, which pleased him amazingly. He gave me his name and the address of his residence at Senglea, and begged that if ever I went to Malta again, I would call upon him. The old gentleman took my arm, and asked me if I was a Catholic. I replied in the negative, when he said, "Catholics and Protestants are all one." It would be well if every one were as charitable in his religious opinions as this priest; it might surely serve to prevent the innumerable contentions and the bitter enmity that reflects such disgrace upon mankind in this and other countries. My good friend told me that he had attempted to climb Vesuvius, which is about one-third of the height of Etna, and that he was too fat to get to the top! He, however, proposed to venture the ascent of Etna, and informed me that if I thought of doing so, three French gentlemen who were staying at the Corona d' Oro, where I had taken up my quarters, would also be very willing to form a party. This was agreed upon, as I had intended ascending alone, with guides, from Nicolosi, and I regarded the prospect of having companions with me as most fortunate, besides rendering the expenses of the ascent considerably less; but I afterwards found that this arrangement did not turn out so fortunate or agreeable as I had anticipated,—but more of this hereafter. We arranged matters so that our survey of the remaining antiquities should terminate at three o'clock, and that after dining at the Corona d Oro, we should all start for Nicolosi at four precisely. After exploring the ruins of the Greek theatre, of which three corridors and seven rows of seats are distinguishable, we turned our steps towards the immense subterranean amphitheatre, erected by the Roman colony which was established by Augustus in this city. It was originally built on the side of a hill, but the various eruptions of Etna have so altered the appearance of things that it has long since been buried under ground, and would most probably have remained so until this day, had not the Prince Ignazio Biscari excavated a large portion of it, in hopes of finding a quantity of Roman antiquities. The circumference is said to be about 1000 feet: several of the corridors are cleared; they are very lofty, and are arched over at the top. The lowest range exhibits vestiges of the dens for the wild beasts, and the doorways through which they were admitted into the arena are also visible. We groped our way through these damp subterranean passages, our guide carrying a large flambeau in his hand, which I made him poke into all the corners and strange places. In one apartment I met with a spring of water that trickled along through the rubbish, and in another part I found some fine remains of the Roman pillars and lofty arched doorways of this magnificent amphitheatre. The ancient baths are situated under the duomo or cathedral, and are entered by a narrow winding flight of stone steps, closed at the top by an iron gate. These are termed "Bagno Caldi," or cold baths. Our guide again lighted his flambeau, and we once more found ourselves in the subterranean chambers of the ancients. These baths are very perfect, and a stream of water still runs along an aqueduct through them, which might easily supply the baths, and make them again subservient to their former purpose. This aqueduct flows under ground for a considerable distance, and then rises again to the surface of the earth near the quay, where it supplies the " nymphæ modernæ " with a clear stream of water for their household purposes. A short walk took us to the remains of the " Bagno Freddi," which are situated on the opposite side of the lava of 1669, and like those under the Duomo, have also been excavated by the Prince Biscari. In these vapour baths the antechamber and furnaces still remain. A small apartment (probably a vapour bath for one person) is tolerably perfect, and the fireplaces are discernible beneath the cisterns for heating the water. Near these furnaces balls of lava have been found, which circumstance has led some persons to imagine that they were used to keep up the heat of the stoves.

Prior to the dreadful eruption of 1669, a castle stood upon the sea-shore near the ancient walls of the city, having at its side a translucent spring of the purest water, but when the lava which ran from Monte Rossi accumulated till it rose above the walls, which were sixty feet in height, it poured over them with great violence, and ran out into the sea, forming the mole which I have before spoken of. Fortunately, however, for the inhabitants of the city, the lava flood left a small opening near the half-buried castle, which enabled the Prince Biscari to excavate it in such a manner that he had the satisfaction of restoring to his countrymen their long lost and valued spring of water. We descended a flight of sixty-three steps, cut in the solid lava, which led us down to the spring. The water was pellucid and clear, and the numerous women and girls filling their stone jars at its source, and the various groups we met balancing their picturesque water-pots on their heads, filled with the water of the Etnæan spring, showed what a boon this recovered spot is to the people. My old companion the priest, now began to feel very tired, and as it was well nigh time that we should return to the albergo, to make the necessary preparations for the anticipated ascent of Mongibello, we hastened back, and bidding my friend a temporary adieu, I ordered dinner to be got ready immediately, and while it was preparing, I packed up my luggage. My dinner was quickly brought up into my bedroom, for it is the custom in Sicily to set apart a room for each guest in an albergo, in which they both eat and sleep, and in short make it their " sanctum sanctorum." During the time the guest occupies this room, the door of it is kept locked by the master of the house, and whenever the occupant goes out, the key is deposited in the hall until his return. My bed-room, like most others in Sicily, was paved with large red tiles, which rendered it very cool and comfortable. The houses in Catania are all built of stone, in a very strong and secure manner, as a supposed safeguard against the earthquake shocks, and the uncertain and dangerous eruptions of the mountain. My repast was simple, and consisted, as usual, of a dish of maccaroni, very nicely cooked, with the native appendage of Tomata sauce, some excellent fish, and, what surprised me a little, a large lump of frozen snow on a plate. My dessert consisted of grapes, walnuts, figs, and apples—these latter tasted very much like peaches, and had a more delicious flavour than any I ever tasted in England. A very large glass tumbler was set on the table with the wine, and I imagined that it would form an excellent wine cooler. I therefore placed a small glass inside it, and filled up the outside with the frozen snow, not knowing at the time what other use to make of this luxury. The wine thus iced was delightfully refreshing, and seemed to quench the annoying thirst under which I had suffered whilst walking in the hot and dusty streets of Catania. The bread I found to be the very best in all Sicily; it is almost as white as the snows of Etna, and is made in the form of oval cakes, baked very crisp. The commoner sorts of bread are made up into large open rings about half a foot in diameter, and numbers of these fantastical loaves may be seen hanging in bunches upon forked sticks on the outside of almost every cottage door.

The arches of the ancient underground structures of Catania are wholly formed of tiles placed alternately between pieces of lava. Ancient bassi relievi are also frequently met with, and several fine examples of this mural sculpture have been discovered in the subterranean baths. The chief trade of Catania is in its exports, which consist of amber, lava, fruit, silk, timber, and snow, which latter article is obtained from the heights of Etna, and supplies not only all Sicily, but likewise Malta and Calabria with this healthful commodity. In perambulating the streets of this fine city, the traveller cannot fail to notice the strange admixture of poverty and splendour which they present. The proudest palace and the lowest hovel may be included in one glance, and the most magnificent buildings, on which no expense whatever seems to have been spared, are hidden or disfigured by wretched habitations being placed beside them. The streets, though wide, and running at right angles with each other, in many instances are not kept carefully clean, and the tottering condition of many of the houses, and the numerous cracks and fissures observable in the walls in the Strada Etnea, which leads towards the mountain, speak in strong and forcible language of the volcanic fires that slumber beneath them, and that perhaps the fiery streams may again burst forth from some new crater, high up in the mountain, and pour down another sulphurous flood of lava upon the fated city. The volcanic eruptions of Etna have taken place at promiscuous intervals for a great number of centuries, and Dr. Gemmellaro of Nicolosi, who has closely watched and examined the mountain, has published a very curious and interesting table, giving an account of all the various eruptions, from the earliest known period of time. For several years past the mountain fires have slumbered, and at the time of my visit not even a wreath of curling smoke was visible at Catania from its lofty and snow-clad summit.

The population of the city is averaged at about 30,000. It is the favourite residence of the Sicilian nobility, and in size ranks as the third city of the island, yielding the palm in this respect only to Palermo and Messina. The women of Catania, especially those of the peasant class, are not so handsome as those of Messina, but many of the boys are prettily featured, and have fine expressive dark eyes. I was much amused by the water-carts of Catania; instead of having holes drilled at the back of the machine, a leathern hose is used with a head attached to it, which a man moves about as though he were handling a watering-pot, and verifying the proverb that "Lazy people take the most pains."

CHAPTER XXVII.

"The Port capacious and secure from wind,
  Is to the foot of thundering Etna joined,
  By turns a pitchy cloud she rears on high,
  By turns hot embers from her entrails fly,
  And flakes of mountain flame that lick the sky."

ABOUT four o'clock, P. M. our party for the mountain was assembled at the door of Abbate's hotel in the Strada del Corso, and a supply of wine, cold turkeys and bread, having been provided for us by our civil landlord, we had only to prepare suitable clothing to protect us from the intense cold which we expected to encounter in the upper regions of Etna. My Maltese friend had doffed his ecclesiastical robes, and three-cornered silk hat, and now looked very jolly in a light shooting coat, and a fur cap, with a variety of warm comfortable things in the shape of worsted stockings, gloves, wrappers, &c. Our party consisted of the three French gentlemen before mentioned, the priest, and myself. We travelled as far as Nicolosi, a small village situated about twelve miles up the mountain, in an open carriage drawn by three horses abreast. A little bare-footed boy stood behind, and served all the purposes of a handsome English tiger. We drove along the Strada Etnea, which leads towards the mountain, from which point its stupendous base begins to rise, and it seems as though, from this spot, one might pursue the path to its very summit. But the illusion soon fades as the traveller advances onwards. Our route now became steep and winding as we journeyed up through gardens of orange and lemon trees, interspersed with the date-palm, the aloe, and the bergamot. The vineyards are fruitful and luxuriant, and the grapes and wine of Etna are by many considered superior to any in Sicily. The country, as far up as Nicolosi, is called the first or fruitful region of the mountain; after which comes the "Bosco," or "Regione Sylvosa;" and lastly the third region, consisting of scoriæ, ashes and snow, which leads to a platform on the summit of which is the crater. From the road which ascends from the Strada Etnea, we looked back for a few moments, and enjoyed a most charming and picturesque view of the city and bay, and the distant shores towards Siragusa. The day had been uncommonly sultry, the afternoon was lovely, and as yet everything looked fair and favourable for our ascent, as the sun set over the plains below us with every indication of fine weather. But the climate in the valleys and in the lofty and exposed regions of Etna is so totally different, that no just criterion can be formed from the one of the other. To the right of the road are the remains of an aqueduct which formerly conveyed some of the streams that take their rise higher up the mountain to the service of the inhabitants that dwell at its base. A sharp turn in the road led us between two fine obelisks of lava; their bases bear inscriptions, but I was unable to learn to what they had reference. They appeared to be modern erections. Here we met a number of female peasants coming down a steep path, laughing and singing their wild musical songs. They carried their oriental-looking jars of water on their heads, balancing them with that dexterous nicety, so gracefully, and yet so carelessly managed by the Sicilian women.

The olive trees at this part of the ascent are very beautiful, and the general aspect of the vegetation in the lower region of the mountain is rich and luxuriant; and although from the long continued drought I saw it to very great disadvantage, yet the immense size of many of the trees, serves to show the fertility and richness of the volcanic soil. Numerous villages lie scattered about this region of the mountain, and the vineyards and olive trees yield their produce to an industrious set of inhabitants, who show more activity and spirit than the people who reside in the less healthy plains of the south, where malaria and the extreme heat of the sun in the summer and autumn months render them very indolent and inactive. In one of these villages, the church dedicated to St. Antonio formed a picturesque object; the spire was gaily ornamented, being composed of painted tiles of all colours, which impart to it a bright and cheerful appearance, contrasting well with the more sombre tints of the surrounding scenery on the mountain. The next village, Praghi, is built of lava, and the gloom it occasions is in a great measure relieved by the opposition of white stone ornaments and porticos. The inhabitants of this region are healthy and strong, and seemed to enjoy the jokes we played upon them as we passed through their sequestered little villages. We reached Nicolosi soon after dark, and could discern the huge shadowy form of Monte Rossi rising abruptly above the village. Over the immense declivity of Etna, are distributed a number of smaller mountains, all having regular conoid or hemispherical outlines, which are frequently covered with trees, giving them the appearance of small parks scattered here and there over the wide ascending surface of Etna. Every fresh eruption gradually forms one of these smaller mountains, and the torrents of liquid lava do not, as is supposed by many persons, burst out from the summit or grand crater of Etna, but after shaking the mountain for some time, and producing volumes of smoke and ashes, the lava forces itself out at some near aperture in the side of the declivity, and the quantities of stones and ashes ejected by the eruption form these conical mountains, which present so curious and important a feature on the mighty steeps of Mongibello.

At Nicolosi we left our carriage and horses, which were to await our return from the crater, to convey us back to Catania on the following afternoon. We proposed to make a night ascent, in order to witness the sunrise, and the magnificent panorama which daybreak would reveal of Sicily and the surrounding shores. Our first object was to obtain mules and good guides, and we proceeded at once to the residence of Signor Gemmellaro, the philosopher of Etna, to whom I bore a letter of introduction from my friend Dr. H—— of London. We walked from a small albergo, where we had alighted, along a path that seemed to our tread, (for it was quite dark, and the moon had not yet risen,) extremely soft, and it proved to be the finest volcanic sand. Our party, as we entered Signor Gemmellaro's cottage, presented a motley and somewhat singular appearance. There were individuals from three different nations, French, Maltese, and English, paying their respective compliments to the agreeable Sicilian, who found it rather puzzling to carry on a conversation which he was obliged to vary in so many different languages. He fortunately understood a little English, and on my presenting my letter, he received me most kindly, and a few words acquainted him with the object of my visit. " It is now seven o'clock," said he : " you must rest for one hour, and in the mean time I will provide guides for you, and we must have five mules instantly." He had just returned from visiting a patient in the village, and had surveyed the appearances of the atmosphere, which he feared would be unfavourable for an ascent, as the wind was howling in the Bosco, and thunder had been heard occasionally to echo in the region of the crater. Nevertheless, we were all very anxious to make the attempt, and a peasant was despatched to procure the mules and a guide. He soon returned, when we found to our dismay, that only two mules were to be had, all the others in the village being occupied at this season of the year in the vintage. But Gemmellaro insisted upon the requisite number of mules being obtained for our party, and the messenger was again despatched with orders not to return until the five mules were procured, besides a sixth one for the use of the guide. The three French gentlemen could not speak one word of English, and but little Italian ; they were pleasant and courteous, and full of the vivacity so characteristic of the French nation. The mules arrived at last, and we all walked round to the albergo, where we found our guide ready equipped, with another man, who was to precede us on foot with a lantern. The moon had just risen, but there was not sufficient light to show us the path over the sharp and dangerous rocks of lava that formed the only road we had to traverse before we gained the woody region of the mountain. The wind grew louder, and we could distinctly hear it whistling among the ilex trees of the Bosco far above us. The priest hesitated; he feared the difficulties of the ascent, but the Frenchmen and myself were not so soon to be dismayed, and we therefore proceeded onwards. As I had neglected to provide myself with any extra clothing for the ascent, Dr. Gemmellaro very kindly lent me a warm Sicilian cloak, which I found of great service, as even at this early stage of our journey I felt the night air very cool, and the sudden change of temperature from the sultry atmosphere of the plains, could not very well be borne in a thin white dress. At half-past eight our cavalcade started from Nicolosi. Our guide, Antonio Massania, a tall, stout fellow, entirely enveloped in a huge Sicilian cloak, rode in our van, the man with the lantern walking by his side; next followed the three Frenchmen and myself; and the good Maltese brought up the rear. We presented a very formidable appearance, as our mules wound along one after another, threading their way amidst the sharp and broken lavas that strew the mountain road between Nicolosi and the Bosco. The dim light of the peasant's lantern was the pole-star by which we directed our steps, and as we found it was in vain to attempt to guide the mules in the dark, we let them take their own course, as they knew the track of the mountain paths far better than we did, and indeed it was well for us that the darkness concealed the dangerous and slippery passes from our sight, which, in our descent, the daylight revealed more fully to our view. Sometimes we stood on the brink of a black and rugged channel of lava, and at other times we were overlooking some fearful and giddy precipice. Nothing presents to the mind a more imposing idea of the vastness and sublimity of this stupendous mountain, than the immense extent of its own bulk when viewed from some elevated spot high up on its ascent. As we scaled height after height, and rock after rock, we could discover, on looking back, the steep sides of Etna alone, spreading out beneath us, whilst its base was enveloped in the dewy mists that extended far over the plains below the exalted situation on which we stood. This gave to it the appearance of a mountain in the clouds, isolated from all connecting or surrounding objects—a vast and mighty temple raised to the Deity—the pure sky and bright stars shining above, with a deep and boundless expanse of space below. I felt that there was something inspiring and elevating to the soul in such a lofty situation, raised above the insignificant turmoils of the myriads who people the wide earth—we seem for the moment to forget our own ephemeral existence, and the soul spreads its pinions, and soars away into higher, and more exalted regions. Can we wonder, then, that the ancients chose this mighty volcano as a fit spot whereon to rear their altars to the Etnean Jove? that they assigned its subterranean fires to Vulcan and Pluto, and entertained the belief that the infernal

Hades lay beneath it, where Phlegethon and Styx rolled their pestiferous waves? Neither need we be astonished that the same faith in ancient lore taught that the fabled Cyclops, those mighty giants who ate men's flesh, and had but one eye in the centre of their foreheads, were the formidable and fearful race, whose abodes were in the recesses of the forests of Mongibello.

We at last arrived at the Bosco, or woody region of the mountain, where the air felt quite keen, and the wind howled and whistled over our heads from the spreading ilex trees that are scattered about in great profusion over this region of the mountain. Beneath these trees the fern and the heather grow in great abundance, and the scenery resembles in its character that of an English park. The soil was sandy, and mixed up with ashes and lava; but the process of vegetable decomposition had produced in many places a light rich soil. We had proceeded thus far on our way very merrily; the excitement and novelty of the undertaking put the Frenchmen into high spirits, and whenever my mule loitered to crop the fern that grew every where in our path, one of the company behind was sure to call out with a jeu d'esprit, desiring me, (the Signor Inglese,) not to block up the pathway, and shouting out all the time, " Bambino! bambino!" But the worst was to come, for whilst we were enjoying the dangers of the ascent, the wind increased in violence, and the distant howling of the wolf and the wild cat, combined with the low melancholy moan of the elements, filled the soul of the pious father with dismay; and to add to his perilous situation, he was ever and anon slipping off his mule behind, and clinging with all his might to the saddle : a feat which only served to increase the fun of the Frenchmen and myself, who followed in the rear almost convulsed with laughter. As the difficulties of our path increased, the priest showed a great unwillingness to proceed, and a long conversation, which took place between him and the guides in Sicilian, but which none of us understood, afterwards proved that he had persuaded them to invent some excuse for abandoning the attempt to reach the " crater."

On our arrival at the " Casa della Neve," or winter refuge, (a stone hut at the top of the Bosco,) the guide endeavoured to persuade us that the weather was so bad that to venture farther up the mountain, would be to hazard our lives; and that we should either be blown by the wind into the crater, or precipitated over the Val del Bue, a precipice of 1,000 feet in height! We all agreed to wait for an hour or two in hopes of a change of weather, and our guides having gathered a quantity of the dried fern and branches, which are kept in this hut for the accommodation of travellers, together with some charcoal which they had brought with them, soon made a blazing fire, around which we all lay stretched on our woollen cloaks. After taking some refreshment, and passing the time in attempting to sleep, glancing occasionally at the state of the weather outside the hut, we so far influenced the priest as to prevail on him once more to attempt the ascent. Remounting our mules, therefore, we again pushed forward, and soon found ourselves completely out of the Bosco, and entering upon the third region, or, "La regione deserta," as it is called, where the vegetation consists of the scantiest herbs and lichens, scattered here and there among the volcanic sand, and huge masses of lava that constitute the surface of this inhospitable region of the mountain. We had now seven miles to go before we reached the next resting place, the "Casa degli Inglesi," and had already left the late place of our bivouac a couple of miles behind us. Here our ascent terminated ; for the priest jumped off his mule, and standing stock still, refused to proceed any further. It was in vain that the Frenchmen and myself expostulated with him ; his only answer to all our arguments and remonstrances was, "non possible ! non possible !" Finding that he was so resolute, we next endeavoured to prevail on the guide to conduct us to the summit, whilst the priest returned to the "Casa della Neve," under the care of the man who carried the lantern ; but this did not succeed either. The guide, influenced no doubt by the fear of the priest, as well as by his own laziness, and knowing that he would receive the same remuneration whether he took us the whole or only half of the way up to the crater, was as obstinate as the priest ; and although we offered him double the sum agreed upon for the other man to act in his place, yet he would not proceed himself, neither allow the other man to do so, alleging that he was not sufficiently acquainted with the mountain. There was, therefore, no alternative ; go back we must, and after a long parley in French, English, and Italian, we reluctantly dismounted from our mules, and commenced descending the mountain. The guide was an obstinate fool, and though near seven feet high, he seemed to have no more courage or resolution than a child. So satisfied were my French companions of this' that we meditated undertaking the attempt to visit the crater by ourselves in the best way we could. But the mists lay heavy and thick along the sides of the mountain, and we soon lost our companions in the deep shadows, as they wound their way down the mountain's side on their return. We shouted and hallooed after them, and at last we were fortunate enough to regain the track we had lost, and soon rejoined them, greatly mortified at the ill success of our expedition. We found the descent in the dark, and on foot, for the space of seven or eight miles, to be any thing but pleasant. We were, however, fortunate enough to arrive at the "Casa della Neve," in the Bosco, without any serious accident, just as the first faint gleam of daylight was breaking in the eastern sky. Tired and weary, we entered the hut, and commenced forthwith devouring our cold turkeys, without the aid of either plate, knife and fork, or any thing that might have served to distinguish us from the Cyclops, who, with their claws, devoured their prey in the caves of Etna. A furious altercation arose between the Frenchmen and the poor priest, and I began to fear that a serious affray would be the result. The guide, in broad Sicilian sentences, was endeavouring to exculpate himself from blame, holding out his clenched fists all the time; a custom which I found is frequent with the peasantry, when engaged in earnest or passionate disputes. Sometimes the attitude is altered; the arms being stretched out, and the hands brought close together, as though the person were holding them out to receive something, whilst all the while the arms are moved up and down, beating time with the voice in a very curious manner. I have repeatedly witnessed this action, and as it appeared singular to me, I have thought it not unworthy of notice. Descending through the Bosco, I observed the cyclamen and the purple crocus in blossom among the fern, and the sweet breath of the morning filled the air with a pleasant freshness in this exalted region. At ten o'clock we reached Nicolosi, and to our infinite regret, we saw the clouds chasing each other away from the upper region of the mountain, whilst the warm rays of the sun fell brightly over the snug little village at the foot of Monte Rossi. We found our friend, Dr. Gemmellaro, in his museum, and consoled ourselves by examining the fine specimens of lava and sulphur which he had at various times collected from the crater. He took great pains in showing us his museum, and his collection of drawings of the mountain, and requested us all to insert our names in a book which he keeps for that purpose. He visits the crater twice or three times during the summer months, and keeps the " Casa degli Inglese" in repair, of which he has the key ; this he lends to strangers on their ascent, who call for it at his house on their way up the mountain. Finding that the mosquitoes had been attacking us, he very kindly favoured us with some ointment that he makes from a herb of Etna, and which I found afterwards to be an infallible cure against their venomous bites. He further consoled us by remarking, " that when intelligent persons wish to ascend the mountain the weather is generally bad, but when *beasts* (as he termed them) attempted it, the weather proved favourable." This we of course regarded as a polite compliment, and thanking our friend for his attention, we proceeded to the albergo, where we rested ourselves after our fatigue, and feasted upon grapes and the delicious figs of Mount Etna. Monte Rossi forms a fine object in the landscape when viewed from Nicolosi, and seems like two conical mountains rising up from one base. In the crater of this latter volcano, there are found small black crystals of lava in some abundance, which resemble good sized garnets. I was presented with some of these by Dr. Gemmellaro, in a box, which he gave me, containing several beautiful specimens of the minerals of Etna. I regretted much that I was not permitted to enjoy a further acquaintance with this amiable man, as his learning and general information would render him a most delightful companion. Bidding adieu to Nicolosi, we returned by the same horses and carriage to Catania, where I arrived at three o'clock, resolving that I would not leave Sicily until I had stood on the highest peak of the crater of the mighty Montegibello.

CHAPTER XXVIII.

ROUTE FROM CATANIA TO MESSINA.

" ULYSSES.—What land is this, and who inhabit it?

SILENUS.—Etna, the loftiest peak in Sicily.

ULYSSES.—And who possess the land?—the race of beasts?

SILENUS.—Cyclops, who live in caverns, not in houses.

ULYSSSE.—And are they just to strangers? hospitable?

SILENUS.—They think the sweetest thing a stranger brings
    Is his own flesh—

ULYSSES.—What! do they eat men's flesh?

SILENUS.—No one comes here who is not eaten up!"

ABBATE, our landlord, regretted exceedingly that we were not able to accomplish the ascent of the mountain ; and he even went so far as to say, that had his hotel not been so full of the visitors who were at Catania, on account of the arrival of the king and queen in that city, he would himself have acted as our conductor. The guides of Nicolosi, though generally preferred to those of Catania, are, in my humble opinion, not always to be trusted ; as they are lazy, indolent, and difficult to manage. Abbate has, at various times, accompanied parties visiting the mountain, and his attentions have invariably been highly spoken of.

I had now no alternative but to return immediately to Messina, where the schooner in which I was to sail for England was shipping her cargo of lemons. Only two days remained before the proposed departure of the vessel. Writing was useless, as the posts in Sicily are very slow and uncertain. No other course was open than going myself to Messina, and although I abandoned for the present undertaking the ascent of Etna, I nevertheless cherished the hope that sufficient time might still be available before the schooner was ready for sea, for me to return to Catania to accomplish my desired object. Not one moment was, therefore, to be lost, and my next step was to hasten on to Messina (a distance of seventy miles) by the first conveyance that proceeded to that city. Most fortunately for my future plans, Abbate informed me on our return from Nicolosi, that a " diligence " or coach as he termed it, was to start in an hour's time from the square of the Elephant; it would travel that night as far as Giarra, and on the following night arrive at Messina. I immediately embraced this very opportune offer, and hastily swallowing my dinner, I settled my account with my landlord (who, by-the-by, was an extremely civil and obliging fellow) and arranging matters with the Frenchmen, who had acted as pursers on our mountain expedition, I bade them all good day, not forgetting our unfortunate companion the priest, who despite the affair in the "Casa della Neve," gave me a very kind invitation to visit him at Senglea, in the island of Malta. Having secured my luggage as well as I was able, I awaited the arrival of the diligence at the door of the albergo. It soon came up, and I looked for Abbate to act as my interpreter to the coachman, who had the appearance of a smart sailor, but Abbate was nowhere to be found. My luggage was immediately seized by half-a-dozen different people, and I fully expected to lose some portion of it, for they commenced carrying it off in all directions. However, my alarm was groundless, as I found all my packages safely deposited in the coach, and in another minute we were driving furiously along the Corso in the direction of the new road that leads to Messina. The vehicle into which I had thus been so unceremoniously packed, resembled very nearly one of the third-class-train coaches on the Great Western Railway. It was divided into two parts, each holding four persons; the roof was flat, and supported by iron rods, from which hung curtains, which might be let down at pleasure, to protect the traveller from the sun and dust, which at this season are very unpleasant in Sicily. I found this mode of travelling to be pretty comfortable, and could almost have fancied myself in a Devonshire jaunting car. The horses, which were harnessed three abreast, were full of spirit, and we galloped off towards Giarra in fine style. My *compagnons de voyage* were four in number, all of them Sicilians, and although I was able to converse but little with them, and that partly by signs and motions, they yet endeavoured to show me those small attentions and courtesies so pleasing to a stranger, owing to the kind motives from which they spring. I soon discovered that one of my companions could speak French, and through the medium of this third language we managed to understand each other very well. He pointed out to me every object worthy of notice by the way, and made himself as agreeable as possible. My companions offered me some cigars, and were quite surprised to find that I declined them, as in Sicily everybody smokes, from the miserable sulphur miner up to the noble at Ferdinand's own table. Cigars may here as in Malta be obtained for a mere nothing, eight or ten of them being purchased for five grana, which is about equivalent to an English penny. The road we were pursuing traversed that part of the country, called the port of Ulysses, which was overwhelmed by the lava of 1669. It is said that this precise spot was formerly a deep and capacious harbour, which Virgil describes as—

"The port capacious, and secure from wind."

It is now entirely filled up, and the broken fragments of lava that strew the sands of this beautiful coast show but too plainly how dreadful must have been the catastrophe of that eventful and fatal eruption, perhaps the most dreadful of any that has burst from the bowels of the mountain which records have handed down to us. By the sea-shore a little farther on, stands the castle of Aci, built on a promontory of black lava and surrounded on three sides by the sea. The next objects of interest, are the Scopuli Cyclopum, or rocks of the Cyclops, at the village of Trizza. They consist of seven islands, a short distance from the shore, though only the three principal ones bear the name of Cyclops. The largest of these is basaltic, and has a kind of substratum of yellow chalk; in form they are abrupt and conical, and are supposed to be the rocks mentioned by Homer, which he describes as being situated near the cave of the cannibal Polyphemus, who devoured the unfortunate followers of Ulysses when they were driven on this inhospitable shore, then the favourite abode of the Etnean Cyclops. Between Trizza and Aci Reale we travelled through groves of orange and lemon trees, along a good road. I found this part of the country to be extremely rich and fertile, and the peculiar beauty of a Sicilian landscape was enhanced by the warm yellow glow that overspread it, mellowing the western hills where the setting sun lay cradled in a gorgeous mass of belted purple and golden clouds. It was at this point that we passed on the sea-shore the far-famed steps of Acis, or the *Scali di Aci*, but the ghost of the beautiful shepherd stole not along the balmy eve, nor did we see any thing of the nymph Galatea. These steps consist of eight or nine layers of lava, of different degrees of antiquity. As there is a layer of vegetable earth between each, a considerable time must have elapsed before a second eruption took place: which fact goes a great way to disprove the notion that all eruptions of the volcano have occurred since the time of Homer; prior to which period, some authors inform us, it was not known as a burning mountain. We reached Giarra shortly before eight o'clock, where we were all to take up our quarters for the night. We were ushered into one general apartment with a stone floor, and which corres-ponded to what we should, in a country village in England, call the "traveller's room," with this exception, however, that it was to form our dormitory also, the beds being supported on tressels around the apartment, which was, to say the least of it, very large and airy. We sat down to our supper in excellent spirits, and with a good appetite. Our waiter was a bare-footed woman, whom I took to be the mistress of the hotel. Our supper was in the true Sicilian fashion, and consisted of eggs, bread, salad, and wine, with a dessert of apples, grapes, and raw turnips. When these latter articles came on the table, I paused to observe how they were eaten, imagin-ing for the moment that they might be some other vegetable used perhaps as a salad. But there was no mistaking the turnips, for there they stood facing me, tops and all!

Presently one of my companions was seized with a friendly feeling towards them, and cutting one in half, placed it on his plate. I most gravely followed his example with the remaining piece, that I might not be deceived by external appearances. After thus philosophically eating my turnip, I was desirous of having some tea, but this is a beverage so very rarely used in Sicily, that I found it impossible to procure it. After a great deal of trouble, however, I managed to get some wretched coffee, for which a lad had been sent half over the town, and this, such as it was, was served to us without sugar in cups as big as thimbles. I now discovered that one of my companions was an amber merchant, who was proceeding to Messina with a quantity of beautiful trinkets, manufactured from this substance in Catania. He amused us after supper with a display of his treasures, amongst which were some superb brooches and necklaces. Our barefooted hostess again entered the apartment, and, having furnished the beds with clean linen, and lit the small shrine to the Virgin which stood at one end of the room, she left us with a good-natured " buona sera." In joining a native " table d'hôte" in this manner, I was astonished to find so great a diminution of my expenditure. I found that for a supper and bed, which, had I been alone, would have cost me nearly half a dollar, I now paid only 8½d. This mode of living is the only one which can give the traveller a good opportunity of observing Sicilian manners in their primitive state, as I found that when Englishmen visit the larger cities where they " put up" at the chief hotels, every pains is taken to wait upon them in the fashion of their own country, and thus it happens, that instead of their being surprised and pleased with novelty of custom, they only see repeated in a very imperfect manner what they find at home every day of their lives.

At sunrise we again started on our journey, one only of our party remaining at Giarra ; his place in the vehicle was supplied by an elderly gentleman, accompanied by a young lady who appeared to be his daughter. They kept the diligence waiting nearly half-an-hour, when they very leisurely seated themselves, and having given their friends a farewell embrace, they made the signal of our departure from Giarra. The morning was a charming one, and our road lay through a most romantic and fertile country, commanding fine views of Etna, whose unclouded summit arose clear and distinct in the brilliancy of an early dawn. The town of Catabiano, perched like an eagle's eyrie, on the summit of a lofty rock, formed a picturesque object on our route just after passing Giarra, and afterwards we came in sight of the mountain of Taormina which is also city-crowned, with the village of Mola overhanging it from a still loftier peak. Taormina, now an impoverished place, was once the magnificent city of Taurominium, built by a Roman colony who settled there. It contains many vestiges and remains of its former splendour particularly the theatre, which is considered, in its present state, to be the most perfect Roman ruin in Sicily. We were, at this part of our route, among the mountains of the Val di Demone, which occupy the north-eastern portion of the island. The whole country to the north of Etna consists of steep and rugged hills and mountains, forming part of a chain called the Nebrodes. Of these, the Monte Scuderi is the most remarkable: on its summit is the ruin of an old building said to have been erected in the middle ages; but the story of an exceedingly cold wind blowing out of the crater, which Brydone relates, seems to have no foundation whatever in fact. Brydone was most probably misinformed by the inhabitants, who, in those days, were much less acquainted with the motives of travellers in making inquiries than they at present are. These mountains are very fertile, and abound in olive and mulberry trees, whilst the steeps, which stretch down abruptly towards the sea, are cultivated by the inhabitants, and groves of oranges, lemons, and bergamots are interspersed among the cottages that enliven the shore. The fruit on the trees was yet green, but when fully ripened, it must present a charming and beautiful appearance. When the lemons have been swelled out to their full size by the rains, they are plucked in the green state, and shipped at Messina, and it is during their voyage that they acquire the yellow colour which we see them have in this country. Most of the lemons for exportation are grown in the mountain fiumaras around Messina; numbers are also grown near Giarra, and are exported from Catania to Malta and other places. These mountains are also famous for the grapes they produce, and even as far back as the age of the elder Dionysius, the red wine of Taurominium was highly esteemed. At the time of my visit, the vintage was nearly over, though occasionally I saw a vine-press teeming with the purple juice of the grapes, as they were thrown in in baskets full, fresh gathered from the vineyard. We met troops of peasants with large baskets on their heads, piled up with tempting clusters, of which they would sell us as many as we could eat for a baiocchi (about a penny.) We halted a short time at the foot of the mountain of Taormina, where I noticed that the peasants were generally a handsomer race than those of southern Sicily, and I found this generally to be the case, as we proceeded farther northwards. In Messina, for instance, there is much more personal beauty than at Syracuse, though this circumstance may, in some measure, be accounted for by the latter place being so very unhealthy, whilst the former is famed for its salubrity, delightful climate, and the bracing air of the straits.

Both the men and women of Sicily wear remarkably large rings in their ears; some which I have seen worn by the women are above two inches in diameter, and of solid gold. The possession of a pair of these rings is an important desideratum with the poorest peasant, and many a more useful and necessary article is dispensed with to become the owner of what they consider so great an ornament. The ear-rings of the men are smaller, and seldom exceed an inch across, whilst all are made of a circular shape, and quite plain. It is also no uncommon thing to see a barefooted female cottager with her fingers adorned by three or four massive gold rings, whilst the remainder of her dress may not be worth as many shillings.

After leaving Giardini the country becomes mountainous and romantic the whole way to Messina ; the road lays along the sea-coast, and in many places it winds round the sides of the mountains, commanding views which are extremely beautiful and picturesque.   The pass of Fort St. Allessio is very fine, and the opposite shores of Calabria add increasing beauty to the scene.   We reached Zia Paola at noon, where we halted for a couple of hours at a small inn by the sea-side.   Here we dined on a rotolo of maccaroni, and the old gentleman who joined us at Giarra, adding to this supply a fine stuffed turkey and some Etna wine, which he very kindly invited us all to partake of, we came off for our dinner much better than we had anticipated.   One of my fellow travellers expressed a desire to drink wine with me, not after the Sicilian fashion, which consists chiefly in touching glasses, but, as he expressed it, in the mode of the " Ingleses.''   Instead, however, of saluting me when I bowed, he seemed dreadfully afraid of not hitting the identical moment, and shouted out " now," with all his might.   This was most probably done to display his knowledge of the English language ; but seeing me smile, and mistaking the cause, he continued at intervals to vociferate " now," during the whole of the time that we were at dinner.   He was very desirous of knowing the English name for every thing, and as he pointed to various articles before us, I gave him the English words for them ; but when he came to the word " fly," he pronounced it as " fry," and after making numberless attempts to improve his Anglo-Sicilian pronunciation, he gave it up as a bad job.   After a very merry dinner, we once more started on our journey northwards, and passed through the village of Scaletta on the sea-shore.   Towards evening we drew near to Messina, having travelled through fields, the hedgerows of which were composed entirely of aloes and Indian figs ; these latter shrubs, which are called by the Maltese " prickly pears," bear a yellow blossom, which in size and shape very much resembles that of the cactus speciosissima, and this as well as the fleshy lobes of the plant is armed with small prickles, whose wounds cause much inflammation, which I discovered to my cost on attempting to pluck one of the yellow flowers for my hortus siccus.   After dark, the lights of Reggio, on the Italian side of the straits, shone brightly through the clear evening air, and after passing successively through several villages, we at last entered the beautiful city of Messina, the Zancle of the ancients.   I alighted at the Britannia Hotel, and after partaking of a cup of excellent coffee, retired to my room quite overcome with fatigue ; my want of sleep preventing me from visiting the quay in search of the schooner until the following morning.

CHAPTER XXIX.

" Incidit in Scyllam, cupiens vitare Charybdim."

On ascending Etna, I found that the sharpness of the cold night air in the exalted regions of the mountain so severely affected my eyes that I was nearly blind; for they had not as yet recovered from the effects of the hot glare of the sun in Malta. During my journey to Messina, I suffered acutely from this species of ophthalmia, and finding it much worse when I awoke in the morning, I resolved on having a pair of spectacles. I purchased these in the Strada del Corso, and hurrying down to the Marina, I commenced searching for the vessel amongst a crowd of others of all nations, Greek, Austrian, Turkish, Russian, Spanish, and Italian, that thronged the quay to the extent of a mile. I soon discovered our rakish little schooner, and found the captain, his wife, and all on board, well. My favourite gazelles, which I had procured from Tripoli when in Malta, were in good condition, and seemed as healthy and playful as when I left them at Valetta. From the captain I received the pleasing intelligence that on account of the want of rain the lemons were not yet ready for exportation, and that another week would elapse before we should finally sail for England. On hearing this news, I determined to start very early on the following morning for Etna, and to make a visit during the remainder of the day to the Faro, from which Messina is only seven miles distant. Having accomplished this, I purposed to engage mules back to the neighbourhood of Etna, and lose no time in making the ascent of the mountain, leaving my survey and description of Messina, till my return.

I set off on a large donkey, which the cicerone of the hotel procured for me; and taking an old man as a guide, we soon got clear of the streets of the city, and entered upon the Faro road, which runs along the sea-shore. The ride was beautifully diversified with villas, and fine spreading trees, which are backed by the fiumaras that descend abruptly from the mountains, down which, in the rainy season, the streams pour with great force and volume, forming numerous cascades in their course. Along the whole road, the view of the opposite coast is very beautiful;

s

the mountains of Calabria rising rugged and abrupt, sprinkled over with vineyards and olives; and the deep blue waters of the straits, winding, like a vast and
mighty river, between Sicily and the continent of Europe.   The distance at this
part is only three miles across, and beneath the clear atmosphere of Italy, objects
appear to be much more distinct than persons residing in less genial climates are aware
of.   Tradition states that Calabria and Sicily were once joined.   Pliny, Strabo, and
even Virgil, all tell a similar story.   The received opinion is, that they were parted
asunder by a violent earthquake; and that formerly the straits were much narrower
than they are at present.   This constant widening of the channel accounts, in some
measure, for the terrors of Scylla and Charybdis having so nearly vanished, the waters
being now less pent up, and their force greatly diminished.   The banks here consist,
in some places, of fine yuccas, interspersed among the aloes.   The prickly pears are of
two sorts; the larger kind, which bears the fruit that forms so large a proportion of
the food of the lower classes during this season, and a dwarf species, more prickly
than the former, that grows close to the sea, and produces only a hard green seed-
vessel of the size of a walnut.   Before arriving at the promontory on which the lighthouse stands, the country is low, flat, and sandy, and the road runs between several
salt water lakes that are flooded at high tide.   I was much amused in passing one of
these lakes to see several birds stuck upon sticks, in imitation of cranes, wading in the
deep water, but for what purpose this deception was practised I could not discover;
it seemed most probable that it was for decoying others during the winter season,
when these birds are taken.

On reaching the straggling village of Faro, we dismounted at a fisherman's hut,
and having tied up our donkey, and procured him some hay, we entered the cottage
to seek some refreshment for ourselves.   In the vineyards around the Faro the famous
Falernian wine was formerly made, but at present none is to be procured.   All we
could obtain was some red wine of the roughest quality, with some black bread,
a few figs, and a dish of olives; the latter detestable and unpalatable morsels were for
my guide.   The wine was served out to us in a monstrous Calabrese vase of so
singular a construction, that my guide very wittily ascribed it to the Saracens, a
nation to whom every thing that is ancient or doubtful is constantly referred by the
Sicilians.   When 1 had nearly finished my repast, the woman of the cottage came in
with a fish on a plate, which my guide informed me that she had just caught.   This
accounted for her sudden disappearance on my expressing a wish to have something to eat, and had not the sea been so close to the door, I should have stood but
a poor chance of tasting the fishes of Faro!   But she had been fortunate in her
capture, and seemed determined that I should enjoy it whilst it was fresh.   She
took her prize into an outhouse, and threw it upon a charcoal fire, and after a few
minutes' frizzling, she brought it in to me upon a trencher, black, smoking, and half

smothered in olive oil. Having finished this delicate and dainty dish, we started off on foot across a sandy beach to visit the lighthouse, the celebrated Pharos of the Greeks, which is situated on the sandy flats of Cape Pylorus. A small fee secured my admission, and the door being opened by a Neapolitan soldier, we ascended several flights of steps, and soon reached the top, from whence I was gratified with a panorama, the beauty of which fully repaid me for the time I had taken to visit the Faro. Northwards, and studding the sea like so many fairy islands, lay Stromboli, Lipari, Panaria, Volcano, and the whole of the Lipari group, with the promontory of Milazzo jutting out into the water to the westward. Whilst looking towards the east, the eye rested with delight on the Calabrese mountains, and the distant shores of Italy stretched along far northward in the direction of Naples. Beneath wound the blue waters, deep and dark, of the Messinese straits, near the centre of which the eddying current that flows in and out of the channel every six hours, points out the direction of the far-famed Charybdis, and jutting out from the opposite shore the steep rock of Scylla rises jagged and abrupt, the waters lashing and foaming around its cavernous base with that moaning sound, that gave rise to the fabled dogs and syrens of the ancients. The rock of Scylla is united to the Italian shore, and is not a detached portion by itself, as some have supposed. On its summit stands the town of Sciglio, containing a castle and about 300 inhabitants. On returning from the lighthouse, I found my magnificent donkey completely invigorated, and engaging a smaller one for my guide, who was much fatigued, we trotted off towards Messina, followed by half the children in the village, begging for a single baiocchi. On returning to my hotel, I called on Mr. R. the banker, an English gentleman residing in this city, to whom I bore a letter of introduction. He received me very kindly, and favoured me with a recommendatory letter to a friend of his at Riposto, a town near Giarra, at the foot of Etna, from whence I was to start on my ascent to the crater. With this essential aid I was enabled to lay down the plan for my route during the few remaining days I was to spend in Sicily, and I therefore abandoned a project whih I had entertained of visiting Stromboli, which was represented to me as impracticable, the boats being sometimes detained there for upwards of a week, owing to the surf, which runs so high upon the beach, that mariners are compelled to wait for a change of wind before they are able to launch away.

CHAPTER XXX.

"I see a chaos of green leaves and fruit
    Built round dark caverns, even to the root
    Of the living stems who feed them; in whose bowers
    There sleep, in their dark dew, the folded flowers.
    Like winged stars the fire-flies flash and glance
    Pale in the open moonshine,—but each one
    Under the dark trees seems a little sun,—
    A meteor tamed,—a fixed star gone astray
    From the silver regions of the milky way."

     *   *   *   *

*   *   *   "And a bird,
    That cannot be a nightingale, and yet
    I know none else that sings so sweet as it
    At this late hour."

AFTER a good night's rest at the hotel, I arose at daybreak, and shortly afterwards found the guide and mules, which I had engaged for my journey to Riposto waiting for me at the door. As the distance was great, I felt very anxious to start as soon as possible, in order to reach Riposto on the same night. Every thing was ready, when I found that my passport, which the landlord of the hotel, Signor Nobile, assured me that he would get signed in time, remained yet unsigned, and that the authorities were not in attendance at the office of the police at so early an hour. As I did not wish to run the risk of imprisonment in any of his Sicilian Majesty's gaols, I did not consider it advisable to run the chance of proceeding into another province without government permission, therefore I set off myself in search of the authorities at their respective dwellings. After a tedious search, which cost me a delay of nearly two hours, we found the officer at mass in one of the suburban churches. Here we had to wait until the old gentleman had finished his devotions, and the moment that the priests had concluded their ceremonies at the altar, he took the passport, and requesting me to step into an adjoining room, where the priests were disrobing, he affixed his signature, for which I paid him the usual fee. We had now to obtain the counter-signature of the head of the police, which concluded the affair. It was nearly ten o'clock before we started from the Corso at Messina. The sun was scorchingly hot, and the glare and dust rendered the roads very unpleasant. Beneath the bright blue sky of a Sicilian autumn day, the peasants, dressed in their holiday clothes, thronged the environs of the city, or followed the paths along the fiumaras, mounted upon mules. It is no uncommon sight to witness a peasant on his mule, with a barefooted lady seated behind him, and a little child clinging to her waist. In this part of the country, the women climb the olive trees, and beat down the fruit with a long stick. In fact, they perform these out-door services in the fields and vineyards with more spirit than the men, whose employment consists chiefly in fishing.

About twelve miles from Messina, my guide, who was running behind the mule, received a severe kick on his breast from the animal, which caused him to faint. We were several miles distant from any village, upon a lonely road by the sea-shore, and I was fearful that the man would be unable to proceed any further. As he did not understand one word of English, I could not discover how much he was hurt; but fortunately, after a short delay, we were enabled to start again, the poor fellow pointing to his breast with a most rueful countenance. In another hour we reached Scaletta, a village on the sea-coast, where we stopped at a cottage to dine. This cottage appeared to be the general shop or store of the place. A number of peasants were seated around an open doorway, and after dismounting in a spacious stable adjoining, I entered the cottage, and seating myself at a small table apart from the rest, I waited whilst the good woman of the house prepared me some dinner. Here again I saw Sicilian manners in all their native simplicity, and the poor accommodation I received was amply repaid by the amusement which the scene afforded me. I was surrounded by three very lean Spanish dogs, which almost devoured me for something to eat; four or five remarkably sleek tabby cats followed their example, and I amused myself by feeding them on grapes until my maccaroni was cooked. As the cats grew more troublesome, they were driven out of the house, and flew scampering away in all directions, whilst the dogs slunk underneath the table. My dinner was by this time quite ready; it consisted of a huge pile of maccaroni, (or "tobacco pipes made easy," as it has been very aptly denominated,) with a dessert of figs, walnuts, and delicious grapes. After I had eaten a few mouthfuls of the maccaroni, I handed it over to my guide, who, despite his kick in the morning, managed to clear the trencher. The maccaroni in the Sicilian cities is good, but the home-made stuff which had been cooked for me was very unpalatable, and, indeed, was only rendered barely eatable by the addition of a sauce of red pepper, or tomatas fried in oil. The son of the landlady, a fine boy of thirteen, soon made friends with me, and when I remounted my mule to start again on my journey towards Riposto, he came with his brother and kissed my hand to wish me farewell, begging me to accept some sweet apples which were the produce of their garden. I took them, and bidding the boys a friendly good-by, resolved to make this my resting-place on my return from the mountain, having met with so kind a reception from these people. The hostess was a merry soul, and little Antonio was the prettiest page I had seen in Sicily. Leaving Scaletta we travelled on till long after dark, and, finding that it was impossible to reach Riposto on the same night, we took up our quarters at the little inn at Giardini, at the foot of the mountain of Taormina. The latter part of our journey was very lonely; it lay along the rocky shores, beyond the pass of St. Alessio, where there is a region of gloomy caves which are the nightly resort of a desperate band of smugglers. Here we were serenaded by the shrill cry of the cicada, whose pining note resounded from every olive tree when twilight had spread itself over the romantic steeps of the Nebrodes, and the light of an occasional fire-fly sparkled among the dark green foliage of the lemon and the bergamot. The accommodations of the inn at Giardini consisted of a moderately-sized apartment, with a bed in each corner; these, consisting simply of mattresses laid upon wooden tressels, are very easily removed. Presently, my old landlord came in, and, bringing me a lamp, laid a book upon the table for my amusement until the supper was ready. This was the visitors' name book, and it was nearly full of autographs in various languages, chiefly English, French, and German, accompanied here and there with droll verses and personal jokes on the old landlord himself, who, ignorant of the meaning, had treasured them up for many years, thinking, no doubt, (good and credulous soul!) that they were all eulogiums on his establishment, and the unremitting attention of himself and two old women, who formed a capital trio for the fun of merry travellers halting in a Sicilian village. Some of the jokes were so ridiculous, that, although exceedingly tired, I sat and laughed outright over the precious volume, until the supper was brought upon the table. The old folks were certainly very attentive, and they did their best to make me comfortable. I had honey from Hybla of the finest kind, and as no milk was to be procured so late in the evening, they beat up some eggs instead in my coffee. After this wholesome repast, for which I was heartily thankful, I slept soundly until four o'clock the next morning. Before leaving, I made an entry in the old man's name-book for the amusement of future guests, and having mounted my mule I started off again with my guide towards Riposto.

For the first hour it was quite dark, but a gleam of light over the Mediterranean gave indications of the approach of sunrise, and soon after the summit of Etna caught the earliest ray, and the dawn gradually spread itself lower and lower, till at last the round red sun itself peeped up above the sea, and the whole plain revealed its wealth of vineyards and olive groves to the cheerful light of morning. We struck out of the main road along a bye path, over rugged lavas and torrent beds, from which I enjoyed a magnificent view of Etna. The bright green vineyards circling its base, were cheerfully interspersed with numerous villages, and white cottages.

About a mile from Giarra, we turned down a sandy lane, and passing through a plantation of canes, we reached the shore. After proceeding for a short distance further on, we arrived at Riposto, which is a place of some trade, though the streets are dirty, and the people present a very miserable appearance.

Mr. Carlhill, the gentleman to whom I bore an introductory letter, received me most kindly; and as the family were just sitting down to breakfast, I joined them immediately, and dismissed my guide, who returned to Messina. The house, which has only been recently built by Mr. Carlhill, is furnished quite in the English style, and is the best I have seen in Sicily, if I except some in Catania and Messina. The dining and drawing-rooms are paved with coloured tiles, and resemble mosaic work, the climate being too warm for carpets. Mr. Carlhill's wine-presses are very extensive, and he is engaged in raising new works upon the premises. After breakfast, Mr. Carlhill, senior, who has resided many years in Sicily, favoured me with an inspection of the wine-presses and distilleries. As the vintage was nearly over, I was unfortunate in not seeing the process in active operation. A great variety of wines, both red and white, are made here, and exported to various parts, more especially to Malta and America. The wines of Etna are very superior of their kind; and there is a richness in the grape growing on the mountain which is said to be peculiar to itself. The *Vino da Dama* is delicious, and exceeds most cordials in flavour, though I was informed by a gentleman of Nicolosi, that it is the pure juice extracted from the grape. Vessels coming to Riposto for cargoes of wine, usually lay off about a mile from the shore, and the goods are carried out to them on rafts constructed especially for that purpose. Smaller vessels are sometimes employed; they are dragged up on the beach, and I have even seen some of fifty or sixty tons, high and dry on the shore, taking in their cargoes at Riposto. As there are scarcely any tides, the vessels are drawn up and re-launched by means of a slip, and their keels are supported by strong beams. It was a pleasant thing, when so far removed from home, to meet with an English family with whom I could hold intercourse. They dwell isolated as it were, at the foot of the great Mongibello, on that charming shore which for ages past has been the scene of classic story; and in imagination, has been peopled with Cyclops, nymphs, and satyrs. Here they live in perfect retirement, Messina being the nearest point of communication with any English family. The pleasure of meeting one's countrymen was in this instance greatly enhanced by the very kind reception which I met with from them. Indeed it was impossible for me to have received more unostentatious kindness from any persons than I did from the friends whom I met at Riposto. As Mr. R., at Messina, referred me to his acquaintances at this place for instructions as to my best means of ascending Etna from hence, Mr. Carlhill proposed that I should start at noon for Nicolosi across the country, taking with me some mules and a faithful servant of his own who had been in his employment and service from a boy.

All things, therefore, being prepared according to this plan, I took a temporary leave of my kind friends at Riposto, and proceeded on foot with my guide to Giarra, where we joined the mules, taking with us a small bottle of rum in case we should require it when we arrived at the summit of the mountain. After a tedious ride of five hours, over rugged beds of lava, and through the most romantic scenery, we arrived at the village of Nicolosi. Our ride lay along steep beds of lava, bordered with rich vineyards. The mountaineers, in groups of ten or twenty, occasionally met us, descending with their baskets of grapes to the vine-presses in the valleys ; but the vintage was nearly over, and these were the last clusters of the season. The peasants of Etna are a hardy, robust, and picturesque race. It is a pretty sight to meet a group of the villagers winding down the mountain passes, men, women, and children, all joyous and merry, singing as they go, at the highest pitch of their voices, and each one laden with a cane basket, piled up with purple grapes, and covered over with a branch of spreading green leaves. It was past eight o'clock ere we reached Nicolosi. The little lane of soft volcanic sand, and the pretty cottage of Signor Gemmellaro, were again familiar to me. I entered and found the philosopher of Etna seated by his well-trimmed lamp, near the open window, and his wife busied in her household avocations. He was greatly surprised at seeing me, and after explaining matters to him, he promised to procure for me a guide who would accompany me to the "Sommo Cratere," without fail. In order to render his promises more secure and certain, Signor Gemmellaro intimated to him from me, that unless he took me to the very top of the crater, he should not receive his stipulated pay. With this precaution I felt satisfied, and agreed to start soon after nine o'clock, on my expedition to the upper regions of the mountain. Whilst resting at Nicolosi, the worthy Doctor regaled me with a supper of conserve of grapes, and the sweet wine of Etna. He accompanied me to the inn where my two guides and their mules, with a third one for myself, were in readiness awaiting my arrival. Before the village bell sounded the hour of nine, we were feeling our way over tracks of volcanic sand, towards the Bosco. It was quite dark, and we groped our way onwards without even a lantern, leaving our mules to follow their own well-known paths, and hoping by-and-by to be cheered by the light of the rising moon. But the wind had brought a heavy mass of clouds from the north and west, and the moon and stars were alike shrouded from our sight. About midnight we arrived at the " Casa della Neve," in the exalted region of the Bosco. Here the wind howled and moaned most dismally, but we only halted for a quarter of an hour, and did not even light a fire, as our grand object was to gain the summit of the crater by sunrise. Added to the melancholy moaning of the wind among the trees, the occasional yell of a wild cat, sounded like the voice of some unearthly demon from the subterraneous abodes of fire beneath us. By-and-by, the clouds broke partially away, displaying here and there patches of the glorious blue canopy of heaven, studded with innumerable stars, shining with a brilliancy peculiar to the clear atmosphere of so elevated a region as the one we were now traversing. It is computed that Etna is upwards of 11,000 feet, or rather better than two perpendicular miles above the level of the sea, though the ascent is more than thirty miles.

We had now passed the limits of vegetation, and after a most fatiguing ascent of seven miles over barren lavas, and sand intermingled with ashes, we reached the " Casa degli Inglesi," or summer refuge, situated on the plain at the foot of the cone. Here we rested for half an hour, and warmed ourselves by a good fire of charcoal which the guides had brought with them. The key of this refuge was lent to us by Signor Gemmellaro, who has lately repaired and improved it at his own expense. It consists of a spacious hut, built of lava, and divided into two apartments. In the innermost one are some straw mattresses, on one of which I threw myself down, and enjoyed the most delightful rest imaginable, though they were frozen completely stiff. The walls of this refuge are covered with ice, and the intense cold of this region renders the " refuge" an indispensable comfort to all travellers visiting the crater. After warming ourselves again at the charcoal fire, and taking a draught of rum apiece, we once more prepared to start. It was now about an hour before sunrise, and leaving the mules in the refuge, under the care of my Riposto servant, I set out on foot, accompanied by the guide, who pointed significantly towards the dim shadowy form that rose high before us, the object of my desire and toil. We had now by far the most difficult part of the ascent to accomplish, and it was still very dark. We were provided with long sticks to assist us in climbing over the sharp and dangerous lavas, and managed to grope on as well as we could. Every now and then I slipped into some unseen cavity, or stumbled over a sharp projecting rock of lava. But with the exception of a gash in my knee, occasioned by falling among some of these, I escaped all further mischief. As we got higher, the steepness of the ascent increased, and with it the difficulty of climbing onwards, for the ashes and cinders, which constitute this portion of the cone, are so loose as to give way at every step, and we sank down sometimes to our knees. The wind was so high and so violent, that in some places we had to stoop down and crawl on our hands and knees to prevent our being completely blown away. The vapours gently curling out through the loose apertures in the lava soil intimated our approach to the mouth of the crater, but our goal was still farther off from us than I had imagined, and it took us another half-hour's industrious climbing before we stood on the sides of the highest or grand

T

crater. Here I sank down on the ashes quite exhausted, but a moment was sufficient for me to recover my breath, and after making another vigorous effort, we stood on the brink of the crater. Vapours, strongly impregnated with sulphur, were arising on all sides. The whole of the immense cone consists externally of lava, ashes, and volcanic stones mingled with sulphur. The basin, or interior hollow, which is, properly speaking, the crater, descends very abruptly downwards towards the bowels of the mountain. We lay flat down and looked over the side into the crater, but the quantity of sulphurous vapour that slowly but continually arose from all sides of its mighty depths, prevented our seeing very far down into it. None who have gazed on the inside of the crater of Etna can ever forget it. The whole descent on every side is thickly encrusted with sulphur and other volcanic productions. The gradations of tint and colour are extremely beautiful; they vary from a fine yellow, which is the prevailing hue, to white, orange, red, brown and dusky grey, and these all blend into each other with the most exquisite softness of colouring imaginable. The wildness and solitude of this vast crater are truly magnificent. All around is sublimity and stillness. The bewildered traveller standing on this vast and isolated peak seems for the moment to forget all of earth and its associations, and is utterly lost in the contemplation of the grandeur of the scene before him. But a peep into the wonders of the crater was not all that I enjoyed on the mighty summit of Etna. There was yet another and a higher peak above us, forming the north-east edge of the crater. This was the loftiest "top" of the mountain, above it there was no object to obstruct the boundless view of all things around. Naked and exalted, the highest pinnacle of the volcano reared its summit into the clear blue space of sky far above the clouds that lay cradled in a thousand fleecy forms over the whole of Sicily. It was on the summit of this peak that I longed to stand, and my guide, who was a very resolute fellow, creeping on first along the edge of the crater, beckoned to me to follow him. The wind was very high, and had we slipped on either side, we should have been precipitated, on one hand into the crater, and on the other over a precipice of three hundred feet towards the Val de Bue. We gained the rock in safety, and, holding by the hand of my guide, I stood on the highest peak of Etna. I felt a thrill of satisfaction at the mere attainment of my desired object, and casting a hasty glance over the dizzy precipices below, my guide joined me in three cheers to the Cyclops, and we commenced our return along the narrow edge of the crater. The phenomenon which delighted me most after the red sun rose above the clouds, that hung like bags of wool over the Mediterranean sea, was the shadow of the cone itself in the shape of a pyramid, resting upon the atmosphere ! At first I mistook this appearance for another vast mountain at a distance, until my guide pointed it out, exclaiming, " *l'ombra, l'ombra.*" As the sun arose in the heavens, this vast shadow decreased in height, and the deceptive appearance grew less. I need hardly inform my readers that this shadow lay to the north-west of the true crater, and was most clearly defined towards the top, whilst the broader base melted away into the dusky twilight that pervaded the lower regions of the mountain. Very soon the whole sky was brightened

by the morning sunbeams, but I was disappointed at not gaining the panoramic view which I had expected over the whole of Sicily. Cloud upon cloud canopied the land, and only here and there, where the massy vapours were disparted, could I gain a glimpse of the earth, that lay extended like a map far, far below, the rivers winding through it like silver threads. To the south and west the eye ranged over the pinnacled tops of crowded mountains, that lay like so many hillocks crouching at the feet of a giant. But to the northward, over Italy, all was shrouded beneath heavy clouds, blown in that direction by the wind. After collecting some specimens of lava and sulphur from the edge of the crater, we commenced our descent, which was accomplished by a series of running leaps, our feet sinking up to our ankles at every step, which prevented our going downwards too fast. By the time we reached the foot of the cone, I discovered that my shoes and stockings were cut all to pieces, and the cinders filled them at every step I took. Happily, however, the most laborious part of our undertaking was now over, and we reached a track of soft volcanic sand, which was quite delightful to the feet after the sharp and pointed rocks of lava which we had just left.

The Torre del Filosofo, or the Philosopher's Tower, at the foot of the cone, was the next object which presented itself worthy of the traveller's notice. It stands to the eastward of the "Casa degli Inglese," a little lower down the side of the mountain. As a visit to these ruins led us out of the direct road, which our mules were to take in their descent, the guide ordered them forward under the care of my Riposto servant, and arranged that they should wait for us at a given spot, in the region of volcanic sand. A succession of flying leaps and slides over a steep descent of loose ashes brought us at last to the Torre del Filosofo. It presents but little to the eye of the inquisitive traveller, consisting only of a few remains of large red tiles, having rude impressions upon their surfaces.   These are scattered loosely about in a quadrilateral form, and in the middle are a quantity of stones, which probably once formed part of the edifice.   Some persons have ascribed these ruins to Empedocles; and others again affirm them to be the remains of an altar to the Etnean Jove, of which there are several in different parts of the mountain.   If the former of these suppositions be correct, the philosopher, indeed, chose a most excellent situation from whence to study the stars that beam through the rarified atmosphere, surrounding this lofty and isolated peak.   A feeling of sublimity amounting almost to terror, pervades such a spot as this, where the buzzard and the eagle venture not, and ages roll by without the sound of any created thing to tell of their solemn and certain flight.   Stern, silent, and alone, Etna rears its snow-clad crater high up into the blue vault of heaven; its eternal solitude broken only by the voice of the occasional traveller on his pilgrimage to the summit of the cone, or when the subterranean fires belch forth from below, by the muttering thunders, and the portentous rumblings that accompany the dense volumes of smoke, and the broad and fiery streams that boil up from the red hot furnaces of the volcano.   It is a remarkable circumstance, that in the numerous and overwhelming eruptions of the mountain, these ruins of the Torre del Filosofo have never been destroyed.   The lavas have swept past them, but their course has been either to the right or to the left.   This might, in some degree, help to confirm the opinion, that the eruptions of Etna but very seldom issue from the mouth of the grand crater, but generally from some pseudo-volcano, which arises during the erup- tion from the sides of the mountain much further down, out of which the streams of lava burst forth, and the quantity of ashes and scoriæ thrown out during the con- tinuance of the eruption form conical hills around the new crater, which after the lapse of ages become converted into a rich soil and are eventually covered with trees. Of this I observed several examples in descending the mountain, and the instance of the terrible eruption of 1669, will suffice to prove the assertion.   This eruption, which destroyed the city of Catania, burst out from the Monte Rossi, just above Nicolosi, which is at least seventeen miles below the principal crater, and flowing in a south-easterly direction, ran into the sea, blocking out the coast with huge moles of black lava in many places between Catania and Aci Reale.   From the Torre del Filosofo, we proceeded to the brink of the Val del Bue; on looking over which we could discern among the morning clouds that hung beneath us, a giddy precipice, and the mouth of a vast crater far beneath us.   After crawling on our hands and knees along the rocks that form the margin of this precipice, to prevent being blown over by the wind, we struck off to the westward across a bed of soft sand, to regain our mules, which we found waiting for us beside an ancient pile of rude stones, which struck me as being more picturesque than the altar of Empedocles.   I could gain no information respecting the history of this pile, but I should imagine it to be a relic having a similar origin to the Philosopher's Tower, at the foot of the cone.

We now mounted our mules; for although the descent was extremely steep and dangerous, I was so overcome with fatigue that I was glad enough to avail myself of this sort of partial rest; and trusting entirely to the superior knowledge of the mules in traversing the broken lavas, I threw the reins on the back of the animal, and enjoyed the beauties of the descent as much as my extreme state of fatigue would allow me to do. We soon arrived at the first stages of vegetation; the air felt sensibly warmer, and I unburdened myself of the huge Sicilian cloak which Dr. Gemmellaro had lent me. On reaching the region of the Bosco, the air felt delightfully refreshing, and the sun was quite warm, butterflies flitted over the fern, and the American cowslip, and dog's tooth violet, enamelled the grass. The trees of the Bosco consist principally of ilexes, cork trees, and a few pines. These latter, however, are principally confined to the northern side of the mountain. On the borders of the Bosco, we passed on our left a huge mass of frozen snow, which is the store that supplies the inhabitants of the plains with this luxury during the summer. I was much surprised at seeing this so low down the mountain, as I had not met with one particle on the crater; and had only observed a few patches on looking down the northern slopes of the volcano. Just as we arrived at the snow, we met a party of peasants, who had come up from Catania, to cut a supply of it, for which they were provided with spades, and large baskets, covered with flannel. My guide procured a lump for me, which I found very refreshing, as the exhaustion I had undergone caused me an intense thirst, and no water was to be obtained. The snow of Etna is a source of considerable wealth to its several proprietors; and I was informed that an individual of Bronte receives a rental of 2,000*l.* per annum for a single patch of it on the northern side of the crater.

Whilst my mule steadily wound his way down the tortuous paths of the Bosco, I became so thoroughly drowsy that I went off to sleep several times, and I was only awakened from my reverie by the shouts of the muleteer. The next most singular effects which resulted from the severe fatigue under which I was labouring, were the strange dreams that visited me. Once in particular, I fancied that I was sitting by a parlour fire in England, and I was not a little startled on awakening, to find that I was yet descending the mountain; and it required some moments for me to re-collect my ideas perfectly. But all my dreams did not end so easily, for I suddenly discovered that during one of my siestas, I had dropped Dr. Gemmellaro's woollen cloak, and my guide told me that we must either go back, or I must pay the owner of the garment five piastres. This latter remedy was one which I did not at all relish, so after prevailing on one of the guides to go back and look for it, I dismounted from my mule, and lay down under an ilex tree to await his return. After a delightful rest of nearly an hour, I saw the man coming down, bearing the lost cloak which I had dropt a long way back ; and as soon as we were all once more adjusted, we hastened downwards towards Nicolosi, which place we reached safely soon after two o'clock, P. M. After partaking of a vile repast of some maccaroni at Massania's inn, for which I paid half a dollar, I called on Signor Gemmellaro to make him a farewell visit. He received me, as usual, most kindly, and presented me with a small box containing a variety of lavas from the crater.   After spending a short time in his museum, I took my leave, and giving a "buonamano" to the guide who had accompanied our ascent, I started for Riposto by the same route as before, with the servant and mules with which I had been provided by the politeness of Mr. Carlhill.   At the end of a tedious ride of four hours, during the two last of which it was perfectly dark, we reached Giarra, and turning down a road that leads to the sea-shore, we soon arrived at Mr. Carlhill's residence, where I was most cordially received, and congratulated on my having accomplished the ascent to the cone under such very unfavourable circumstances.   Mr. C. remarked that he had been watching the state of the weather during the day, and, as the summit of the mountain was entirely shrouded by masses of cloud, he had feared that my expedition would terminate unfortunately.   Had any of my friends in England seen me on entering the portico of Mr. Carlhill's dwelling, they would have been not a little amused at my appearance.   My white dress was torn and dirty, and my shoes and stockings as ragged as they could well be.   Dr. Gemmellaro's huge green spectacles succeeded admirably in imparting a sober dignity to the whole; for as I was still half blind with the ophthalmia from which I had suffered in Malta, the philosopher of Nicolosi had kindly lent me these spectacles, which I found of great service.   After supper, one of the young gentlemen showed me two ancient leaden crosses, which had been discovered during some alterations in the premises a short time before.   They were found enclosed in some earthen jars of considerable size, which the workmen broke to pieces.   They are supposed to have been the workmanship of the primitive Christians, as they bear evident marks of great antiquity.   Mr. C. begged in the kindest manner that I would accept of these crosses, and I still retain them among my other curiosities ; the one measures five, and the other seven inches in length.   In the course of our conversation, one of the ladies observed that very few of the indigenous flowers of Sicily were remarkable for their perfume, which gives a complete contradiction to Brydone's remarks, as well as the fable of Diodorus Siculus, who tells us that hounds lost their scent in hunting, from the excessive fragrance of the flowers that studded the Sicilian plains.

CHAPTER XXXI.

VISIT TO THE CASTAGNO DI CENTO CAVALLOS.

" Prodigious Etna bore a wondrous tree—
A chestnut, whose vast hollow may contain
A well-sized band of horse."
                              "One mighty tree
Was there.   Even on the edge of that vast mountain,
Upheld by knotty roots and fallen rocks,
It overlooked in its serenity
The dark earth and the bending vault of stars."

On the following morning I bade farewell to my kind friends at Riposto, from whom
I had experienced such genuine hospitality, and taking with me the same servant
and mules as before, I set off for the Castagno di Cento Cavallos, or chestnut of a hundred horse, a gigantic tree, or rather the remains of one, situated some way up on the
eastern side of Etna above Giarra.   As so much has been said of this wonderful tree
by travellers in Sicily for ages past, I could not pass so near without paying it a
visit.   It is particularly marked in an old chart of Sicily, near three hundred years
since, as the " giant tree," and has borne off the palm for being the largest chestnut
tree in the world.   It is said to derive its present name from the circumstance of the
Queen of Arragon having taken refuge during a storm, attended by one hundred
horsemen, within its enormous trunk ; but this account may probably be fabulous.

We left Riposto about noon, and passing through Giarra, struck into a beautiful
and wildly variegated torrent path that led towards the mountain.   This path, though
in many places very steep and dangerous, amply repays the wanderer who pursues
its track by the beauty of the scenery which it presents in every direction ; on one
side of the road lay a deep glen, bordered with caves, and overhung by spreading
chestnut trees : the larkspur, flos adonis, wild thyme, and golden rod, grew upon the
banks, and the blackberry blossom attracted my attention by its deep and rich
colour.   After passing by a pretty village, about half way up, the path became still
more rugged, and the only footing for the mules consisted of blocks of slippery lava,

worn smooth by the mountain torrents that flow down these ravines during the winter season.   After pursuing this wild and lonely path for six or seven miles, we at length arrived almost unexpectedly before the famous tree.   At the first sight, I must confess to my readers that I was rather disappointed; but when I stood within its aged limits, and examined the five massy and tortuous stems that now form its only existing remains, I could not fail to be struck with the magnificent appearance which such a tree as this must have had when in its pristine growth and vigour.   Former writers have not inaptly styled it " the glory of the forest."   The Castagno di Cento Cavallos has now lost its principal attraction; the huge trunk has been destroyed by decay, and the wood cut away in large quantities for fuel when age rendered it easy to chop the bark off, so that, at the present day, instead of rearing up one large stem, the traveller sees five trees, all, indeed, noble in themselves, but surrounding a hollow space affirmed to have been once occupied by the main trunk.   Many young saplings have shot up around the parent stock, and the boughs of the five trees still bear a tolerable supply of chestnuts ; some of these, which had been blown down by the wind, I gathered up.   Through the centre of the trees passes the road, or rather mule-track, and a stone wall connects two of the stems on the northern side.   One reason which leads me to entertain the opinion that these trees were all joined together at no very distant period of time, is from the fact that the insides only of the trunks were hacked and cut away, while the outer surface of the bark remains rugged and untouched.   Every traveller who visits this tree takes the liberty of obtaining for himself a bit of the wood of the " Castagno," and in a small hut, a few paces off, a hatchet is kept for this purpose by an old woman who works in the adjoining vineyards.

Whilst engaged in making a sketch of the tree, a few heavy drops of rain fell, and these were almost immediately afterwards followed by unceasing peals of thunder and vivid flashes of lightning.   After a five months' drought this sudden change of weather was most delightful and welcome to the inhabitants, and the old woman smiled and blessed the saints for so genial a shower, whilst we (mules and all) took refuge in her humble shed.   Fortunately, there was an abundant supply of hay, which satisfied the hunger of our mules, but for ourselves there was nothing but some " carruba," or locust beans, besides the chestnuts we had gathered from the great tree. The vintage being over, the winepress that filled the greater part of this hovel was emptied of its contents, as the juice of the grape, when expressed, is carried in small kegs to the manufactories, slung across the backs of mules.   Whole troops of these animals thus laden were familiar objects of encounter in the mountain pathways, followed by a troop of boys and girls singing their wild and careless songs to the god of the grape.   Instead of abating, the storm increased ; the lofty peak of Etna was shrouded from our view, the wind howled loudly, and, as it swept by, it

From Nature & on Stone by George French Angas.

Day & Haghe, Lith'rs to the Queen.

IL CASTAGNO DI CENTI CAVALLO, ON ETNA.

bent the slender stems of the mountain ash and the sorb tree, and laid the tangled vines level with the ground. The thunder, as it rolled above our heads in the fearful region of the crater, sounded like a discharge of artillery, and the lightning danced out of the black and gloomy clouds in many a wild and arrowy fork. For two hours we were patient occupants of the hut, thankful for having so tolerable a protection from the pitiless storm that raged with unabated fury around us. By-and-by the heavens grew clearer, the clouds rolled away, and the sky smiled as blue and as serenely fair as though no tempest had ever obscured its arch of brightness, and the wind sank down again in silence as suddenly as it arose. But the wide face of nature underwent a universal change; the drenched flowers raised up their petals, refreshed with the genial moisture; the cicada sang more loudly in the green canes, and every watercourse, that was before parched up and dry, now became a swollen stream, murmuring on its way as it leapt from rock to rock on its downward mission to the sultry plains. As the clouds vanished from the top of the mountain, they disclosed the peak of Etna, clear and cutting sharply against the azure sky; but it had undergone a greater change than any other object. Its lofty summit was crowned by a zone of dazzling whiteness, and its brown sides had already put on their winter mantle of snow. This momentary change in the appearance of so conspicuous an object as that of Etna surprised me not a little, as only the day before I had stood on its loftiest crag, and searched in vain for an extensive patch of snow.

Near the Castagno di Cento Cavallos there are other trees of an enormous growth; but as the delay occasioned by the storm prevented our visiting them, I am unable to say whether any of these are as remarkable as the one in question.

Our ride back to Giarra was unusually pleasant, and the freshened air was delightfully cool. Another shower overtook us, and I was much amused at meeting a number of peasants who had come out to gather up the chestnuts which were blown down from the trees that lined the ravine, with enormous umbrellas of coarse sailcloth, painted red and yellow, in size and shape not unlike those of some of the market-women of Covent Garden. On reaching Giarra we turned down a path that led us around the outskirts of the town, instead of passing through it, as we should have done if we had been returning again to Riposto. Our place of destination being Giardini, this road formed a short cut, leading from the mountain fiumara into the coach-road to Messina, on which Giardini lies, nestled at the foot of the mountain of Taormina, with the blue waves of the Mediterranean kissing the doorsteps of its scattered cottages, and the distant shores of Italy bounding the view to the eastward. To this secluded village we now bent our way; the path behind the walls of Giarra consisted of shining particles of volcanic sand, strewed here and there with the whitening skeletons of mules, that gave the spot the semblance of a deserted charnel-house. White cottages, with their trellised vines overhanging the doorway, beneath which the inmates sat enjoying the cool pleasant air of sunset ; the women spinning their native cotton, and groups of dark-eyed children merry in their evening gambols, chasing each other among the dark foliage of the lemon trees.   Fields of the cotton-plant, with its red and yellow blossom, fragrant from the moisture of the genial rain,—hedgerows of aloes and Indian figs, olives with their purple berries, golden vineyards, mulberries, date-palms, and locust trees, were among the varied objects that met our view on this charming coast, as the golden rays of sunset streamed far across the western heavens, busting from behind a barrier of dense and heavy clouds, and producing an effect that even the pencil of Turner might have striven in vain to portray, so wildly beautiful, and yet so evanescent is the evening sky in Sicily.   Many of the cottagers greeted me as I passed with a good-natured " Buona sera," that owed much of its charm to the gracefulness of manner, and playful glance that accompanied it ; though in this fair land there is much of misery, want, and woe, arising from various political causes, yet traces of beauty and loveliness still exist among its children, and the clear dark eye, and finely moulded form of the half-clad Sicilian boy, may even compete with the rosy cheek and flaxen hair of the blue-eyed Scot.

We reached Giardini at eight o'clock ; it was quite dark, and the shrill cry of the cicada, and the plaintive song of the night-bird, had serenaded us from every olive tree during the last hour of our journey.   We halted, as before, at the little inn which had afforded me so much amusement ; but alas ! it was locked up.   The landlord, and his amiable partner in life, had retired to rest on the opposite side of the street. My guide, who appeared to understand this state of affairs better than I did, knocked up the old folks, and presently both Punch and Judy came down in dishabille, and unlocking the door of the albergo, commenced making preparations for my supper. In less than half an hour this meal was before me, and I was satisfying my hunger upon coffee, bread and honey, grapes, and fishes of the eel species, with their tails stuck into their mouths, reminding me of the fable of the wise serpent in a similar position, emblematical of eternity.   The visitors' book was again duly laid before me, and acted like a dose of nitrous oxide, when just at that moment my illustrious landlord came in with his long red nightcap on, looking more like Punch than ever.   As I anticipated a very long and tedious journey on the morrow, I bade him good night, and quickly retired to rest, giving orders for every thing to be in readiness for a visit to Taormina at day-break.

From History & co. Stone by George French Angas.

Day & Eyge Lith^d to the Queen.

REMAINS OF THE THEATRE AT TAORMINA.

(Etna in the distance)

CHAPTER XXXII.

" The heights of Mola, city-crowned,
   Look on Taormina's classic steep,
   Beneath, the sapphire deep
   Rolls on through its accustomed bound ;
   And, far above the ocean foam,
   Like eaglets perched on eyrie home
   The rock-built cities rise !"

No sooner had the first beams of day spread themselves over the blue waters, than aroused by my civil landlord I hastened to ascend the mountain of Taurominium ; and bidding adieu to the snug little village of Giardini, my guide and myself remounted our mules, and slowly wound our way up the steep sides of the hill. The situation of Taormina is most singular and picturesque. It is beautifully placed on the summit of wild and lofty rocks, in a salubrious air, and immediately overlooking Giardini, from which it is about two miles' walk, though the real distance is a mere gunshot, and the merry shouts of the children from above are clearly heard in the village beneath. This now inconsiderable place was once the splendid and magnificent city of Taurominium, built by the Zancleans and Hybleans, in the time of Dionysius the First. It still contains several valuable and interesting remains of antiquity, amongst which the theatre is by far the most perfect.

We arrived at the summit of the hill without meeting with any accident, though some tourists have not been so fortunate, as I found from an inscription in my old host's book at Giardini, in which a gentleman who with his guide visited Taormina on asses, writes thus :—" The donkeys here are shocking. I would also advise people to beware of a young lad who pretends to act as a guide to Taormina, for he is a very great rogue. I have been thrown head over heels three times, and if my skull had not proved uncommonly thick, I should certainly have been killed !" Such are the miseries of most persons who ride on asses, from the cockney who falls gracefully on the green turf at Hampstead or Blackheath, to the more perilous adventurer along the mule paths of

Sicily. We passed through a gateway in the ruined walls of the ancient city, and entered the streets of the modern town, to visit the theatre, which stands in a hollow of the rock above the town. Still higher than this, and crowning a loftier peak, the village of Mola rises above the theatre, from which it appears to be totally inaccessible ; its white buildings contrasting against the azure sky, cluster around its topmost peaks, and look like some impregnable castle of fairyland, from whence its inhabitants may look down upon one of the most enchanting panoramas on the earth. A narrow and dangerous path along the edge of a precipice, led us to the theatre, where we dismounted from our mules, and proceeded to examine the interior of these spacious ruins. A Neapolitan artist, who occupied a small lodge near the entrance to the theatre, acted as our guide, but unfortunately he chattered so fast and so unintelligibly in Italian, that I could scarcely comprehend any thing he said ; I, however, made it appear that I perfectly understood him, and he was quite satisfied. The form of the theatre is semi-circular, and from the remains of the columns it would appear that its architecture was Corinthian : the walls were coated with white marble, and the whole building composed of very small terra-cotta bricks, of a dark red colour. The Scena is nearly perfect, and appears to have had three entrances. On each side of the Scena are large saloons with arched roofs, which are nearly entire ; and below the theatre is a reservoir, with channels for water ; a subterranean gallery runs beneath the Proscenium ; the tiers of seats are almost obliterated, and a quantity of soil, overgrown with grass and wild flowers, occupies their places. The walls are in excellent preservation, as are also many of the ornamental decorations on the front of the edifice. Fragments of rich Corinthian capitals lay scattered about, and portions of columns of granite, Porta Santa, Cipollino, Giall, and beautifully variegated African marbles, are now being removed from among the ruins by order of King Ferdinand. Many valuable vestiges of its former magnificence have been dug up amidst the ruins, and every fresh excavation brings some new treasure to light. But the view alone from this spot, is more than sufficient to repay the traveller for the delay of a visit to so elevated a situation. Let him gaze on the village of Giardini, nestled at the mountain's base ; on the ruined aqueduct, and the modern town just beneath him ; then let him extend his gaze onward to the site of the ancient Naxos, and trace the line of coast past Riposto, Giarra, Catania, and Aci Reale, as far as Siragusa. Northward, the distant shores of the Faro of Messina, with that city itself, its white domes glittering in the sunshine, and the narrow thread of silver running and winding between Europe and Sicily. The dim and distant mountains of Calabria, and the thousand picturesque hills of the Val di Demone, clothed with their wealth of olives, vines, and mulberries ; before him is stretched out the vast bosom of the Mediterranean, that looks as though it were formed of one molten sapphire, so pure, and deep, and lovely is the colour of that faithless, yet fascinating sea. Whilst to complete the scene, Etna towers proudly in front, mingling his snow-capped summit with the clouds. Surely when Taurominium was in the height of its glory, this must have been a truly imposing sight for its inhabitants to enjoy, when they gathered together on the marble seats of the vast theatre, beneath a serene and placid sky, their attention, no doubt, being often attracted towards the mighty Etna, belching forth flames and smoke, and adding a terrific reality to the excitement of some Greek tragedy of thrilling interest. Such was Taurominium; but its grandeur is gone, and its battlements are forsaken. The flowers expand their lovely petals in rich clusters on the ruined walls of the theatre; the lizards bask beneath the prostrate marble columns, and lonely as the spot itself, the keen-eyed eagle sits on its loftiest pinnacle, and broods in silence over the forsaken city. Below the Theatre are the vestiges of a chapel belonging to the primitive Christians, and two quadrilateral sarcophagi are visible in the valley, which lies to the northward of the hill. Leaving the theatre, we descended on the opposite side to that by which we had come up from Giardini, down a path exceedingly steep and rugged, bordered with oleanders, and strewn with blocks of green and red marble, over which the winter torrents gush and murmur on their downward course, amongst bushes of myrtle, syringo, and laurel. On arriving at the foot of this path, which, in some places, was so slippery and perpendicular that we were obliged to dismount, and even our mules seemed fearful to venture, we entered a deep glen, and shortly afterwards found ourselves close to the sea-shore. Passing the romantically-situated fort of St. Alessio, and other remains ascribed to Count Ruggiero the Norman, we arrived at Ali, where there are some famous medicinal baths, but the accommodations would hardly suit the fastidious and delicate invalids of Great Britain.

We halted to dine at the village of Scaletta, at the same cottage where I was so much entertained on my journey to Riposto; and I had no sooner reached the door, than I was warmly greeted by little Antonino, who came running to welcome me on the strength of our late acquaintance. Inside the house, the hens, chickens, and turkeys appeared more numerous than ever; and the dogs and slim tabbies beset me the moment I entered. When seated, the good woman turned out a rotolo of maccaroni into a large dish, which I expected was intended for me; but to my surprise and astonishment, the whole family surrounded it instantly, and began to demolish it with wooden forks, cramming as much into their mouths at first as possible, and then dexterously pushing in the depending filaments with their fingers. This is the true Sicilian mode of eating maccaroni, though certainly not the most polite. After the family meal was over, there was a second dinner prepared for me, which my hostess served on a trencher, and, without any ceremony, or even consulting my taste on the subject, she poured over it some tomata, or red pepper sauce, fried in oil, and then scattered the salt over my plate with her fingers. Presently Antonino brought me in some delicious figs and grapes, which were worth all the maccaroni in the place, and we soon entered into a conversation in which his "mamma" took a part. He sadly wanted me to take him to Messina, and said, in the prettiest voice imaginable, in broken English, "Antonino go to England, but mamma no permitti." My hostess now left the room, and in another quarter of an hour re-entered, not in her rustic petticoat of blue serge, and neat white handkerchief pinned over the head, but decked out in a rich boddice of scarlet silk, with a gay stuff skirt of a bright green colour, platted into immense folds; a profusion of lace about her head, and her fore finger adorned with three massive gold rings. This was her gala dress, which is similar to those worn by most of the peasants on holiday occasions, excepting only that the red and green are often varied by yellow, purple, or scarlet stuffs. As she was going with her husband to pay a visit to some friends, who lived in the mountains, they seated themselves on a mule, the lady riding behind quite conscious of her finery, and trotted off in style towards the nearest fiumara. I also took my departure from Scaletta, and left Antonino Chrysofalo all alone as housekeeper, till his good mamma returned from the mountains. The day was now delightfully cool, and as we approached the suburbs of the city of Messina, we met crowds of people all abroad on some festive gala; some were dancing in careless groups around the doors of the cottages, to the discordant notes of the bagpipe, and the jingling of the tambourine; others, mounted on mules and donkeys, were thronging the dusty roads, whilst their clear voices broke the stillness of the evening air. As we neared the city, we met numerous carriages rolling rapidly along, filled with gaily dressed ladies and gentlemen. As I passed one of these, an elderly gentleman put his head out of the window, and asked me if I had been to the mountain, to which I replied in the affirmative, when I recognized him as one of my fellow travellers from Giarra. Before it was quite dark, our mules' hoofs were clattering over the pavement of the Strada del Corso, and in another minute I was comfortably lodged in my quarters, at the " Grande Bretagne hotel," overlooking the Marina, and the opposite shores of Italy.

CHAPTER XXXIII.

" The Italian shore
And fair Sicilia's coast were one, before
An earthquake caused the flaw."

" How beautiful is sunset, when the glow
Of heaven descends upon a land like thee,
Thou paradise of exiles—Italy !
Thy mountains, seas, and vineyards, and the towers
Of cities they encircle."

NOTHING is more delightful and picturesque than the situation of Messina. Brydone happily termed it, " an enchanted semicircle," and no description can do justice to its beauties. According to tradition, this city was founded 1600 B. C., and was named *Zancle* (which signifies a sickle) by the Greeks, on account of its crescent-like shore, which projects into the sea, in a form somewhat similar to that instrument. The climate is most salubrious ; and owing to the constant current of air blowing up and down the straits, it is cooler than any other part of Sicily. That singular atmospherical phenomenon, the Fata Morgana, is sometimes witnessed here, aud its illusions are described as most surprising. The houses in Messina are large, elegant, and spacious ; but, owing to the prevalence of earthquakes, the splendid row of buildings stretching along the Marina, for more than a mile in extent, has been left unfinished, and instead of capitals, their broken columns are covered with a rude tiling. A modern writer on Sicily, gives the following account of the great earthquake that befel this city in 1783 :—

" The plague in 1743 swept away fifty thousand of its citizens, and the earthquake of 1783 nearly destroyed its magnificent quay, and most of its superb edifices. The splendid crescent of houses fronting the Marina was reduced to a pile of ruins, and the narrow streets were universally blocked up by fallen buildings, though some of the public structures, owing to their solidity, remained standing, and amongst these was the cathedral. The shocks succeeded each other from the 5th to the 7th of February. The first was the most violent; providentially, however, an interval of a few minutes between the first and second enabled the inhabitants to escape from their tottering houses, and take refuge in the country. At the entrance of the straits of Messina on the Calabrian side, a violent shock of this earthquake being felt about noon, the people of the neighbourhood fled to the sea shore, where they remained in safety until eight o'clock at night, when, owing to another shock, the sea swelled immensely, and suddenly precipitated its waves on the beach, engulphing upwards of one thousand persons, and the same tremendous swell sunk the vessels in the port of Messina, and destroyed its mole. The dogs in Calabria appeared to anticipate this awful convulsion of nature by howling piteously; the sea-fowl flew to the mountains, and a noise like that of carriage-wheels running round with great velocity over a stone pavement preceded the first shock of the earthquake, while at the same moment a dense cloud of vapour arose from Calabria, gradually extending to the Faro and the town of Messina. The loss of property was incalculable—splendid churches, works of art, libraries and records being all involved in the common ruin."

The public gardens situated at the end of the Corso are well worthy of notice, and though small, they are yet arranged with a great deal of taste. The trees consist principally of mimosas, pimentos, and various kinds of locusts, oleanders, and other flowering and ornamental shrubs. Near the entrance there are some palms, (phœnix dactylifera,) and under the shade of the trees rustic seats are placed about, for the accommodation of the people, who make this a favourite lounge on a sultry afternoon. Water is introduced, though scantily, in an artificial grotto, and a stork and a purple gallinule occupy small aviaries on the left side of the gateway. The Cathedral, or mother church, is a fine old pile, situated on one side of a square, and well repays the trouble of a visit. The high altar is embellished with rich marbles and columns of lapis-lazuli, above which is an enormous picture of the Trinity. The capitals of the columns supporting the nave are richly gilt, and there is a vastness and grandeur about the whole edifice which cannot fail to impress the mind of the beholder. Above the outer door is a chastely coloured fresco, and the entire front is magnificently ornamented—the altar plate is by Guevara; and the pulpit, which is of marble, is the work of the famous Gagini.

Whilst passing along the Strada Corso, groups of people leading little children, attracted my notice, all moving towards the church of St. John of Malta. As the crowd entered through two underground doorways beneath the church, the walls of which were gaily decked with flowers and ribbons, I imagined that there must be something extraordinary going on below stairs, and went down also. It was the centary and festival of St. Placido; and I soon found myself in a low but extensive subterranean chapel, or grotto, brilliantly illuminated with tapers. The roof was covered with gilding and festoons of artificial flowers ; and urns, relics, and images of saints, were aranged around the walls. In the centre of the floor stood a simple marble shrine containing the bones of St. Placido himself, whilst at the gorgeous altar three priests were performing various ceremonies, gabbling rapidly in Latin over a mass which seemed to be addressed to every saint in the calendar in succession, each ejaculation being devoutly responded to by the deluded worshippers, who knelt in clusters on the cold floor of mosaic work. Some were bending over the shrine in reverence, and others silently counting their beads, whilst one old woman actually fell prostrate on her face before the altar. All this time music sounded sweetly from unseen choristers, and all seemed so engaged in the rites that I passed out unnoticed. At the end of a corridor I saw a small altar-piece for the little children ; a beautiful painting of the infant Jesus and the Virgin, stood above it. Here I waited for a short time and watched the mothers bringing their young children, and even little babies, teaching them to bow before the picture of Christ, and sprinkling their foreheads with the holy water, which is contained in a font of verd-antique, near the door. This constitutes nearly all their religion. On the outside of the church door, a number of small cannon were being fired off, which caused an echo in the surrounding mountains, producing an effect not unlike incessant thunder. Messina is a place where the church is all powerful, and this may easily be supposed from the number of priests, monks, and friars, that are constantly met with in the streets. The Senate-house is a fine building, having one entrance in the Strada Corso, and another principal one from the Marina. The Marina itself is a beautiful promenade, ornamented with fine statues and fountains, and overshadowed with pimento trees. After sunset this promenade is a most delightful one. Vessels from all parts of the world throng the whole line of the quay, close to which the water is very deep, and so clear, that every pebble at the bottom is readily discernible.

The castle, situated on the extremity of the curved promontory of the harbour, seems to stand midway between Sicily and Calabria ; and the panorama of mountains, clothed with wood to their very summits, rises around the straits in picturesque beauty. But the view from the convent of St. Gregorio surpasses that from the Marina, and the scene when gazed upon from the heights of the telegraph above the city, approaches to the description of the appearance of Constantinople, and the shores of the Bosphorus, from the burial place of Scutari. The coral fishery is carried on here, and the straits abound with excellent fish of all kinds. It is a beautiful sight on a dark evening to observe the process of fishing by torchlight in the Faro. They carry a large flambeau at the prow of the boat, and its light attracts the fish, which are speared with a small harpoon when they rise to the surface of the water. The streets of Messina are much superior to those of Siragusa, and the whole place has an air of bustle and cheerfulness which is wanting amid the wretchedness and ruin of that city. Most of the tradespeople, as in Malta, carry on their occupations either outside the doors, or around the open entrances to the stores and bazaars. The jewellers' shops are worth notice, and the display of Neapolitan trinkets is sure to attract the eyes of a foreigner. Beautiful shell-work may be purchased in this city; and a man who resides on the Marina, assisted by his daughter, manufactures most exquisite models in cork of the various antiquities on the island, as well as figures of the native costumes, which may be obtained at very low prices, though the duty imposed on them in this country is so enormous as to deter many persons from bringing them home. The cafés and ice shops are equal to those of Valetta, though not so numerous, and the Rosolia, and other cordials made here, are delicious. The Grande Bretagne hotel, where I staid whilst in Messina, is a magnificent and spacious building, excellent in every respect, and the charges moderate; the landlord, Signor Nobilé, is a very polite and civil Italian, and speaks English well. I must not forget to mention the great kindness which I experienced from my friends, Messrs. Rew and Rynd, to whom I bore letters of introduction. On the morning before I left, I walked with Mr. Rynd and his brother to the Capuchin convent, which stands on the hill where Brydone saw the dancers treading their " light Sicilian measures," of which he speaks so poetically. Lupins grow wild around Messina, and the road towards Palermo is shaded with fine carob trees. The view from this spot is, like all others around the Faro, enchanting, and I was truly disappointed at being obliged so soon to cut short my sojourn in this delightful city. But the long-horned oxen dragging their ponderous and clumsy wagons along the Marina, piled up with boxes of lemons, warned me that the time of my departure was nigh; and before sunset I bade adieu to the shores of Sicily, and re-embarked in the schooner " Prospero," for England. She was now stored with a full cargo of lemons, every nook and corner being filled with them; and the paraphernalia of passports, health-bills, and manifests being finished, we lay off the quay ready to set sail, waiting only till the current turned in our favour for passing the dangers of Scylla and Charybdis. The market boats were our last visitors from the shore; they were laden with fruits of all kinds,—oranges, grapes, figs, walnuts and pomegranates, of which we laid in a fair stock for our voyage.

The excitement of my tour was over; the blue and smiling sky, the golden vineyards, the fertile plains and sunny mountains of Sicily, were about to be exchanged for a dreary and dangerous voyage to a less genial clime, and the dark storms of winter seemed already to whisper their melancholy music in the passing tempest that succeeded to this sultry day. But memory had wreathed a many-coloured garland of flowers to cheer me over the dreary ocean; and though years roll by, my brightest visions and fondest recollections shall be of those sun-lit isles that lie cradled in the bosom of the Mediterranean.

CHAPTER XXXIV.

VOYAGE FROM MESSINA TO ENGLAND.

" I go towards the shore to drive my ship
  To mine own land, o'er the Sicilian wave."

———

" The sea-world shook beneath a mighty storm,
  Each billow on his brow had bound a wreath
  Of white foam-flowers; and every moving form
  Of spectral Typhoon and sea-monster rose
  To battle wildly with the deep wild sea."

A VIOLENT storm of wind, accompanied by torrents of rain, prevented our leaving the port last night. The water soon collected from the mountains, and pouring down the fiumaras, or torrent-beds, swept with resistless violence onwards to the sea, carrying every thing before it. In one of the streets of Messina, leading down to the Marina Quay, a poor mule was taken off its legs by the force of the torrent, and washed along by the flood, which carried away the contents of its panniers. The drowning animal was, however, at last rescued by its owner, having been stopped in its career by a projecting wall. The Sicilians appear to be quite accustomed to these heavy rains, and during their prevalence, they lead a kind of aquatic life; they run skipping along the streets without shoes or stockings, their trousers turned up to their knees, and an enormous umbrella carried over their heads. During the night the rain partially abated, and when the morning broke, the sun burst through the clouds, (which still hung on the mountain-tops,) with its wonted brilliancy, shining along the hilly slopes, which looked greener and more beautiful after the storm. At six o'clock we left the quay, and were soon in the midway channel between Sicily and Calabria; the high and rugged mountains of the latter country seemed still as so many attractive points for the storms; and their black precipices contrasted well with the hills of Sicily, over which the sunbeams were shining a long farewell, perhaps for ever. I much regretted leaving Sicily, where I had passed so many pleasant days in exploring her ruined cities, her shady groves and wild flowery glens; her scattered monuments of former greatness, that silently speak to the musing beholder ; and last, though not least, her lofty and romantic mountains, with the giant Etna, towering majestically above all, capped with a zone of pearly snow, that gleamed white in the sunshine as we receded from the lessening shores.   To our right, the rock and castle of Scylla, formed a conspicuous object ; and several small villages skirted the foot of the Calabrian mountains.   As to the whirlpool of Charybdis, nothing now remains but a few occasional breakers ; and I fancied that the current sometimes took an eddying course, but neither corresponded with Virgil's terrible description in the voyage of Eneas :—

> " Dextrum Scylla latus, lævum implacata Charybdis
>   Obsidet, atque imo barathri ter gurgite vastos
>   Sorbet in abruptum fluctus rursusque sub auras
>   Erigit alternos, et sidera, verberat unda !"

Having escaped the dangers of Scylla and Charybdis, whether real or imaginary, and got clear of the Faro, our pilot left us, and put back in his little boat, telling us at parting, that we should have a fair wind, or, as he termed it, a " cracker levanter," and promised to pray to St. Antonio for a good voyage for us.   This kind offer was made in the hopes of getting an extra dollar added to his pay, a trick which often succeeds with these men, though whether they really use their pretended influence with the guardian saint, is a fact of which I am rather doubtful.   The Neapolitan steamer passed us in the afternoon, and a gentle breeze carried us past Monte Stromboli, the most eastern of the Eolian or Lipari Isles.   Though this volcano is said to be always in a state of ignition, I could not discover any appearance either of fire or smoke, although it might, perhaps, have happened that we were at too great a distance from it, for this to be visible.   It has the appearance of a huge cone rising very abruptly out of the sea ; it is upwards of 2,000 feet in height, and nine miles in circumference, and is about thirty-two miles distant from Sicily.

Monday.—Instead of the " cracker levanter," promised to us by our weather-wise pilot, the sea this morning was as calm as a lake ; the distant shores of Sicily were visible at Milazzo, and the top of Etna could be seen towering above the clouds. About breakfast time a fishing boat from the shore came, and rowed twice around our vessel ; this is a plan adopted by the natives in order to attract the fish, which they suppose lie under the ship's keel.   In the afternoon some light airs carried us within sight of Volcano, and several more of the Lipari isles, Salina, Lipari, and Panaria. The night was calm and beautiful, and the stars beamed out most brilliantly through the clear, still air.

Tuesday.—Almost a dead calm ; another boat came around us again this morning, but they did not appear to catch any fish.   The islands of Alicudi and Felicudi bore north of us ; they somewhat resemble Stromboli in form, but they have been extinct, as volcanos, for ages.   Volcano is still active at times ; the crater, which is situated in the centre of the island, presents a superb and magnificent spectacle, and the whole island abounds with pumices, salts, and sulphur.

Wednesday.—A calm all day.

Thursday.—Towards evening a breeze sprang up, and we passed Ustica, the most westerly of the Lipari Isles, situated nearly opposite to the city of Palermo, in Sicily, and far remote from the rest of the Lipari group. A large eagle soared around the vessel about sunset, and a thrush was caught on the rigging. Several quails, which I brought from Malta, unfortunately died. I rather think that they committed suicide, or *felo de se*, by strangling themselves between the wicker work of their cage.

Friday.—Almost calm again. We were amused in the course of the morning by watching several pilot-fish swimming under the keel, and accompanying the vessel for some miles; they are about the size of a large mackerel, and beautifully striped with broad bands of black and white; these fish are said to swim before the sharks, and act the same part for them which the jackal is supposed by many to perform for the lion. When attacked, the sailors affirm that they swim down the shark's mouth, where they find a safe retreat. At sunset a wild duck passed us, apparently winging his weary flight towards Sicily; it reminded me of Bryant's lines to a water fowl.

Saturday, 23rd.—To-day I was gratified with the sight of a number of beautiful dolphins. I almost feared that we should leave the Mediterranean without seeing any of them; but to-day they seemed determined to show themselves, and sported around the vessel in high style. Whilst swimming they appear to be of a deep blue, with a golden-coloured tail, and gleam with a rich metallic lustre on every change of light; they are said to be much more beautiful when they are out of the water, but we were not fortunate enough to catch any, though we made many attempts. We even put poor " Prinny," the dog, overboard, with a rope made fast around him, for a bait; however, we afterwards substituted a large piece of pork, which had the effect of drawing them near, and the captain succeeded in striking one with the grains (a weapon used for fishing,) but it was so far under water that he found it impossible to hook it. These fish are said to be the forerunners of a strong breeze, and are therefore favourites with the sailors.

Sunday, 24th.—We have been fortunate enough to have a fair wind all day, which, of course, the men attributed to the dolphins, for sailors, though generous and good-natured, are the most superstitious set of men imaginable.

Monday.—After a fine breeze all day, we passed the island of Sardinia. The high land of the south-east coast is visible at a great distance.

Tuesday.—This morning we were out of sight of Sardinia, as it had blown hard all night. Dark clouds from the south-east seemed to portend a storm, and it was not long before we were suddenly visited by several white squalls, or gusts of wind, which are every where dangerous, but are particularly dreaded in the Mediterranean.

At eleven o'clock the captain, who was on the look-out, observed one of these squalls approaching ; he lowered all the sails immediately, and made every thing as snug as he possibly could.   He had just time to do this as the squall reached us.   It lasted about five minutes, accompanied with a flood of rain, but happily passed off without doing us any serious injury.   However, a much more alarming accident awaited us, which would in all probability have proved fatal, had not a merciful Providence pro-tected us.   After the first squall had passed away, the sky appeared much clearer, and all sails were then immediately hoisted, to make the most of the breeze.   Not an hour had elapsed ere another squall overtook us, quite unawares, just at the instant that the men were hauling back the sails.   For several minutes the wind raged furiously, accompanied by a loud thundering noise.   So sudden was the onset of the tempest, that the captain was unable to get down a single sheet of canvass.   We were blown quite over on one side, so as to bring the vessel's keel completely out of the water, and we were within a hair's breadth of being upset.   It was impossible for us to do any thing to save ourselves, as all the hatchways were open, and the captain was on the point of cutting away the boat, when the squall as suddenly abated, and the vessel regained her previous position in the water.   Mrs. B. and I were below, and whilst drifting along in this dangerous position, I saw the waves, which appeared all of a froth, high above our heads, and threatening to overwhelm us through the skylight of the cabin.   The remainder of the day was stormy, but as most of our upper canvass was taken in, we were comparatively out of danger.   The thunder, however, increased, and towards evening it blew a heavy gale, which raged during the whole night.   We were now running under double-reefed mainsail, and the rolling of the ship had over-turned all the boxes, &c., in my bed cabin, which prevented my getting in, as during the gale it was impossible to attempt stowing them away.

Wednesday, 27th.—Wet, cold, and miserable, I lay all night upon the steerage floor, where I remained during this day, and all the next night, the gale raging during the whole time with unabated fury.   With a hard biscuit and a few cold potatoes I satisfied my hungry wants, and lay thinking of the pleasant scenes in Sicily I had so recently left, and all the comforts of an English fireside to which I was approaching.   As hour after hour passed drearily by, and no appearances seemed to prognosticate the ces-sation of the storm, I tried, but in vain, to get a little sleep, for the water constantly pouring down over my head, and the strange manner in which I was rolled about over the floor, rendered it quite impossible.

Thursday, 28th.—Though the wind still continued to blow with great violence, yet the sky was as blue as a summer's morning, and the sun shone brightly, seeming to mock our pitiable condition.   The waves ran mountains high, far higher, indeed, than ever I had seen them before.   It was a truly grand sight to see their mighty crests rolling on each side far above our heads, looking as though they would engulph us in their fathomless depths. But our little vessel floated like a cork on the water, now riding on the summit of a vast wave, and then sinking down its sloping sides into a deep and yawning abyss. When the waves rose against the sky, the light shining through them produced a lovely transparent blue colour, which, contrasting with the snowy foam breaking over their summits, formed a strikingly beautiful effect; and as though we were to lose no portion of so grand a sight, a large man-of-war (the *Hastings*) came close upon us. Her spacious decks were covered with men, and the Royal Arms of England, with the motto, "England expects every man to do his duty," shone conspicuously, whilst every now and then she rose on the top of one of these mighty waves, as though she were a mere nutshell upon the waters. We sailed alongside of her for some time, and whilst our little vessel was drenched with spray, her lofty decks were quite dry. One of the officers gave us the longitude, which we found to correspond pretty nearly with our own. By-and-by she kept more to the leeward, as though going to Minorca, and we soon lost sight of her. During the afternoon a bottle drifted close past us, sealed up with red wax, and having several barnacles on it. It exactly resembled the one which I threw overboard during our outward passage to Malta, and I doubt not but it was the same. Could we have secured it to ascertain the fact, it would have been strange indeed.

Friday, 29th.—During the night the wind had much abated, though it still blew a pretty strong breeze. In the afternoon we managed to take tea upon the deck, when we passed the island of Minorca. We saw Port Mahon quite distinctly. It appeared to be a charming place, and the whole extent of coast is sprinkled with houses and villages. The sky had a remarkably wild appearance, but the sunset was one of the most resplendent I ever witnessed. Bank upon bank of molten clouds lay piled up in the golden sky, glowing like the embers of a furnace, whilst huge storm clouds, black as night, mingled in the scene, and caught the radiant gleam upon their dusky sides. It was altogether a scene of sublime magnificence, and after watching it till the last amber streak died away, I could not help regretting the transient nature of so grand and glorious a spectacle. It reminded me of Byron's exquisite description in "The Island."

> "The broad sun set, but not with lingering sweep,
> As in the north he mellows o'er the deep;
> But fiery, full, and fierce, as if he left
> The world for ever, earth of light bereft,
> Plunged with red forehead down along the wave,
> As dives a hero headlong to his grave."

Saturday, 30th.—During the night we passed Majorca, and this morning the islands of Iviza and Formentara were in sight, though very distant. To-day we have had several more squalls, but we were prepared to meet them. They were, however, nothing to be compared with those we had before experienced. After sunset the full moon shone remarkably clear, and its orb was surrounded by a double halo of uncommon brilliancy. Whilst at the mast-head, the captain caught a redstart in his hand; the poor little bird had been flying about the vessel all day, and seemed totally exhausted. We put it into a cage with some birds which one of the men had brought from Sicily, but on the next morning we found that it was dead.

Sunday, 31st.—The weather still continues very squally and unsettled, though at times it is almost a perfect calm, whilst at a short distance off we can see as much wind as we could wish to have for sailing. About noon I observed a waterspout for the first time. A very black cloud hung over the sea, in the direction of Africa. It had attracted my attention several times as I sat reading upon deck. At last I observed a long cylindrical column projecting downwards from the under surface of the cloud, and at the same time the sea beneath became violently agitated, and drew itself up until it met the column from above, forming a line of communication between the cloud and the sea. Several other spouts showed themselves in different parts of the horizon, all presenting similar grand and extraordinary appearances, till one after another they dispersed from among the clouds, and the waters beneath grew calm as before. Soon afterwards we saw a beautiful rainbow, and not far off a heavy squall appeared, which seemed to disturb the waters with a violent agitation, and cover their surface with a sheet of feathery foam; whilst around our vessel, the sea's surface was calm and still, and not a breath of wind disturbed a single sail. In the afternoon we made the coast of Spain, at Denia, the tops of the mountains looking like islands above the horizon. The evening was calm and pleasant, and we took tea upon the deck.

Monday, Nov. 1.—This proverbially dreary month was ushered in by a brilliant morning, and during the day we passed the longitude of Greenwich, which made us think of getting nearer home, though we had still nearly 1,800 miles to traverse across the fathomless ocean.

Tuesday, 2nd.—Made Cape de Palos. In the evening we again took our tea on deck, illumined by the glow of a beautiful sunset; quite one of Claude's in its way. The Spanish hills lay bathed in its warm light, whilst the calm sea and purple sky caught rich orange-coloured reflections on the breast of every emerald wave, and the bosom of every sleeping cloud. The sea had a most singular appearance, ribbanded, as it was, with alternate colours of green and orange, which I had never observed so distinctly before. After dark the water became extremely phosphorescent, a phenomenon which is said to be the forerunner of a southerly wind. The wake of our vessel glowed like a sheet of flame, and the waters were luminous for some distance around us, particularly in the ripple of the waves.

Wednesday, 3rd.—A fair wind blowing from the south-east has carried us past

From Nature & on Stone by George French Angas.

GIBRALTAR FROM THE MEDITERRANEAN.

Bearing WNW

Day & Haghe Lith^{rs} to the Queen.

Cape de Gat, and all day the Spanish coast was in sight; the high mountains of Granada, covered with snow, were visible at a great distance, and presented a magnificent appearance from the sea. The air was delightful, and the sun shone clear and bright, reminding one of the warm sunny days of spring. Eight or nine vessels were in sight, and about four o'clock, P. M., we overtook a small French schooner from Marseilles. As we ran close past her the French captain cried out in great terror, "Que voulez-vous?" the poor fellow no doubt taking us for pirates, as he seemed desperately frightened. We soon glided past them, for the "Prospero" is what they term in nautical language a "clipper," and before dark they were only as a speck on the water. The thermometer at noon was 63°.

Thursday, 4th.—At sunrise the rock of Gibraltar was in sight, as we had run during the whole night before a fair wind. At nine o'clock, A. M., we passed the rock, and hoisted our colours out of compliment to the British Government. The wind became stronger as we entered the straits, through which it generally blows with great violence. Most fortunately it was in our favour, as it also was on the passage out; so that instead of having to lie off Gibraltar for two or three days, we ran past with a most favourable breeze. Numbers of vessels, which doubtless had been waiting for a fair wind to help them through the straits, were now all running on, crowded with as much canvass as they could safely carry. Perhaps such a fleet had not sailed past Gibraltar for a long time, and it certainly was a sight of no common interest to see from eighty to a hundred vessels all sailing by, and taking advantage of such a favourable wind. We passed close to the rock, so that I was enabled to obtain a very good view of it. Some parts appear to be uncommonly picturesque, particularly where the villas of the officers, and other British residents, are situated, towards the western side of Europa Point. Further in stands the town of Gibraltar, and the bay crowded with men-of-war and other shipping. The garrison amounts to several thousand troops, and the whole rock is very strongly fortified. At the foot of the precipices on the eastern side, are a number of caverns, against which the waves dashed with great violence; the stone is of a mottled reddish colour, and bears a remarkably fine polish. About half way along, on the eastern side of the rock, there is a small fishing town most snugly situated at the foot of a deep ravine. As we rounded the lighthouse, we stood close in to the land, and I distinctly saw the aloes with their long flower-stalks growing around the houses, as well also as several soldiers of the 42nd regiment of Highlanders coming down a narrow defile in the rock, reminding one of those lines of Sir Walter Scott's:—

> "But if beneath yon southern sky
> A plaided stranger roam,
> Whose drooping crest and stifled sigh,
> And sunken cheek and heavy eye,
> Pine for his Highland home," &c.

Y

I saw the hill on the Spanish side of the boundary that commands a view of Gibraltar, where the queen of Spain sat during the siege of that fort, and vowed that she would neither eat nor drink until she had seen the Spanish flag hoisted above that of Great Britain, on the heights of Gibraltar.

Leaving the town and bay of Algeceiras on our right, we passed Cape Carbonaro, where there is a sunken rock called the Pearl. On looking at the chart, we found that we had passed it pretty closely, but fortunately we had avoided coming into contact with it. Vessels are sometimes lost upon this rock, as it lies at no greater depth than ten feet below the surface of the water; and in blowing weather it is very difficult to be discovered. The high hills between this point and Tarifa, are richly cultivated with vineyards and orange groves, and the hedges are composed entirely of aloes, and the cactus opuntia, or prickly pear. Several old watch-towers guard the coast, and we passed so near that I amused myself by looking through the telescope at the men, the oxen, and other objects on the shore. I noticed several of the inhabitants engaged in ploughing, and watched for some time two Dons who were mounted upon mules, travelling along a narrow path, until, at last, a projecting rock hid them from my sight. I was particularly pleased with a little dell at the foot of the mountains skirting the sea shore, filled with luxuriant trees, where there was a small chapel to the Virgin. It was a spot where one might lie musing for hours on the magnificent works of nature, far from the busy hum of crowded cities, and the chilling influence of cold and selfish men. As we neared Tarifa, we flew rather than sailed, and ran past the lighthouse at the rate of fifteen knots an hour. The sea was covered with foam, and the current of the waves served also to help us along. Two priests were sitting on the rocks that jut out beyond the lighthouse, watching, no doubt, the numerous vessels gliding by, and perchance also staring with amazement at the little " Prospero," for she outran every vessel that was in sight, and before dark we had passed them all. As fast as we came in sight of one, we overtook her, and then came up with the next, and so on, until we got entirely clear of the straits, which was about two o'clock. Tarifa is a fine old town, surrounded with a high wall, and the lighthouse forms a conspicuous object in the distant landscape. The African mountains were shrouded in a thick misty haze, and Cape Spartel was only just visible. We ran quite close to one of the vessels we passed; she was the " Alchemist," of Whitby, and had lost part of her bulwarks in the late gales. Presently we overtook another very fine brig, who hoisted her signals to know who we were; we consequently returned the compliment, and hoisted ours, when she proved to be the " Cassandra." After this we passed Trafalgar, where Nelson received his fatal wound, and as we got clear of the straits we gained a glimpse of Cadiz, and then steered away direct for Cape St. Vincent.

Friday, 5th.—Having run all night at the rate of ten or eleven knots an hour, we expected at daybreak to make Cape St. Vincent, when we found to our astonishment on the captain's reckoning that we had run about thirty miles to the westward of it, and were still advancing into the Atlantic Ocean. Directly we found out our mistake, we tacked to the northward, and by-and-by we made the mountains of Monchique, bearing east. The wind had blown pretty strongly all day, and we progressed at the rate of ten knots an hour during the whole time. It is Guy Faux day, and we have not forgotten the sports and amusements which it is no doubt affording to many a merry school-boy in old England, whilst we are breasting the broad Atlantic. About dinner time a bale drifted past us, apparently full of goods, and must have escaped from some wreck during the late storm.

Nov. 6.—In the night we passed Lisbon, and I came on deck to get a moon-light peep at the rock for one minute, and then jumped back again into bed. At day-break the Berlings Islands were in sight, and a vessel, supposed to be the Isabel, (a very fast-sailing schooner that left Messina on the same morning that we did,) and a steam-ship also, appeared on the distant horizon. The atmosphere was fine and mild, and several swallows flew around our vessel. The mate caught a large locust in the hold, which probably had come out from amongst the lemons, just to get a breath of fresh air. In the afternoon the captain put me at the helm, to see if I should be lucky enough to "bring a breeze," as the sailors term it. After steering for about an hour the wind freshened, and I, of course, was considered lucky. It annoyed me sadly, for hereafter I shall always be called to the tiller in calm weather, when whistling is of no avail.

Nov. 7.—Off Oporto; the sun shone as warmly as it does on a summer's day in England. During the morning I was again called upon to steer for a breeze, and, indeed, I expect now to be created nothing else than chief helmsman. Latitude 42° 13. In the afternoon we passed a large brig bound in an opposite direction to ourselves; she hoisted the signals, but we could make nothing of them. The captain was fortunate enough to spear a young pilot fish, which we fried for our tea; we found its flesh to be white and very good, only there was not enough of it. After dark I saw what I considered to be a large fire on the Spanish coast, and called the captain to look at it; he, however, thought less of it, and returned to the cabin grumbling, and saying, that it was only two or three old Spanish women sitting round a farthing rushlight! so I took care not to call him up any more to interpret my observations.

Nov. 8.—Off Cape Finisterre, distant about thirty miles; thermometer 67°, and the weather warm and fine. Towards the afternoon it became nearly calm, and the water appeared to be full of small polypi and jelly fishes, some of which were single, whilst others were in clusters of twenty or thirty, and some had the appearance of snakes. We spoke the "Eliza," of Weymouth; her master, W., proved to be an acquaintance of Capt. B.'s, and they held a long conversation together. We invited him to come on board and dine with us, but unfortunately the boat was being painted, so that we had no means of communication, and the distance between the schooners was too wide for a leap. I was much vexed at this, for he offered us some nice salt fish, which would have been a great treat.

Tuesday.—During the night a very copious dew had fallen. The dews of Spain and Portugal are much heavier than those of Sicily, hence the greater luxuriance of vegetation in those countries. To-day we spoke the " Water Lily," of Bideford, from Alicant, bound to Falmouth. In the afternoon a very thick fog hovered about us, which soon spread around on all sides, and rendered the air very sharp and chill.

Wednesday, Nov. 10.—There is a great swell in the bay, though only a light air is stirring. The morning is very fine but rather chilly; the " Eliza," of Weymouth, is still in sight to the windward; the thermometer at nine o'clock stood at 59°. During the afternoon we had the wind from the east, but in the night it changed to the south-west, which of course was fair for crossing the bay.

Thursday, 11th.—Lat. 45° 57', long. 9° 14'. A large vessel passed us this morning, outward bound, probably an American liner; the day was throughout very fine and clear.

Friday, 12th.—Spoke the " Isabel" at last; she sailed from Messina two hours after us, and when Capt. B. saw her, he lay-to till she came up with us, and then we sailed along together; the sea very rough, and the vessels running along at from nine to ten knots an hour. The captain of the " Isabel" was much pleased to see us, and I was greatly amused at hearing our captain invite him to come on board and have a slice of his ham; for before we left Messina, he made us a present of a couple of very fine ones. Towards evening the sky grew fearfully wild and stormy, and flocks of sea-gulls skimmed around our vessel, uttering their melancholy and boding cry. All night it blew a strong gale, and before midnight we were abreast of Ushant.

Saturday, 13th.—At daylight we made the Start Point. I started at hearing the captain say, as he came down into the cabin, that the English land was in sight, and hoped that a happy termination would soon be put to our voyage. Ere long we passed the Bill of Portland, and as the evening shades fell around us, we could discern St. Catherine's lighthouse in the Isle of Wight.

Sunday, 14th.—In the morning we were off Dungeness, the air was intensely cold, and the wind blowing strong. A great number of vessels were leaving the Ness Roads, and several Boulogne fishing smacks were cruising about. Eleven o'clock, A.M., off Dover; the pilot cutter came up with us, and put a pilot on board; we hoisted a yellow flag as a signal that we were in quarantine, and by noon we were anchored in the Downs. We had no sooner cast anchor than it came on to blow a dreadful gale from the north east. The storm increased every hour, and we dragged our anchors, and expected to lose them altogether; our last resource was the remaining anchor, which had in some way got the chains entangled; and after a great deal of trouble, the captain was obliged to have fifteen fathoms of heavy chain dragged through the cabin. We were altogether in a state of great suspense, but our remaining anchor was good, and the cables strong. The aspect of the sea was terrific, and the sky above our heads seemed all on fire. Several vessels drifted from their anchors, but fortunately almost all the ships had left the Downs early in the morning. At six o'clock, P. M., it blew a perfect hurricane, but at midnight the storm lulled, though the sea still ran high, and there was a very heavy swell. Towards morning some boats came off from Deal, to know if we had lost our anchors, and at daybreak a smack passed us, towing along a beacon which had been blown down off the Goodwin-sands during the gale. The "Isabel" anchored alongside of us, but owing to the stupidity of our pilot, she got under weigh two hours before us, which exceedingly mortified the captain, as he had only lain down to get an hour or two of sleep, having had none for several previous nights, and desired the pilot to be sure and not let the "Isabel" get the start of us. This man was a source of great trouble to us during the time that he was on board, and so obstinate was he, that he would move for nothing; indeed the captain had to take the entire management of the vessel himself, whilst the pilot lay snoring in the cabin! During the storm, three *ignis fatui* rested on the vessel; they arranged themselves very fairly, for one alighted on each topmast, and the third on the gib-boom end.

Monday, 15th.—It was almost a calm the whole of the day, and the "Isabel" was nearly out of sight. We passed Ramsgate and the North Foreland, and anchored for the night at Pansandhole. The sky looked very wild and stormy, and we lay expecting another gale before midnight.

Tuesday, 16th.—The threatened gale of last night fortunately passed over to the eastward, and on going on deck this morning, I saw the shores towards Margate covered with snow, whilst those which were abreast of us had entirely escaped. We weighed anchor at breakfast time, and reached Sheerness by noon, where we had to enter Stanley Creek to get product, and to be released from our state of quarantine. The Doctor came alongside, and our whole company had to arrange themselves on deck to show him that they were well, and free from all stain or spot of plague. Our ship's papers were taken from us by a pair of tongs, and carried back to the shore in an iron box to undergo the process of fumigation. After they were examined the captain went to the product-ship, and obtained our release almost immediately. The same afternoon we got out of the creek, and anchored for the night about a quarter of a mile below the Nore light.

Wednesday, 17th.—Early this morning we fell in with a steam tug, and by noon we had reached Gravesend, where the Custom-house officers came on board. By two o'clock we were safely anchored at Fresh Wharf, and in another moment I was on shore, moving amongst the busy thousands of the metropolis, on my way homewards.   After a stormy and dangerous voyage of thirty-one days, I was truly glad to set foot again on terra firma, and to bid farewell for a season to the lonely and murmuring ocean. When the dark storm and the howling blast sweep with their wintry pinions over its troubled bosom, I shall think of the rocking ship and the tempest-tossed sailor, whose home is on the faithless sea.   And my thoughts shall wander on till they revisit the fair forsaken shores of Sicily, and trace every well-known spot on memory's glowing chart—spots once seen, but never again to be forgotten !

THE END.

Tyler & Reed, Printers, 5, Bolt-court, London.